With A Little Help From My Friends

JOE COCKER

With A Little Help From My Friends

The Authorised Biography By J. P. Bean

OMNIBUS PRESS

LONDON · NEW YORK · SYDNEY

Edited by
Chris Charlesworth

Cover and book designed by
Lisa Pettibone

Front cover photo by
Clayton Joye

Picture research by
J. P. Bean

Typeset by
Selectmove

Printed in England by
St Edmundsbury Press Limited
Bury St Edmunds, Suffolk

ISBN 0.7119.2360.4
Order No. 46044

Exclusive distributors:

Book Sales Limited
8/9 Frith Street
London W1V 5TZ, UK

Music Sales Corporation
225 Park Avenue South
New York, NY 10003, USA

Music Sales Pty Limited
120 Rothschild Avenue
Rosebery, NSW 2018, Australia

To the Music Trade only:
Music Sales Limited
8/9 Frith Street
London W1V 5TZ, UK

Contents

Foreword

I would like to thank the author for his extensive research on this book. Many of my old friends must have been well surprised by this sudden intrusion into their lives, and for me he certainly sorted out some doubts about the period from 1973 to 1978.

Right now Pam and I are happily married and touring the States with the Band of Doom. I'm very pleased that Chris Stainton is back on keyboards. He's played a very significant role in my musical career and is a great friend.

Looking to the future, I just want to stay healthy and keep rocking and recording.

See you down the road somewhere.

Cheers,

JOE COCKER
New York, July 1990.

Introduction

JOE COCKER, enjoying a quiet drink with friends in December 1986, did not hesitate when I asked for his agreement to this book, the first full account of his life and career. Although we had been introduced to each other only minutes earlier, and he knew hardly anything about myself or my work, he laid down no conditions, saying that a biography was a nice idea and he would help all he could. He kept his word and asked for nothing in return.

I first saw Joe perform live in 1965, fronting his short-lived Big Blues. My lasting memory of that evening, a church hall youth club dance, is of Cocker swaying on the edge of the stage, a crate of beer at his feet as he wailed on the harmonica and sang his heart out on numbers like 'Hoochie Coochie Man' and 'Georgia On My Mind'.

From a distance I watched as his career, after a few hiccups, gathered momentum:- The Grease Band, 'With A Little Help From My Friends', Woodstock and Mad Dogs and Englishmen. Then it all went wrong and for the rest of the 1970s the only news about Joe Cocker seemed to be bad news.

Yet he kept making albums – albums that sound as good now as they did when first released. His life was in turmoil but the quality of his records did not waver. Songs like 'Guilty', 'The Moon's A Harsh Mistress' and 'You Are So Beautiful' – songs that have become Cocker classics – all came from the dark days of 1973–4.

By the beginning of the 80s Cocker's career appeared to have reached the terminal stage. More than three years passed without an album. Then along came The Crusaders who invited him to join them on the specially written 'I'm So Glad I'm Standing Here Today' and suddenly everything looked brighter. The lyrics of the song said it all – Joe Cocker was not, as had so often been predicted, destined to join the long and star-studded roster of rock casualties. The knockers and prophets of doom had reckoned without the stubbornness and resilience that had taken him from gas-fitting to the top flight of rock, against the odds, in the first place. From that point on he has never really looked back.

The basic research for this book began several months before I received the subject's blessing. It had been suggested to me in the early stages that, even if Joe did agree to the book, there would be some areas of his past that he would not like to talk about. Friends who had been close to him in the post – Mad Dogs era said there was no way he would discuss that tour, or its aftermath. Likewise, other less than happy periods were considered to be potentially hazardous. I can only say that whatever questions I asked he never took exception, nor did he shirk an answer even when the memories were clearly painful to recall. On the road in West Germany in '87 and '88, on several short trips to England and on transatlantic telephone he patiently gave up many hours of his time to be interviewed. For his trust, co-operation and generosity I am deeply grateful.

Special thanks too to Pam Cocker, Joe's wife, for all her kindness and encouragement, to his brother, Vic, and to his father, Harold, who gave me unlimited access to the treasury of memorabilia collected by his late wife, Madge.

Michael Lang, who rescued Joe's career – and more – deserves a special mention. His assistance and the time he has given me are greatly appreciated.

Without Ray Stuart, who arranged my first meeting with Joe, and Jim Foster, who eased my introduction to the Cocker touring party in West Germany in 1987, I doubt that this book would have materialised.

For their enthusiasm and help in so many ways I thank: – David Beal, Dave Berry, Skip Blauner, Ray Capewell, Bill Carr, Mike Chambers, Rita Coolidge and her manager, Tim Goodwin, Denny Cordell, Phil Crookes, Nigel Cross, Rick Cunningham, Gerard De Kovel, Bob Everson, Tommy Eyre, Kevin Falvey, Reg Featherstone, John Firminger, John Fleet, Rick Gilbert, Charlie Giordano, Cliff Goodwin, Phil Grande, Rick Grech, Dave Green (Big Blues), David Green (tour manager), Maxine Green, David Halliday, Malcolm Hill, Nicky Hopkins, Dave Hopper, Neil Hubbard, Pete Jackson, Phil Kaufman, Jim Keltner, Marty Kersich, Albert and Karen Lee, Jeff Levine, Rod Libby, Danny Louis, Mareike Malzkörn, Larry Marshall, Marshall Arts, David McPhie, Dave Memmott, Frank Miles, John Mitchell, Stuart and Monica Moseley, Jerry Moss, Vernon Nash, Ray Neapolitan, Eric Parker, Bernard Pendry, Jeff Pevar, Rüdiger Plegge, Bruce Rowland, Gin Saw, Glyn Senior, Carolyn S. Shaw, Janice Singleton, Kenny Slade, Alan Spenner, Chris Stainton. T.M. Stevens, Liz Stuart, Tom Sullivan,

Nigel Thomas, Terry Thornton, John Troy, Carla Vaughn, Mick Weaver, Heide Woicke and Frank White.

For their help with newspaper items relating to Joe Cocker, thanks to: Express Newspapers, The Japan Times – Brian Harrell, Los Angeles Times, New Zealand Herald, Rolling Stone, San Bernadino Sun, Sheffield Newspapers Ltd – Tony Fry, Alan Powell and Keith Strong, Sydney Sun-Herald, Time-Life International, Toronto Globe and Mail, Vancouver Sun, Western Australian and Winnipeg Free Press.

A final thank you to my agent, Mic Cheetham, and to my family and friends for their patience and support throughout the writing and research of this book.

J.P. Bean
1990

"I Wish I Could Be Up There"

NUMBER 38, Tasker Road is a stone semi-detached house in Crookes, a suburb of Sheffield which lies towards the highest point of one of the city's seven hills. Built in the last century, the house has been Harold Cocker's home since he and his late wife, Madge, were married in 1937. Victor, their first child, was born there in October 1940, only weeks before Sheffield was blitzed by German bombers, and on May 20 1944 came John Robert. At the time Harold was away, serving in the Royal Air Force, and the new arrival would be three months old before his father saw him.

How John Robert became Joe is a tale of early childhood. Joe has explained that it came about through "just playing cowboys as a kid— Cowboy Joe", but one of his friends of the time is more specific. Says John Mitchell, who lived across from the Cockers at 47 Tasker Road, "It came from an old window cleaner called Joe who we used to giggle at as he went about with his bucket and his ladders. We called each other after him—I became Joe Mitchell and he became Joe Cocker." Whatever, the name stuck and from there on John was Joe.

His family, not surprisingly, took longer than his friends in getting round to the change of name. Madge was the first to begin calling him Joe while Vic carried on addressing him as John until "it got confusing at concerts, people didn't know who I was talking about." Only Harold has stood firm. Even today when the phone rings at Tasker Road, from some far corner of the world, and the familiar voice says "Hi Dad, it's Joe", Harold will usually reply "Never heard of you."

1

* * *

Everyone who knew Joe Cocker in his early years remembers him as a warm, friendly boy. Happy-go-lucky, always cheerful and exuberant and possessing – as one schoolfriend describes—a magnetic personality, Joe was never short of friends. His brother, Vic, recalls their school days when he was in the juniors and Joe in the infants: "When they let them out at playtime there was one person who was always first in the playground with a tremendous roar – Joe! He must have been about six at the time."

Harold Cocker, now in his eighties, remembers the extrovert side of his younger son from family holidays in the early 1950s. "We went to various places but his favourite was Great Yarmouth. He loved it there—he liked waffles and the swimming pools—he used to watch those blokes who dressed up in funny clothes and messed about on the top splash. When we came home we wouldn't be back more than a quarter of an hour before he'd be outside with an audience of kids and he'd be re-enacting all he'd seen—high diving off the garden wall and all that sort of thing. He seemed to be very popular with all the kids, both at school and at home."

It was a happy, comfortable childhood in a family where Joe's developing personality seems to have been positively influenced in different ways by each parent. Harold Cocker had a secure job with the National Assistance Board, administering financial aid to the unemployed. A quiet, forthright man, he believes that Joe inherited from him the stubbornness and single-mindedness which helped see him through some of the rockier periods of his career. Harold's interests were, and still are, gardening and listening to music—his own father was an amateur singer in the days when people entertained themselves in their own homes and he himself has always liked what he calls "the old music". Harold was also a Mario Lanza fan and Joe would later recall creeping into the house late at night to find his father sitting on the settee, singing along at the top of his voice to Lanza records, as well as accompanying his parents to the cinema to see the singer in *The Great Caruso*.

Joe's mother, Madge, who died unexpectedly in December 1984, was more open and out-going than her husband. She is spoken of with great affection by all those who met her—friends, musicians and Joe's fans from around the world who were always sure of tea and cakes no matter when or how they arrived on the doorstep at Tasker Road. Says Vic Cocker: "My mother always encouraged both Joe and myself to do the things that we wanted to do. There wasn't any overt influence . . . it was just general support."

In the years to come, when the craziness of the rock 'n' roll world became too much to bear, it would be to his parents' cosy home in Crookes, Sheffield that Joe returned time and time again.

2

* * *

In July, 1987 Lonnie Donegan, playing some of his favourite records as guest on BBC Radio's 'Sounds of the Sixties', introduced 'Delta Lady', a Cocker hit from 1969, with the simple statement, "Joe Cocker is the best white blues singer in the world." Praise indeed from the former skiffle star who, three decades earlier, had been the young Joe Cocker's first musical hero.

Joe was eleven years old when the skiffle explosion hit Britain in early 1956. Like almost everyone else between the ages of eight and eighteen he was swept up by the simple, shouting, strumming music—and by the king of skiffle himself—Lonnie Donegan. He spent all his pocket money on Donegan's records, eagerly buying 'Rock Island Line' and all the follow-ups as soon as they were released—78's like 'Stewball', 'Don't You Rock Me Daddio' and the singer's two consecutive British number ones—'Cumberland Gap' and 'Putting on the Style'. He was one of the first kids in Crookes to join the official Lonnie Donegan fan club and proudly wore the club badge, a small guitar, at all times. He quickly learned the words to all the songs and was frequently to be found in front of a mirror, using a tennis racket as a guitar to imitate Donegan.

Not surprisingly perhaps, school held little interest for Joe. Says his father: "He was always doing something else, instead of what he should have been doing." When he was eleven Joe left Lydgate Lane Juniors to go to Western Road Secondary Modern. The last days at Lydgate in July 1955 were celebrated by Joe's class performing the operetta, *Prince Ju Ju*. Joe, as one of the princes, had a comedy routine and was, by all accounts, quite a hit. A photograph of the cast shows him, plump and smiling, in an Aladdin—style costume, holding a ukelele.

At Western Road, where he spent two years before moving on again to the Central Technical School in Sheffield's city centre, Joe seems to have concentrated less on the curriculum than on developing his fine sense of rhythm. A former classmate recalls him . . . "always beating on his desk . . . always! His hands and feet were continually going!" Bob Everson, who lived close by to Joe and had moved to Western Road with him, remembers the half mile or so walk home from school: "We used to have non-stop nick-nack sessions all the way home . . . singing the old skiffle songs. Everyday."

* * *

In mid 1956 Vic Cocker did what thousands of other fifteen year olds in Britain were doing at the time—he formed a skiffle group with three friends. The Headlanders, Vic on washboard, his pal on banjo and two others on guitars, took their name from nearby Headland Road and set about rehearsing the skiffle repertoire in each other's homes. They played the occasional interval at teenage dances and a few youth clubs around Crookes where, not surprisingly, Joe was a keen spectator. It was at such a youth club, in Fir Street, Walkley, that the call came.

Vic Cocker: "Dave Brooksbank, the banjo player and one of the leading lights, said he thought Joe had got a good voice and he got him up to sing with the group. He was about twelve and a half at the time. That was when I first became aware of it."

From that night on there would be no turning back, but the path was never smooth and set-backs lay ahead. Shortly afterwards The Headlanders entered a talent competition at the Sheffield Empire. The compère was Jim Dale from '6.5 Special', Britain's first rock and roll television show. At such a prestigious event, a showcase for the cream of Sheffield skiffle, there was no room on stage for the washboard player's little brother. Joe had to be content with a seat in the audience. "I remember being at the Empire and thinking God, I wish I could be up there. I've often wondered if it would have been my claim to fame."

Thirty years on Joe remembers clearly how he felt at that early disappointment, along with another event which occurred after he had moved on to the Central Technical School when he was thirteen. "They had a skiffle group at Central Tech and I remember the headmaster saying 'We have a bunch of boys who are going to play for you today . . . some dreadful music but I'm sure you'll enjoy it.' And this guy got up and started . . . 'Hey Lawdy . . . Lawdy Lord' . . . I was sitting on the front row and I was just . . . bubbling inside, I really wanted to just get up there and join in. I was like a nervous kid who wanted to do it. I knew I'd be great—but something held me back."

Even more than the disappointment, Joe recalls his sense of frustration, curious considering his outgoing personality and popularity among his friends. "I could never just push myself. I've always had a weight problem, ever since I was a kid, and that made me a bit self-conscious over the years, just being tubby. It always made me very shy with girls and all that stuff. It's like a reservation . . . a reservation that people wouldn't like me."

However, when he got the chance to meet Lonnie Donegan, Joe did not let his reservations get in the way. It was at the stage door of the Sheffield Empire and Donegan was at the height of his fame. As he signed his autograph for the young schoolboy he would later acclaim Lonnie asked, "Well, what do you do?" Joe did not hesitate. "I want to be what you are," he said.

* * *

4

"It was healthy stuff . . . youthful musical interest"—Phil Crookes was fourteen in 1958 when he first met Joe Cocker, as they both went about their newspaper rounds. "We used to meet up at certain points on the round and have a cigarette and we just got talking. Joe was a very talkative guy in those days. I'd picked up a bit of guitar from a guy in the next road, and Joe was listening to records. Eventually it got into me getting a cheap guitar and going round to Joe's house. That was the first time we did anything about it."

Although, like Joe, Phil Crookes was a member of the Lonnie Donegan fan club, skiffle was beginning to wane and both had started to pick up on the American rock and rollers—Elvis Presley, Chuck Berry, Eddie Cochran and Gene Vincent – who Joe first discovered while sitting in Crookes Picture Palace. "All of a sudden 'Be-Bop-A-Lula' came over the air—and I'd never heard anything like that! Gene Vincent blew me away and then a few days later I met Phil and we actually put down a tape. It was a primitive tape machine that my dad bought me—you attached it to the record player. I remember we did a version of a Big Bill Broonzy tune and Phil's guitar playing really impressed my brother's skiffle group."

Big Bill Broonzy had visited Sheffield City Hall earlier in 1957 and both Joe and Phil Crookes were in the audience. One of the great surprises which lay in store for Phil when he went round to Tasker Road was finding Joe had some records by the Mississippi bluesman. The tape recorder, too, was a rarity for those days. It was one of the first Phil Crookes had seen and many an hour was spent recording Elvis Presley impressions on it—seeing who could put down the best Elvis voice.

Phil Crookes has vivid memories of Joe in those formative years. "He used to eat music. I mean, he was a real scoffer, Joe, and his mum used to really look after him . . . Joe this and Joe that. I'd go round and he'd be eating his dinner but he'd be listening to records all the time . . . Big Bill and early Elvis . . . Carl Perkins. Once Joe had heard the music it kind of took a hold on him. It was like something really grabbed him. It was all new, all precious stuff then you know."

Besides Big Bill Broonzy Joe caught other notable American visitors to Sheffield in the late 50s. Buddy Holly was one—"I remember him having that huge guitar lead, a long cord that stretched the length of the stage—but he didn't impress me. Now Jerry Lee—he knocked me sideways! It was the first time I'd heard a piano amplified—all he had was a 30 watt Fender amp but he stuck a mike in the top of it. He did 'Move On Down The Line' and we stormed that stage!"

There were other visiting rockers that Joe went along to see and there were countless other records that he listened to—vital influences that he would absorb and filter into what was to later become his distinctive style. But the

5

one man who would do most to shape that style—the man who even today Joe Cocker still calls 'The Genius'—was yet to enter his life.

*   *   *

In 1959, ten years after he made his first records for small-time, obscure labels, Ray Charles finally hit the mass market with his own composition, 'What'd I Say'—a song he had first improvised to fill in time in a Midwest dance hall. A compulsive, rhythmic, raucous declaration of love, 'What'd I Say' was banned by some American radio stations, who considered it too suggestive. It was Ray Charles at his best—playing the hard-driving fusion of Church gospel and bar-room blues which was to become catalytic in the development of American black music.

Joe Cocker first heard 'What'd I Say' on the transistor radio he always carried about with him. It was a hot summer's night and he was wandering around Crookes with a small gang of friends, as fifteen year olds do. "I was well into rock 'n' roll records by then but there was some magic that came out . . . his voice just did something to me. I rushed out and bought it, and the follow-up, 'I'm Movin' On'—it was the B-side of that, a song called 'I Believe To My Soul' that made me realise that Ray had it . . . that it wasn't just smash and bang . . . that there was a bit more to rock 'n' roll."

Ray Charles became an obsession with Joe. He bought his album 'Yes Indeed' and went into a phase of listening to Charles' music to the exclusion of almost everything else. Years later he told John Mendelsohn of the *Los Angeles Times* "When you do that long enough you reach a point where it's all in the back of your head, where the influence becomes part of you and you sing a particular way without thinking about it. When I sing now it comes out the way it does—without any conscious effort on my part to sound like Ray Charles."

*   *   *

In the winter of 1959–60 Joe Cocker and Phil Crookes formed their first group. It was a gradual development from their sessions around the tape recorder in the front room at Tasker Road. They did not have to look far for the two other members of the group, which would become known as The Cavaliers.

John Mitchell had been a friend and neighbour of Joe's since their earliest schooldays at Lydgate Lane. At thirteen his father bought him a banjo and he and Joe spent many happy hours sitting out on the garden wall, singing skiffle songs. Switching to guitar, he took up a rhythm role to Phil Crookes' lead. Bob Everson, with whom Joe had sung all the way home from Western Road School, made a bass guitar in the cellar of his home. The only missing

6

link was a drummer—and they were hard to find in Sheffield in 1959, not least because of the expense of a kit. This problem was soon overcome when Joe acquired a snare drum and cymbal and took on drumming duties as well as those of lead vocalist.

Amplification was a priority and the first member of the group to get an amplifier was John Mitchell, who had to take his mother along to sign the agreement when he bought a 14 watt Watkins on hire purchase. Both he and Phil Crookes plugged into this and then Bob Everson bought his own—"10 watts for the bass—the speaker got hammered to death!" They were almost there when Joe bought a clip-on mike, though he still had no means of amplification. John Mitchell: "He bought the mike in town and I said 'Where are you going to plug it in Joe?' He said 'I don't know' but I did—it went in my amp even though it was already overloaded with two guitars. But we were okay."

Harold Cocker recalls: "They used to practise in our living room. We had to retire in the other room. They had drums and amplifiers and all the lot . . . made the place shake it did! It's a wonder our neighbour didn't complain, but she was a widow and she used to go out nearly every night so she probably never noticed. They used to practise a lot!"

All former members of The Cavaliers remember spending a great deal of time rehearsing at Joe's, virtually living there once they had the group. There was never any problem with Mr and Mrs Cocker about the nightly invasion. Harold took it all in his stride and Madge was always, says Bob Everson, "So easy-going it was untrue."

* * *

After much practice, The Cavaliers were booked for their first public appearance—a youth club review at Wesley Hall, Crookes. They arrived on the night, complete with equipment. While they never expected star treatment the reception which awaited them did come as something of a surprise. "We had to pay to get in!" recalls Phil Crookes. "It was three pence . . . We told the guy on the door 'We're playing' but he said 'Yes—and you're paying.' We had to pay or they weren't going to let us in!"

Following this dent to the ego there was another surprise when the producer of the review insisted the group wear make-up. Eventually they made it to the stage, going on after a girl who sang 'Ave Maria'. They played 'Johnny B. Goode', the first song they had learned as a group, plus 'Move It', 'Twenty Flight Rock' and 'I'm a Man', with Joe doing double duty on vocals and snare drum. Throughout the set Phil Crookes insisted on standing with his back to the audience. "Phil didn't like the limelight at all," says Bob Everson. "From the outset he was brilliant. We were all picking the instruments up and learning and he was accomplished—into Chet Atkins at sixteen." After Wesley Hall the group played a few more youth clubs and then they acquired what every aspiring group of the day could not be without—a manager.

Ray Capewell had all the credentials to be manager of The Cavaliers. He was four years older than the members of the group, he had 'contacts' and—most important of all—he had the use of the firm's van overnight. He worked for a Sheffield television rental firm, where Bob Everson was an apprentice and, after hearing all about the group, went to Joe's house one night to listen to them playing in the front room. He liked what he heard and said he would help them get bookings in the Sheffield workingmen's clubs, where he knew people through his father, a concert secretary. The lads were delighted—they had a manager and he had a van to carry them and their gear about. Business cards were printed and the first booking was arranged. The Cavaliers were on their way.

Meanwhile the vocalist-cum-drummer was having problems. "I remember the band saying 'Joe—you can't sing and play drums. It's unheard of'." Phil Crookes reveals a more technical insight: "Joe had real difficulty playing the snare drum and keeping the voice going. So—and this is funny, isn't it—we decided to get a singer in . . . a good looking guy, can't remember his name."

Amazingly, none of the former Cavaliers can recall the name of this temporary usurper, although it is generally agreed that he looked good, wore fluffy carpet slippers on stage and could not sing. He was there when The Cavaliers made their first workingmen's club appearance at Heeley Green, a cold prefabricated building where the concert room was half-full and children lay asleep on chairs as the group played. They got a reasonable reception but on the next couple of gigs they did not fare so well and the singer became disenchanted. As he faded out Joe resumed vocal duties. Ray Capewell recalls Joe "really captivating" an audience at Sheffield Trades and Labour Club with 'Blue Moon'; the same night the group emerged from the club to find all the tyres on the van had been let down.

Ray Capewell's period as manager of The Cavaliers came to an abrupt end when he was involved in a road accident which wrecked his van and broke both his legs. The group visited him in hospital and afterwards as he convalesced at the home of his wife's parents. "They'd all come and be sitting round the bed, playing records. My mother-in-law used to get really annoyed because Joe was drumming with his hands and feet all the time and they could hear him downstairs, above the telly." The most vivid memory Ray has of those early years is that of The Cavaliers playing at his 21st birthday party, held in a tiny flat in Sheffield. "All the group was there with their amplifiers and Joe singing and playing the drums. That was a night to remember!"

* * *

The Cavaliers lasted a little over a year as a group. Much of that time they spent in the front room at Tasker Road, practising their instruments and learning new material. Their repertoire was made up of Elvis Presley, Cliff Richard, Eddie Cochran and Chuck Berry songs, along with the occasional Shadows instrumental. From the Shadows they got the idea of wearing dicky bows on stage—a touch always appreciated in workingmen's clubs. So far they played very few Ray Charles numbers—he was still considered too 'underground' by everyone except Joe—although he did manage to introduce 'Georgia On My Mind' once the threat to his role as vocalist had been removed.

Even when they were not rehearsing or playing, The Cavaliers spent much of their time together. One of their regular haunts was a chip shop at Crookes, another was Tiler's, a herbalist shop, where Joe had a lot of friends and followers who congregated on Sunday afternoons to drink sasparella. On Saturdays the group always went down the hill from Crookes to Sheffield city centre, where the afternoon was passed in record shops. John Mitchell: "Joe used to spend all his money on records. He'd come back home and he'd listen to a Chuck Berry song twenty times. We'd get fed up but he'd say, 'Well I like to listen, that's how I get the words'. He was crazy on music."

And, if he had been out for the evening, the neighbours always knew. "He used to go on Crookes, singing at the top of his voice," says Stuart Moseley, a local piano player whose friendship with Joe began around this time. "You could hear him streets away! He'd bellow down Crookes and they'd say 'Eh up, Joe's walking home!'"

Meanwhile, in the Summer of 1960, Joe officially left Central Technical School. Officially, because he had not bothered to attend for a long time beforehand. When he first went there, at thirteen, he had applied to do engineering studies, but instead he was placed on a building course. Unimpressed by school in any event he spent much of his time in class either day-dreaming or drawing pictures of his rock heroes in school exercise books. When, in his last year, Sheffield bus crews came out on strike, it was a golden opportunity to opt out—on the grounds of not being able to get to school without transport. "We thought the bus strike was great" says Joe. "When it was over all the kids stoned the first bus up Crookes!" As he never returned to school he was expelled. His parents were none too pleased but to a sixteen year old with a head full of rock and roll it did not really matter at all.

Chapter Two

1961 — 1963

Vance Arnold & The Avengers

VANCE ARNOLD and The Avengers was a stylish name for a Sheffield rock and roll group in 1961. It sounded much snappier than The Cavaliers and established the fact that the group had a featured vocalist. As to where the name originated, Joe always explained to those who asked that it was the idea of the local newspaper. Even the other members of the group believed this until, in a 1982 Radio Hallam interview with an old friend, Ray Stuart, Joe revealed that he had thought up the name himself. "It was just something flash for the times," he said. "Joe Cocker wasn't a very acceptable name back then. It was always my big secret that I could never own up to anybody that I called myself Vance Arnold."

The first public appearance of the newly-named group was at the Minerva Tavern, a small pub in the centre of Sheffield. They went down well enough to secure a regular booking on Friday nights—when it was customary for the audience to celebrate the oncoming weekend by fighting as the group played. It got so bad sometimes that the landlord had to shelter beneath the bar while he phoned the police and it was normal for the concert room floor to be covered in blood and broken glass by the end of the evening. One night Phil Crookes was head-butted on the nose by a man who accused him of looking at his girlfriend, another time he had to dodge a pint of beer, thrown at his head as he played on stage.

Joe recalls the Minerva with great affection: "They were fantastic days man, they really were. To be young—what else could you ask for?" Certainly not money—the gig was worth £5 and Joe—by now handling the bookings

10

as well as drums and vocals—had to pay £2 each way for a van and driver, leaving only £1 to split among the four members of the group. On one memorable occasion they had to haul their equipment to the gig on public transport. "That was the night Joe forgot his snare drum," recalls Bob Everson. "He'd hung it out on the washing line to tighten the skin up and he forgot to take it off! He only had the drum and cymbal to remember and he forgot the drum."

From the Minerva, where physical survival depended on a willingness to play cover versions of such current hits as 'Let's Twist Again' and 'Here Comes Summer', Vance Arnold and The Avengers moved up a step to another pub booking, at the Fleur De Lys, on the outskirts of Sheffield. At a time when the area had a thriving pub rock scene, with dozens of venues and up to a couple of hundred groups eager to play them, the Fleur De Lys was a prestige spot. Phil Crookes: "That was a top venue, where all the bands played. When we first played there we thought 'Oh great—this is it'. We were all nervous—the gig was advertised in the paper."

The Fleur De Lys audience, in the main, preferred music to brawling and Joe and the band soon built up a following at their weekly booking. Ray Stuart, rock and roller turned local radio disc jockey: "It was at the Fleur around '61 that Joe really started to get noticed by people . . . other groups saying 'Hey, have you seen Vance Arnold and The Avengers?' It was him and the material—he was doing numbers by Ray Charles, who very few people had heard of, and the Chuck Berry stuff was little known in Britain in the very early '60s. Joe was hooked on that sort of music but everybody said 'Oh, that'll never take off'."

By now Vance Arnold and The Avengers' set included 'What'd I Say', as well as 'Georgia' from Ray Charles, quite a few Bo Diddley numbers— 'Diddy Wah Diddy' was a favourite-and a selection of Chuck Berry rockers. As a complete contrast, Big Bill Broonzy's song of racial prejudice, 'Black, Brown and White', always went down well but on other numbers Joe was again finding it increasingly difficult to play drums and sing at the same time. "We did things like Jerry Lee's 'Move On Down The Line'. It was hard work singing and playing—I'd always be getting my sticks crossed!" This time the solution was much clearer to see. A friend, Steve McKenna, was brought in on drums and Joe swapped his clip-on mike for a hand mike and moved up front for good.

He soon had a close rapport with the audience, chatting and joking between numbers, with humour and imaginative flow given free rein. It was at this time that he adopted the imaginary guitar playing movements that would become a trade-mark in later years. Phil Crookes remembers how that began: "Joe never got on with the guitar . . . he never actually got round to playing it but he always wanted to. So he used to kind of imagine he was playing it—I tried to show him a few things but he always ended up imagining he was playing and that was probably good enough for him."

In their dark suits and bow ties, Vance Arnold and The Avengers were soon appearing in pubs and workingmen's clubs all over Sheffield and further afield in to the pit villages and steel towns of South Yorkshire. With their drummer and a new rhythm guitarist, Graham Bower, who had replaced John Mitchell, all was going smoothly—until the night Joe walked out on the band. "We'd played somewhere near Rotherham and I'd lost my voice, which is a pain to any singer but it doesn't happen to me too often. What happens is—you get over-enthused and tend to blow out too much energy. And they were going 'Joe, you're useless' so I got on the bus and left them! About six weeks later they came round, knocking on my door . . . saying 'Joe, we can't find anyone else! So . . . ALRIGHT!' Back in business!"

* * *

But life was not all rock and roll. In the Summer of 1960, once he had officially left school, Joe got his first job—as an apprentice gas fitter with the East Midlands Gas Board in Sheffield. He began by helping an older, qualified fitter to install gas fires and repair cookers in customers' houses, did a three month stint in the showroom, and attended a local college on one day each week, where he learned the theoretical aspects of gas-fitting.

It was on this day-release that Joe met Pete Jackson, another sixteen year old apprentice from the Gas Board. Pete lived next door to the Fleur De Lys, where, from the age of fourteen he had been a regular drinker. He also liked to listen to good groups. He and Joe hit if off immediately.

After working separately for about eighteen months, both Joe and Pete Jackson passed the intermediate part of the college City and Guilds exams. This was a significant step because it meant that, instead of having to always be accompanied by an older fitter, they were issued with their own tool kits and could go out alone. "Quite frankly," says Pete Jackson, "we didn't do a lot of work. We weren't supposed to work together, but we did. I had a car at seventeen so we drove to the jobs in that and we'd finish by about 11.30 am and go to the pub."

This arrangement worked well for a long time, in spite of the close attentions of Joe's foreman, an elderly chap named Skinner who drove about in a gas van trying to keep an eye on him. Many were the occasions Joe and Pete were obliged to hide down cellars, up alleyways and behind walls, until one day the keen foreman discovered what was happening and Joe was suspended from work for a week without pay.

On the nights that Vance Arnold and The Avengers did not have a gig, Pete Jackson would pick Joe up at home, in his white open-top Ford Consul, customised with blue flames down each side, and they would drive out into the countryside to watch rival groups play in the pubs around Bakewell. Joe: "We had some fantastic times together me and old Pete. We'd go out and terrorise Derbyshire, dressed up in black leather—the Gene Vincent look. We used to wear this night tan—you rubbed it in and it made you look sunburnt. The only trouble was—I'd go to work the next day and I'd have forgotten to wash it all off. They'd say 'Eh—what's that brown patch behind thi ear?'"

* * *

Another young man with whom Joe became friendly at this time was engineering apprentice Bill Carr. He first saw Vance Arnold and The Avengers in September 1962. "It was the standard Shadows line-up and yet they sounded quite different, verging on the Chuck Berry and Bo Diddley. He was doing one or two of the more obscure numbers, which he would have had to be an aficionado of the record collections to have learned the songs." Already a serious collector of blues records, Bill Carr had found a method of obtaining American imports via a mail order catalogue in Norway. He had been into Ray Charles for a couple of years and bought albums by artists such as John Lee Hooker, Lightning Hopkins and Muddy Waters.

Although the Avengers were playing a few numbers by such artists, none of the group were as deeply into the music as Joe, so when Bill Carr started talking to him one night in between sets at the Staniforth Arms pub, Joe welcomed a fellow enthusiast. "To meet someone who had the same things in common—discovering the blues—was pretty novel."

Equally novel was the unbounded extent of their enthusiasm. Joe: "I remember, Bill called me at two in the morning. He said 'Joe, it's come'. I said 'What has?' He said 'Muddy Waters'. We'd sent off for this import and I got a late-night bus and went right down to his house at Darnall to get it. Wow, was it worth it too! Blew me away that album—'Best of Muddy Waters'. It was original, a Chess pressing. It cost about £5 to import . . . a lot of money then, but I was knocked out with it."

Other revelations were to be found at Violet May's, a second-hand/specialist record shop in Sheffield. The proprietor, a small bespectacled grandmother, catered for every musical taste imaginable and, realising there was a bit of interest, began to stock imported blues albums. However, her knowledge of the music was not as strong as her business acumen, as Joe discovered when he bought an album by the gigantic American bluesman, Howling Wolf. "It was a re-packaged album with just a picture of a girl on the front. Violet took my money, looked at the cover, and said 'Such a nice singer, Howling, isn't she!'"

Influences on record were steadily increasing but there were few opportunities in Sheffield to hear live rhythm and blues. Most groups were content to bash out the hit parade past and present, even though by 1962 rock and roll had given way to a diluted, sentimental form of pop music.

One of the very few exceptions was Dave Berry, then a leather-clad rocker who played around Sheffield with his group, The Cruisers. Berry didn't only take his name from his hero, Chuck—his first hit was a cover version of "Memphis Tennessee". Joe would later acknowledge the live inspiration that Berry, a few years older than himself, provided in the early years.

Dave Berry went on to considerable chart success in Britain and Europe and became particularly noted for his cobra-like stage act. He looks back on his own discovery of the blues: "I think we were all a bit disillusioned at the end of the 50s. We'd heard all these rockers and then the whole thing got really watered down with all the Jimmys and Johnnys and Billys. I personally was disillusioned and instead of moving on I started delving back to see where it all came from. I used to get up at half past five in the morning to listen to American Forces Network radio—they had a half hour blues show and I started listening to the black acts . . . Smiley Lewis—and thinking Ah, thats where Fats Domino came from is it? Big Boy Crudup—so that's where Elvis got that sound! Now the special thing that I've always felt about Joe is that we were both looking at the same sources for our influences. So instead of watering our stuff down we went back and started playing Sonny Terry and Brownie McGhee—as opposed to Adam Faith. And in a place like Sheffield, where everybody else was pop, it was that which took Joe and myself away from the pack."

Dave Berry and The Cruisers were one of the first groups to appear at the Esquire Club, when it opened in September 1962. Situated in a converted factory in a Sheffield backstreet, decorated by art students and furnished from junk shops, over the next few years the Esquire would be a stopping-off point for almost all touring blues acts—and British rock superstars in the making.

The club was run by Terry Thornton, a thirty year old draughtsman. He remembers clearly the night Joe approached him and asked him to book Vance Arnold and The Avengers. "He said he was a singer and I looked at him and I thought 'He's never a singer in this wide world'. He was such an unlikely character . . . we were used to rock and rollers being brash and full of confidence, but Joe was so shy . . . such a kindly lad. I hedged and finally I agreed that he could have a try-out for a fee of £5. He grew ten foot tall!"

Vance Arnold and The Avengers went down well and soon had a regular weekly spot at the Esquire, which was to become a local mecca for the growing contingent of rhythm and blues fans. There was no alcohol on the premises, so the customers were only there for the music—an ideal situation for Joe and the group, who could play blues numbers at the club that would have got them booed off elsewhere.

14

Trouble was virtually unknown at the Esquire. So when the club was raided by a large contingent of police one Monday in 1963 it came as a surprise to everyone present—especially to Vance Arnold and The Avengers who had just taken the stage and were halfway through their first number when a policeman climbed up to join them, took the mike off Joe and announced "This club is under police jurisdiction. Stay where you are." Three hours later, with all exits blocked and no one allowed even to go to the toilet, the police finally finished checking the membership and let everybody go home. "I think they had all been reading too many detective stories," said the proprietor, while Vance Arnold and The Avengers were left to ruminate on a performance which only involved half a song but got them a large mention in both local newspapers.

One visiting band to the Esquire that made a big impression on Joe was the Graham Bond Trio. Bond, previously a jazz altoist, turned to Hammond organ when he struck out on his own and his trio was completed by Jack Bruce and Ginger Baker. Graham Bond opened Joe's mind to the soul/jazz organ sound of Jimmy Smith and Jimmy McGriff and he immediately went to Violet May's and bought all the Blue Note albums by these artists that she could find.

A few weeks earlier, in February 1963, The Beatles made their first appearance in Sheffield at the Azena Ballroom. Joe went along, "I remember 'I Saw Her Standing There' and thinking how tight they sounded," he says. "It was like they'd been working at it for years."

But the biggest event of the period came in the summer of 1963 when Ray Charles made his first visit to Britain. The nearest show was about forty miles away in Manchester. Fellow enthusiast Bill Carr decided to make a day of it and took an early train. "I spent the day going round the record shops and I remember when we met up at the hall I'd got the 'Jimmy Reed at Carnegie Hall' album. Joe was a bit sick because he'd looked all over and couldn't get it." That apart, all concerned were totally knocked out by Ray Charles live.

* * *

In early 1963 Joe began to take his girlfriend, Eileen Webster, along to the group's bookings. Eileen, who was two years younger than Joe, lived with her family at Crookes and worked as a clerk for the National Coal Board. They first met around the time The Cavaliers were playing Wesley Hall Youth Club, where Eileen was a member, but they did not go out together for a couple of years. Eileen had a profound effect on Joe, as Pete Jackson recalls; "The only hang-up Joe had was Eileen Webster—he was always in love with her and she played him about a bit. It was a very on-off relationship because she had two boyfriends, Joe and another lad from Crookes, and she kept switching from one to the other. Every time she went with the other lad Joe went into a sorrowful mood for a considerable time—until she came back. Eileen affected him quite a lot."

This would be the state of things for a long time to come. Joe's friends and musicians from the early days recall frequent rows between Eileen and Joe, but all are agreed that he was very much in love with her. Some years after they finally parted for good Joe told an interviewer that he had only ever been in love with one girl—back in Sheffield when he was sixteen. Today he looks back and says, "I don't know, we grew up in that big rush . . . it was just that young, manic kind of relationship."

On the nights Eileen went along to gigs she travelled with Joe and the group in their hired van. Still handling the bookings, in the absence of a manager, Joe also dealt with the hire of van and driver—which took a large slice of the eight or ten pounds they were paid most nights. So when Bob Everson, the only member of the group who could drive, bought a battered Bedford Dormobile, the group now not only had their own transport, but they were also a little better off financially.

Meanwhile Vance Arnold and The Avengers continued to practise at Joe's house, Bob Everson even keeping his equipment in the garden shed between gigs. Madge would sometimes escape the noise by going dancing and Harold slipped off to his allotment on light nights, but when they were both in the house there was no complaint. On occasions Harold even bore the brunt of booking complications, like the time Joe booked the group into two different places on the same night. "This headmaster phoned up . . . the group had been booked to play at his school dance and they'd not turned up. He went on and on, wanting to know what I was going to do about it, threatening to sue and all sorts. I took it for so long, until I'd had enough, and then I told him 'It's not my group you know'."

It was around this time that a new drummer came onto the scene. Dave Memmott was an apprentice joiner who knew Joe from day release at Sheffield Technical College. At lunch times they went to the pub together, often as not never returning to the college. Memmott also played drums for The Falcons, a Crookes group with a singer whose mother would not let him go out more than two nights in succession. Occasionally, Joe was called upon to deputise, which he did if he was free, and Memmott was not slow to notice the difference in commitment. "I was getting fed up with The Falcons . . . going round to pick up the singer and his mother saying 'He can't come tonight' . . . so I pushed out Steve McKenna, who was a mate of mine, and took his place. I could see the potential with Joe so I muscled myself in." As he was a better drummer than his predecessor, Memmott's arrival met with full approval from the group.

Besides pubs, occasional dances and the Esquire, the group often played weekends at workingmen's clubs, where they were paid better money than the pubs. But workingmen's club audiences were more interested in beer, bingo and a bawdy comedian than a group who played obscure music which was totally unknown to them. Dave Memmott: "The times we played noon and nights—and got paid up at lunchtime—don't bother coming back to-night lads. They'd always be shouting out—'play something we know'."

Before too long Joe realised that the workingmen's clubs were a road to nowhere. Audiences wanted only music they were familiar with and even then preferred to talk and drink rather than listen. By contrast Vance Arnold and The Avengers had built up a loyal following in the Sheffield pubs and at the Esquire—fans who were serious about rhythm and blues which, by the autumn of 1963, was gaining a strong foothold in Britain. Before his own crowd Joe could sing what he wanted to sing—without making compromises.

*　　*　　*

While the Esquire was the main haven in Sheffield for rhythm and blues, two other clubs also catered for the teenage market. The Black Cat and Blue Moon were based in old church halls and run by Pete Stringfellow, a twenty one year old salesman, together with his nineteen year old brother, Geoff. It was the Stringfellows who had booked The Beatles in February 1963 and in the following months they had watched with great interest as the Merseybeat phenomenon mushroomed.

In October the Stringfellows showed the sort of initiative that was to take them from Sheffield church halls to the nightspots of London and Manhattan. They hired Sheffield City Hall, booked the top local groups and invited record company executives to witness first hand the city's talent. Among the ten acts were Vance Arnold and The Avengers—playing before three thousand fans in a hall ten times bigger than anywhere they had played before.

The following month the Stringfellows did it again—but this time they booked as bill toppers The Rolling Stones. The Stones were on the up-and-up. 'I Wanna Be Your Man', their second record, was out and their wild image was already attracting outraged reaction, helped considerably by the attention of the national press.

Joe Cocker has vivid memories of that evening back in November 1963. Pete Jackson picked him up at Tasker Road—by now he had changed the Ford for a Daimler sports car, which he had duly customised with flares all over the bodywork and eight carburettors sticking out of the bonnet. Pete drove down to the City Hall but, instead of stopping the car for Joe to get out, he kept going. Joe: "He drove round the City Hall not once, but about four times. I'm saying 'Pete, give over man.' There was a huge queue, everybody waiting to get in, and we were in the open top . . . he kept driving round and round again."

Backstage, Joe met up with the rest of the group and his girlfriend, Eileen, who made a beeline for The Rolling Stones, much to Joe's embarrassment. "She walked up to Mick Jagger and she said 'You're rubbish!' I said 'Leave him alone' but she said 'No, I'm gonna tell him, he's rubbish.' And I'm saying 'Let the man alone.' I always remember she said to him 'You're a big 'ead, you!'"

On a bill that also included Wayne Fontana and The Mindbenders, Joe and the group went on second. They did 'Hard Headed Woman', 'I'm A Man', 'You'd Better Move On' and 'Georgia On My Mind', during which Bob Everson remembers "You could have heard a pin drop." They left the stage to tremendous applause.

The local papers of the following day raved about the City Hall Show, the *Telegraph* describing it as . . . "One of the most entertaining and value for money shows ever seen in Sheffield." The Rolling Stones—"five raving beat boys from London who look like Neanderthal men"—received due acclaim, but it was Vance Arnold who took the honours. "He is surely a star of the future," said the *Telegraph*. "It is doubtful whether even Liverpool can offer a better singer in his class than Vance Arnold." The *Sheffield Star* was equally impressed—"For sheer showmanship and style Vance Arnold is undoubtedly top of the list. On this showing he must be one of the country's top rhythm and blues artists. Fantastic!"

Chapter Three

1964

Big Blues

ONE FREEZING MORNING in late 1963 Vance Arnold and The Avengers climbed aboard Bob Everson's old van and made a hazardous journey across the Pennine hills. Their destination was the Southern Sporting Club in Manchester and awaiting them was Dick Rowe, A & R man of Decca Records. For six months the group had eagerly anticipated this day, since making a tape of some of their numbers in Joe's front room. Joe sent the tape to Decca, who had already signed Sheffield's only other R and B singer, Dave Berry—by this time in the Top Twenty with his first single.

Atmosphere at the audition was as solemn as the club was cold. The group had to be fortified with tots of rum and pints of beer before their fingers could thaw out sufficiently to even tune their instruments. Dick Rowe introduced Mike Leander, a producer who he had brought along to take a look at the group, and Joe—like a fish out of water, without a crowd in front of him—shyly announced the first number, 'Sixteen Tons'. This was followed by a ballad, 'You'd Better Move On', a stomping 'Got My Mojo Working'—on which Joe turned purple—and, finally, his favourite 'Georgia On My Mind'. There was little reaction—Dick Rowe hinted that he might call the group to Decca studios for a recording test, then they packed up their instruments and went home.

A few weeks later Decca summoned Vance Arnold and The Avengers to London. This was a journey into the unknown for all of them, especially in that pre-motorway age. "It was like going to another country," says Joe.

19

"London was so far away in those days—and we never knew if the van was going to collapse. But we got there." Only just—they ran out of petrol in the centre of London and ended up having to push the van through the West End.

It was an uneasy recording début. Overawed and intimidated by the clinical surroundings, so different from the live atmosphere in which they were used to playing, none of the group was able to relax. Mike Leander tried to spur them on but his efforts served only to highlight the gap between local and studio musicianship. Dave Memmott: "He asked me to play something a certain way and I said 'Oh, I don't know whether I'll be able to do that.' He said 'Give me the sticks' and he sat at the kit and did it. We just weren't good enough. In those days we must have looked very raw."

In all, four tracks, including 'Georgia On My Mind' and 'Got My Mojo Working', were recorded. The group listened to a playback and then returned to Sheffield to await a decision as to whether or not they would be offered a recording contract.

When the news came it was good—but only for Joe. Decca wanted to record him as a solo artiste but they were not interested in the group. Joe signed to make a single, in the meantime working by day at the Gas Board and by night, with the group, on the usual round of local gigs.

Among the pubs and youth club dances there were a few plum jobs that winter. In late January '64 the Stringfellows promoted another sell-out show at the City Hall, with Vance Arnold and The Avengers alongside Wayne Fontana, Dave Berry and The Cruisers and The Hollies. Three weeks later Joe especially had a rare delight when he and the group supported Sonny Boy Williamson—one of the earliest bluesmen to tour Britain—at the Esquire Club. They also appeared at the Sheffield 'Top Stars Ball', an event organised by the local newspaper, whose teenage monthly 'Top Stars Special' had begun to give Joe a little coverage after the City Hall shows.

Interviewed after the Top Stars Ball, Joe revealed that plans to release 'Got My Mojo Working' as his first single had been dropped due to several other British artistes bringing out records of the same song. He told the paper that he had recently been to London to record eight more songs and that he was very anxious to find a new name for the group. "Vance Arnold and The Avengers has too much of a tinge of the Presley rock era to go down well these days," he said, inviting readers' suggestions for "something really original".

The early months of 1964 saw the departure of Phil Crookes from The Avengers. For a while he had felt that the group was becoming too bluesy, while his own interests were moving more and more towards the country music of Hank Williams, George Jones and Grandpa Jones, the banjo-playing hillbilly whose 'Make The Rafters Ring' album Phil tried to get Joe to listen to. "He couldn't get into that at all! I wanted the group to be lighter but Joe was getting stronger and stronger into the blues. He had this commitment—I think he's followed it all the way down the line. I don't think he's ever really strayed from it."

* * *

Still only nineteen years old, with a large following of local fans and a contract to make a record, Joe's future looked even brighter when, in April 1964, he was offered a management contract with Martin Yale and Terry Thornton. Yale, a Cleethorpes businessman with an interest in dance halls, was generally credited as the man who discovered Dave Berry, while Thornton, a fan of Joe's for over a year, owned the Esquire Club.

The legal agreement between "Vance Arnold"—there was no mention of Joe's real name—and his managers was impressive for an apprentice gas-fitter who had never earned more than a few pounds a night. It appointed Messrs Yale and Thornton as his managers and personal representatives in business itemised as:

a) Vaudeville and Circus
b) Motion pictures
c) Legitimate theatre
d) Radio and television broadcasting
e) Concerts, private parties and cabarets
f) Phonograph recordings throughout the world for a period of five years.

If Joe earned more than £25 per week he was to pay 12% commission, if he earned less then he was to pay 10%. There were the usual clauses about each party doing their best and a schedule for a parent to sign, as Joe was still under-age in the eyes of the law.

The contract was instigated by Martin Yale, Terry Thornton's name being added at Joe's insistence when he learned that there had been disagreement between Yale and his earlier protégé, Dave Berry. But the Esquire owner was reluctant to become involved in management, feeling that the commission rate was too high and that he could not do Joe justice as well as run the club, so Yale took up sole representation.

In June Joe went along once again to Decca's West Hampstead studios, where he recorded what was expected to be his first single—'Georgia On My Mind'. Hoagy Carmichael's great composition was given the full Ray Charles treatment by Joe, with a strings arrangement and a 22 piece orchestra. The recording has never been released. Dick Rowe—the man who had earlier turned down The Beatles—was head of the A & R panel and he thought it had no commercial potential.

Another session was booked for the following month, with Mike Leander producing.

On July 28, 1964, in a three hour session Joe recorded 'I'll Cry Instead', a Lennon/McCartney song from *A Hard Day's Night*, with Big Jim Sullivan and Jimmy Page on guitars, and The Ivy League providing backing vocals. A 16-piece band was brought in for what was to be the B-side of the record—'Precious Words', a song first recorded in America by The Wallace Brothers.

Accompanied at the session by Martin Yale and a publicity man, Joe was in good form, announcing that Vance Arnold was in the past and "from now on I'm Joe Cocker again." Asked by a reporter, who had travelled down from Sheffield, what he would do if he made a lot of money, he said, "The money side of this business doesn't worry me—I don't view this business in a commercial light. What I really want is to be a respected singer. Music is all I care about." As long as he had enough to buy a few pints of beer and could keep adding to his already extensive record collection—Joe was happy.

Then and now, in Joe Cocker's life, materialism has always been secondary to music.

* * *

For some time life had been hectic. Singing six nights a week with the group and gas-fitting during the daytime meant Joe had to dash home from work, quickly eat his tea, race off to the gig and on most nights not get to bed until the early hours. "The problem was getting him up the next morning," says his father. "He'd be leaving the house at the time he should have been arriving at work." In mid-August, with the release of 'I'll Cry Instead' only two weeks away, Joe decided that the time had come to hand in his tools and concentrate on full-time singing.

The Gas Board were most understanding. Rather than terminate his employment for good they gave him six months' leave, with the offer of his job back if things did not work out. At home Madge was happy enough to let her youngest son decide his own future, but Harold was not so sure. "His mother used to think 'Let him do what he wants', but I had stronger views than she had. I didn't like it at all—I told him to stop and get his final City and Guilds so that he'd have something to come back to. But he handed in his notice."

A significant factor in Joe's decision was the offer of a spot on a package tour due to begin shortly after his record was released. Manfred Mann, The Merseybeats and Little Eva were on the bill, which, it was announced, would tour Britain for seven weeks. Joe had been singing in pubs and clubs for over four years but in all that time he had rarely strayed far from Sheffield. Now, with a record due out and a tour lined up it looked as if he was finally knocking on the door of national recognition.

*   *   *

Despite the pop style of his forthcoming record, Joe was, by mid 1964, totally immersed in the blues. In his own words he "got very purist minded about it", dropping all the Chuck Berry numbers and performing material strictly by the likes of Muddy Waters, Jimmy Reed and, of course, Ray Charles. His own harmonica, which he had introduced on stage only a few months before, added a new dimension to the group's sound, but what he needed was musicians around him whose feel for the blues was something akin to his own.

Dave Hopper, Phil Crookes' replacement on lead guitar, fitted in perfectly. A musician whose proficiency extended to doing party-piece impressions of other guitarists—both the famous ones and his local contemporaries—Hopper was heavily into Buddy Guy and the Chicago blues. Dave Memmott was okay—he provided the solid beat that Joe liked to hear behind him, but for Bob Everson and Graham Bower, both of whose musical commitment was not so definite, it was the end of the road.

The last survivor of the original Cavaliers and a friend of Joe's from the age of eight, Bob Everson's exit from the group was harsh, if effective. "I went round Joe's house and Madge said he's down at the Esquire rehearsing. I couldn't understand that so I went to the Esquire. The door was locked and I couldn't get in but I could hear them playing. I was devastated." There had been no inkling of what was to happen and nothing was said, before or afterwards. Looking back Bob Everson says, "I was bitter when he sacked me but I realised later that what he was doing was way beyond me. I always admired Joe for sticking to his guns. Those years with him were the highlight of my life."

Dave Green came in on bass guitar. He had played in various Sheffield groups and had been looking for a job with Joe for a while. Completing the new line-up—to be known as Joe Cocker's Big Blues—was Vernon Nash, an eighteen year old pianist who Joe discovered one night in the pub next door to the Esquire club. "I was playing boogie woogie and blues and Joe just walked in and said 'You're hired'. I said 'Look, I haven't played with any bands—I'm straight out of the front room' but he gave me a job on the spot." Vernon was about to embark on a music teacher's course at Huddersfield. He had a grant, lodgings were arranged and he was due to leave anyday. He never made it. "I went straight out of the front room to play with the best band in Sheffield."

*   *   *

23

'I'll Cry Instead' was released on September 4, 1964. It got a few radio plays on the BBC, Radio Caroline gave it a spin and Jimmy Savile, on Radio Luxembourg, went so far as to describe it as "a really great disc", adding, "Joe Cocker is a name you'll be hearing again and again."

Press releases for the record gave as much publicity to Joe's gas fitting abilities as to his singing, Decca declaring "Joe looks certain to become a big star on the pop scene but should anything go wrong, it would seem that Joe is as good a gas-fitter as he is a singer." Martin Yale issued a handbill headed "IT'S A BIG GAS MAN", prophesying that the singer "is either going to become BIG JOE COCKER or JOE COCKER THE GREAT or go back to fitting Yorkshire gas cookers." Joe was described as having "shaggy brown hair and a face like the back of a Sheffield Corporation bus"—not the subtlest exercise in image-making from a manager who was to insist that Joe cut off the shoulder-length hair he had been growing for months and also arrange for him to be manicured!

'I'll Cry Instead' flopped. A typical beat number of the era it was quite unrepresentative of Joe Cocker's style and offered only the merest hint of his vocal talent. Joe, who in the future would interpret other Lennon/McCartney compositions with great distinction, never wanted to record it in the first place. As he would later say, "It was anything to get a break in those days."

* * *

While Joe had no high hopes for his début record, he was very optimistic about the Manfred Mann tour and the exposure it would bring for Big Blues. With a contract from the promoters, he and the band were promised £30 a week each. Pre-publicity for the tour claimed that the show would be very different from the usual run of pop packages—'Special care has been taken with the set design and choreography.' In the event it was a disaster.

Manfred Mann never even made the opening night. A dispute between agents ensured that. No one ever heard why Little Eva—of 'Locomotion' fame—failed to materialize. The Merseybeats, a moderately successful Liverpool group, were left to top the bill, which was filled with a selection of unknown Northern groups, with Joe Cocker's Big Blues way down at the bottom.

The tour opened on September 13 at Sunderland Empire, before a small audience who slow hand-clapped Joe as he sang 'Georgia On My Mind'. Dick Rowe, had he been present, would perhaps have nodded, knowingly, especially as Joe refused to sing 'I'll Cry Instead' on live gigs. It moved to Hull, Newcastle and Edinburgh, where at the Usher Hall the compère urged the handful of people present to move forward to the front row. The next night in Watford was a similar story. "And then we got the news that the tour was over," says Vernon Nash. Stranded, with hardly any money, the band members struggled back to Sheffield as best they could, leaving their equipment to be collected later. They saw none of their promised wages. Five days on the road had turned a dream into a nightmare.

However, Joe Cocker's Big Blues were not the sort of band to let a simple fiasco get them down. At the Esquire, where they had made their début before setting out on tour, the band was tremendously popular and pub gigs soon came in to fill up the lost dates. Martin Yale began to book the band further afield, as rhythm and blues clubs were springing up all over. It was the age of "Put out the lights, hang a skeleton on the wall and you'd got an R & B club," recalls Vernon Nash. Martin Yale's connections were mainly in small Lincolnshire outposts like Cleethorpes, Grimsby and Louth Town Hall where, besides having to carry their equipment up to the fifth floor, all who played there faced constant danger from country hicks who liked to listen to city groups, but liked even more to beat them up with big sticks afterwards.

A more civilised audience could be found at the Twisted Wheel in Manchester, a club run on similar lines to the Esquire. Here, on an all-nighter, Joe recalls. . . . "A classic night. I had a real hoarse throat but it was the best gig the band ever did." Wherever they went, to Cleethorpes, Chester or even as far as Carlisle, they always drove back the same night. Dave Memmott had taken over van duties from Bob Everson some time before the end of Vance Arnold and The Avengers and, no matter how great the distance, nor how much beer had been consumed, Joe always liked to get back home as soon as possible. "I was such a homebody in those days—I couldn't take staying away from home for one night."

A month after the ill-fated tour, Martin Yale somehow wheedled Joe Cocker's Big Blues on to an ITV variety show, *Stars And Garters*, which was set in a studio decked out as a pub. It called for four days' rehearsal in London, which the band greatly enjoyed, living in digs, having a run-through their song once in the morning and once again in the afternoon, and spending the rest of the time in the pub. The only problem was Vernon Nash's electric piano. His father had greatly disapproved of him giving up his studies to join Joe and would have been horrified to find his son had committed himself to buying an electric piano on hire purchase. Going on television would mean he would see it—so Vernon arranged for four large female extras to dance in front of the piano, and his father was none the wiser.

Stars And Garters must rate as one of the more incongruous performances Joe Cocker has made in his long career. On a show featuring crooners, monologuists and a camp host who announced he would like to stuff his settee with Joe's flowing locks, Joe sang 'Shame, Shame, Shame' by the Chicago bluesman Jimmy Reed, while the Big Blues mimed to a backing track. Any excitement about being on television quickly disappeared when they learned there was no payment—Martin Yale claimed the entire fee as settlement for unpaid commission.

* * *

With his Big Blues Joe had achieved a long-held ambition to have a band committed to playing uncompromising blues. Elsewhere in Britain there were other bands playing similar, if not so direct material—The Animals, Yardbirds, Manfred Mann, Them and, of course, The Rolling Stones, who had failed to impress Joe at Sheffield City Hall because "their version of the blues wasn't ours." Having made it, some of these bands were moving away from their R & B roots, a point Joe had in mind when he talked to *Top Stars Special* in late 1964. "We know we are coming in on what might be the end of the r & b craze, but that doesn't worry us. Our stage act is secure for a long time. I feel sure of that, especially with the electric piano, played by Vernon Nash. It's a great new sound." In the same interview he re-iterated his motivation. "We don't particularly want to be big. We want a group to be proud of with a sound we can work on."

Without a doubt Joe Cocker's Big Blues was already a group of which he could be proud, a fact proved by their popularity in the pubs within a twenty mile radius of Sheffield. Dave Memmott: "Everywhere we went the place would be packed—and with the same faces. At that time—'64 to '65 Joe couldn't put a foot wrong. The crowd might have been waiting since seven o'clock and we might turn up at ten—but they knew him you see. It was a very easy, laid-back situation. Everybody else tried to please the audience—Joe never did that. Whenever we performed he always did what he wanted—not the audience. A typical night—other groups did the last session with rockers, belting it out—he never would. They'd be shouting out but he'd say 'No, later'. The last number on most nights he'd do a song from John Lee Hooker."

Dedicated as he was, Joe's attitude to the blues was never solemn and he was not averse to adapting songs to make them more relevant to the audience. "He was quite witty and explicit," recalls Bill Carr, who rarely missed a Big Blues gig, "especially on the twelve bars. He used to hear the basic song then make up his own words, perhaps keeping the chorus—whereas other performers would do numbers verbatim."

The result was a large following of discerning fans—but little financial reward. With a manager who was based eighty miles away in Cleethorpes, Joe still looked after the business of collecting money from gigs and paying the band's wages. It was a straight five-way split, after Dave Memmott's petrol money was taken out. According to bass player Dave Green, who kept a record of such matters in a small cashbook, "The most we ever got was £18.10 shillings a week each. Joe held the money through the week and on Friday we used to go up to his house, have fish and chips and get it organised. Then we went to the pub."

Pubs featured prominently in the life of Joe Cocker's Big Blues. All keen drinkers, when they were not playing together they were usually drinking together—and lunch times on Saturdays they never missed the Stone House.

To the Sheffield music scene the Stone House was not just a pub—it was an unofficial labour exchange. Here a group whose drummer had left them in the lurch could find another merely by standing up and enquiring if anyone fancied the gig. "Guitarist wanted tonight" someone else might announce. "Who wants to go to Aberdeen for two and a half quid?" All the local bands would be there on Saturday lunchtimes, each at their own table.

Joe and his Big Blues sank a lot of pints in the Stone House. "We'd arrive at opening time, 11–30," says Vernon Nash, "and by the time 3pm closing time came round we'd have had five or six pints each, maybe more. Then we'd set off for Cleethorpes or wherever we were playing that night . . . have a 'slurp' (a transport café fry-up) and have another four or five pints before we set the gear up. Once we'd done that we'd have another two or three and then we'd have a drink on stage. A lot of people thought we were unprofessional but it was nothing to do with show business really, we were just playing for ourselves. The instigator was Joe. You can't think of Joe Cocker in the early days without thinking about large amounts of booze."

Terry Thornton winces at the memory. His Esquire Club had no bar so Joe and the band made sure they were suitably fuelled-up before they arrived. "We'd have booked him for eight o'clock—no chance. Nine o'clock I'd look at my watch—not a sign. Everybody would be asking 'Is he coming? Are you sure?' Then about ten there'd be a right racket downstairs—they'd arrived. I can see it now. Eileen would be there—she was always with him, they were like one—she'd be helping him up the stairs—pushing him up. He'd be reeling about the club—the band as well—they'd be hardly able to stand. I'd say 'Joe—why are you doing this to me?' But you couldn't take exception—he was such a nice bloke."

*   *   *

For Joe, 1964 had been an eventful year. There had been so much hope—a record, a nationwide tour and a television appearance, none of which turned out to be real opportunities. There had been talk of Joe recording a second single—a cover of Chuck Jackson's 'I'll Keep Forgetting' was proposed—but it did not materialize and his contract with Decca lapsed. Philosophical about such matters, he knew that at least he was appreciated on his home ground. Joe Cocker's Big Blues ended the year by playing a long Boxing Night session at the Esquire. Dave Berry and The Cruisers were there, and many fans and friends. Joe went down a storm—and at six o'clock the following morning the Esquire was still full to capacity.

Chapter Four

1965 – 1966

Le Petit Ray Charles

THERE WAS ALWAYS a lull in work after the Christmas season and New Year 1965 looked as if it would be worse than previous years. Since turning professional five months earlier Joe and the band had struggled to make ends meet on gigs that paid as little as £8 and never more than £20 a night—between five of them. Times were hard but a lifestyle that involved not having to get up in the mornings, together with the great camaraderie that existed within the band, meant there were few complaints.

Dave Hopper recalls the banter in the van on the way to gigs, and in particular Joe's impressions of comedian Peter Sellers, whose album he learned by heart. "Cocker was very good at mimicry. He could do all the funny voices and he knew all the material. It was a non-stop laugh all the way there and back, no matter how far away the gig was."

But one night in January the laughter stopped. It was a snowy Friday and they had played a Martin Yale gig at Louth. As they drove back home along slippery country roads Joe dropped a bombshell. "He suddenly said 'I'm sorry lads but I'll have to disband the band'," recalls Vernon Nash. "We were stunned. He said 'I've got no more gigs.'" They returned to Sheffield in dismay.

That weekend was a bad one for Joe Cocker's Big Blues. From being proud members of the best band in Sheffield they were faced with the prospect of a mundane future in conventional employment. And then, late on Monday night, just as morale was at its lowest, Joe received a telephone call from Terry Thornton.

The Esquire man, concerned at the band's plight, had been on the phone all day trying to muster up work to keep them in business. Through one of his many contacts he had heard of a band needed to play American Air bases in France. There was six weeks work—but they had to leave the following day.

Joe lost no time. He telephoned Dave Memmott and Dave Green immediately but the first Vernon Nash and Dave Hopper knew about it was the following morning when they were hauled from their beds. "Joe said if anybody wants to pull out, no hard feelings," said Dave Hopper. "We all went."

With all necessary arrangements completed within a couple of hours, including the obtaining of passports, Joe Cocker's Big Blues set off for France in Dave Memmott's Thames van. They arrived at Dover in the evening with just enough money, loaned by Terry Thornton, to pay for the ferry and petrol to get them to Orleans, their destination. They discovered the next ferry was not due to leave until the following morning so they had to spend the night in the van, parked in a football field. It was January and cold—but they were so excited they hardly noticed.

*   *   *

When the band arrived at Calais the following day an unforeseen setback lay in store—French Customs demanded a surety of £450 before they would let them in the country. At that time group equipment was scarce and expensive in France and some British groups had been taking two sets over, selling one at a profit before they returned home. Disregarding all pleas and protests the Customs officers were adamant—no surety, no entry.

There was only one route to take—back to England. Scraping together all their remaining money they returned on the next ferry. They had only been out of the country a matter of hours. Joe made a late-night call to Terry Thornton—the first of many over the next few weeks—and he agreed to wire the necessary money, on condition that a member of the band slept in the van to guard the equipment every night.

However, the following morning, having spent a second night in the van on the same football field, they decided to adopt a different tactic. This time they travelled by ferry to Ostend, in Belgium, where the customs condition did not apply. They were allowed in and drove straight through Belgium, but on the French border a new problem arose when a customs officer decided that a linear amplifier looked like a radio transmitter. Bribery, in the form of a packet of cigarettes, removed this obstacle and they were allowed on their way.

They eventually arrived at Orleans, without any money and knowing only the name of the agent who had booked them, Ted Easton. They found the air base and went to see the Entertainments officer at the Enlisted Mens Club. Joe: "He said, 'Do you do Beatles songs?' We said 'No'. He said 'They'll murder you'. We got up the first night, I went into the harmonica intro for 'You Got Me Running', the old Jimmy Reed number, and they all stood up – went crazy. I thought 'Oh no—this is death'. But they loved us!"

The American airmen, tired of hearing groups who all played the same material, found Joe Cocker's Big Blues a refreshing improvement. The band were bought drinks, tasted their first real American hamburgers- and then realized that they had no accommodation. Once again they slept the night in the van.

*   *   *

At first the audiences who filled the club each evening were mostly white, but word soon spread among the black airmen and they began to arrive in large numbers. Joe: "It was scary because at that time there was still segregation and whoever walked in the room first decided which colour was going to sit on that side of the room that night. So, if he was white a black person would walk in and sit on the opposite side. And we saw terrible fights with prostitutes. They'd never cross territory—if they were designated for blacks, that was their game. They'd go in the toilets and beat the shit out of each other. I once tried to run in there after them and the M.P.s came and grabbed me and said 'Keep outa this'. I said 'It sounds like somebody's dying in there'. . . . 'It's none of your business' This girl . . . they stripped her . . . humiliated her."

There were revelations, too, of a different kind. "I never straightened up so much in my life. A guy introduced me to Bourbon and I said 'Where we come from we get Scotch whisky—two of them would put you on your ass.' And this guy said 'Well try this'. I had a tumbler full and I put it away and they all looked at me—totally flabbergasted—saying 'God man . . . you can. . . .' Next minute I was out. Boom! No show tonight!"

Without accommodation, and with no money to pay for any, Joe and the band continued to sleep in the van. It was cramped and freezing cold but at least the equipment was safe. In the mornings they all went to the public baths in Orleans, paid a franc each and stood under the hot shower for an hour, warming themselves after the cold night in the van. There was no word from the agent, Ted Easton; everyday they tried to telephone him for an advance of wages. "He was untraceable" says Vernon Nash. "He lived in Chateauroux, about a hundred kilometres to the south, and he only came out to see us once—with his bodyguard, a big black guy. We were supposed to get fifty dollars a week (about £20 at that time). We thought it was a lot of money until we found out how we were living."

Once, Joe did manage to make contact with the elusive Easton. "Everyone was saying 'Joe, we're starving'. We had no money at all. So I called this guy and he came up with a great promoter's excuse. 'Ah! My wife, she has just had a baby. I'm so in love. I'm so excited . . . I will call you back later'."

Desperate telephone calls were made to Terry Thornton back in Sheffield – reversing the charges. "I got phone calls nightly. I thought 'Oh dear, old Joe, he's not a trouper'. You see he wasn't used to being away from home. He'd ring—'I'm coming home'—'No. Stick it out' 'Will you send some money?' I kept sending money over and they still kept ringing up. It cost me a fortune in telephone calls!"

* * *

After a couple of weeks the band were told they were moving on to another, much bigger camp—Forest Base. "We went to the Enlisted Men's Club and walked into the concert room," says Vernon Nash. "And this guy called Sergeant Devore came out. I'll never forget him. He said 'What are you guys doing here?'

'We're the group.'

'Whaddya mean? A group of what . . . you shits?'

'We're the group . . . The musicians . . . The band.'

'Okay. You're the band. Yeah . . . Okay. So where's the moose?'

'Moose?'

'Come on . . . where's the pig?'

'Pardon? What do you mean . . . the pig?'

Anyway he reeled off about eight American words and when he got to 'broad' we realized he was talking about a girl.

'Ah! No. . . . we've got a male singer.'

'Well you can't play on this club without a girl singer.'

'But we've come all the way from England.'

'This is nice . . . but you're not playing here and you won't play anywhere else without a girl singer—because the boys won't come up.'"

Joe Cocker's Big Blues retreated to the nearest bar, where they decided to despatch a telegram to Terry Thornton. 'SEND GIRL SINGER. URGENT.' Then they waited for the reply. 'GIRL SINGER ON WAY—START PLAYING'. They went back to Forest Base, showed the English telegram to Sergeant Devore and did their usual spot that night. The following day, says Vernon Nash, "this incredible Marilyn Monroe type . . . big bosomed, dyed peroxide blonde woman comes walking in. And in a broad Sheffield accent she said ''ELLO LUV—where's Joe Cocker?'"

The girl was Marie Woodhouse, daughter of a Sheffield publican. She had sung in a few workingmen's clubs under the name Billy Rae. "She was a right laugh, but she wouldn't rehearse or anything like that. She had a couple of numbers . . . 'Blueberry Hill' . . . but the repartee between her and Joe . . . if that could have been recorded. She was a total comedienne—and the Americans loved her. She later married a sax player who she met out there . . . he was the guy who gave Joe his first joint."

* * *

Once they had a girl singer the band began to play a circuit of American bases around Orleans, moving on to a new one each week. They played an hour on stage, fifteen minutes off, from 7pm to 1am every night. The black servicemen followed Joe from base to base, amazed that a white man could sing like he did. A favourite number was a slow, jerky blues—James Brown's 'I Don't Mind'. One night it lasted twenty-five minutes. The long sets were filled in with instrumentals—featuring Dave Hopper's guitar, Chuck Berry rockers which Joe had seen fit to revive, and numerous Ray Charles songs. In the early evening they played a few Carl Perkins type numbers—'Matchbox' was one—to appease the white servicemen who mostly preferred country and western to the blues. Later Joe would get into the Bo Diddley type raps and improvised twelve bars—changing the words, just as he did back home in the pubs.

Some nights American servicemen got up to perform, in between the band's spots. Dave Hopper: "Joe once fetched us from the bar—'come in here, quick' . . . and there's three black guys standing there. They started singing and it was like a choir." Other servicemen got up to jam with the band. "That was great" says Dave Hopper. "There was a guy that sounded like Sam Cooke – and a fellow called Billy Baldwin—sounded just like Jerry Lee Lewis. Another fellow . . . Jimmy somebody . . . said he'd been in Frankie Lymon's Teenagers. He used to get up with us. I often wonder what they're doing now."

* * *

All this time the band were still sleeping in the van, living on a hamburger a day but managing to scrape and scrounge enough to buy cheap white wine most days. Joe: "I lost about fifteen pounds—I came home and my girlfriend was so impressed—'Joe—I've never seen you so thin!'" Dave Green, always thrifty according to the others, managed to survive on a packet of peanuts a day, although they recall him drinking twice as much as everyone else!

33

Unexpectedly, their accommodation difficulties were solved. One night between sets a Hungarian, known only as Monsieur Jacques, came up and made an offer—if the band played at his night club after they had finished their gig on the base, he would provide them with accommodation and as much free drink as they required. The deal was struck immediately and so every night after playing for six hours on an American base Joe and the band loaded up their equipment and went to the night club, where they played until around 5am.

Monsieur Jacques lived with a woman called Madame Suzie and their club was situated in an old dilapidated building in Orleans. When they had finished their night's work the band climbed to the top storey, to an old servants' quarters, where they slept. The roof leaked and the toilet smelled so bad the band used the garden instead, but it was better than a Ford Thames van. And as for the other half of the deal . . . Vernon Nash: "Can you imagine offering us free drink. As much as we could drink? One night we'd been on the base and it was someone's birthday. We'd got a bottle of Tequila from somewhere and we'd been drinking wine all day. The club was quite full—half U.S. servicemen, half French gold diggers—and we were doing 'Makin' Whoopee'. Well, we started . . . Joe came in 'Another bride, another June, another sunny honeymoon . . . Another season, another reason for makin''—and he spewed up all over the mike and collapsed—bang on the word 'whoopee'. So we've got no singer . . . but we nod to each other and say 'let's make it into an instrumental.' I do a piano solo and while I'm doing that Hopper collapses—he didn't drink as much as us, but we'd all been at it that night. So we're a trio—and then Dave Green faints. The number finished with just piano and drums."

The original six weeks engagement was extended to two months, so successful were Joe and the band. Among the black servicemen Joe had a following similar to that back in Sheffield—they travelled from base to base to hear him, even to Monsieur Jacques' night club. The French called him 'Le Petit Ray Charles', 'Joey Charles' or 'Joey Cockère'. The whole band look back on the trip as a great experience, despite the lack of money, the hassles and the cold.

The anxiety about getting paid lasted right until the final moments. With the van loaded and having bid their goodbyes, the band had an appointment to collect the money from Ted Easton. He was late, and with the ferry to catch they were rapidly losing what hope remained of getting their money, but at the very last moment, he arrived, and they were paid.

* * *

For a self-confessed "homebody" the two months in France widened Joe's horizons in a way he could never have previously imagined. It had not been an easy time by any means, but on stage—where it mattered—he had gained the great respect of people who knew all about the blues—black Americans. The reception they gave him from the first night in Orleans was a great boost to a young man who was still unconvinced within himself that he could be, as he puts it, "star category". Evenings spent drinking with the servicemen, between sets, and afternoons sitting in barracks discussing soul music and listening to records contributed immeasurably to Joe's musical outlook, as did the drafted musicians who jammed with the band on many nights. Looking back more than two decades later Joe says, "It was an incredible life experience. It didn't teach me to fly but it taught me to flutter. It was like a mini intro to America."

*　*　*

Back home in Sheffield the gig situation was worse than it had been before they left. Joe was lucky to get one gig a week. A cut-throat price war for bookings was in existence with fewer venues and more part-time groups willing to play for fees that did not even cover expenses. Reputation and quality counted for nothing and Joe Cocker's Big Blues, refusing to cut their already minimal fee, found themselves sidelined.

Dave Green was the first to throw in the towel. "We had a few cross words, Joe and I. We were coming back from a gig and he hadn't got any more work, so I said 'Well, I can't carry on like this—I'll have to blow'. And Joe said 'Well if that's your attitude I don't need you. And I don't need anybody – I'll make it on my own'."

Prophetic words, spoken in the heat of the moment but at the time Joe was not nearly so confident. "I remember talking one night", says Dave Hopper, "and Joe saying 'I've got no chance of making it'. I asked him why and he said 'Because I'm too fat'. He was very conscious of that image thing."

A new bass player, John Fleet, came in. "We did a few pubs, the odd Esquire gig and I remember dying in a dance hall in Hull. His voice was superb but he didn't look like a rock star. I don't think anybody at that particular time thought he'd got a cat-in-hell's chance of making it big."

The situation went from bad to worse. There was hardly enough work to keep a part-time band together, let alone one whose members had no other income. Martin Yale drifted out of the picture but the final straw came when Dave Memmott, unable to keep up the hire purchase payments on his van, was forced to sell it. At that point everything collapsed.

*　*　*

Early in 1966 Joe decided to go down to London. "I had a couple of friends who'd been to Sheffield University and they said I could stay at their flat in Golders Green. I went to scout out, to see if I could maybe get a gig with a band. I went along to Klook's Kleek and Zoot Money and his Big Roll Band were on but again . . . this is where my shyness or whatever let me down. I knew I could sing as good as those other cats I'd seen . . . but something stopped me from walking up and approaching them and having a go at it."

Unable to make contacts, Joe returned home after only a week. "I went into the Stone House and it was like 'How'd you go on?' I just felt so embarrassed that I made up this story that I'd got up and sang with Zoot Money, and everyone was so impressed. It's something I've lived to regret to this day. I think they all knew I'd lied but they felt sorry for me."

With no gigs and no day job Joe passed the time as best he could. Back at Tasker Road he painted the outside of the house, and the house next door. Although his six months' leave from the Gas Board had long passed, he could have applied to be re-employed. He chose not to. "There was a bit of pride in not going back . . . I think they would have given me a job even though I never passed my final exams—there were two grades and I got the first one . . . But my mind was never really on the job—I was dead keen on making it as a singer."

Finally, after weeks without money, he took a job with W.H.Smith's, the wholesale newsagents, working in their Sheffield warehouse. He stayed for almost a year—a period which he has rarely mentioned in press interviews. "I just got known as the gas-fitter who turned rock and roll singer . . . It was hard work loading and unloading newspapers . . . and for the first three months you had to work nights. I could never get used to that – I carried on as normal—went out and had about nine pints before I went to work."

Nor could he get used to not getting up on stage every night. There had been so much hope—a record, a tour, a television appearance and the great acclaim he had enjoyed both in Sheffield and in France, but it had all come to nothing. Dispirited and disheartened that nobody recognized the style or sound he was trying to achieve, he was reduced to what he called the 'constant collar' of a dreary job that he hated. Vernon Nash, who had enrolled on a business studies course, kept in touch: "He used to complain how he hated the monotony. One thing that kept Joe going with music was the hatred of the sort of monotonous jobs that most people have to do. He was too intelligent, too hip to see that you have to do that for the rest of your life."

But musically, at the time, Joe Cocker looked down and out. Today, thinking back, he recalls how he refused to accept that fate. "I still felt that I could make a living, singing . . . I was so convinced that it had to be my life. A lot of hearts were broken down the road but I think the reason I by-passed a lot of the guys . . . they didn't have the conviction that I did."

Chapter Five

1967 — 1968

With A Little Help . . .

FOR A YEAR Joe never did a gig. He lived a conventional existence—working in the newspaper warehouse, drinking with his mates, and going out with his girlfriend, Eileen. He even took driving lessons—and passed the test first time. Occasionally he talked about putting another band together but he made no moves to do so. His conviction was intact—but his confidence had been badly shaken.

The first ray of hope for local fans came in autumn 1966. Dave Hopper: "Joe called me across in the Stone House one Saturday lunchtime. He said 'I've got this gig at the University tonight. I've got to do it because I promised'." Hopper needed no persuasion. Vernon Nash had already agreed to do it and a bass player and drummer were recruited on the spot in the usual Stone House way. "We all went along—no rehearsing, we just did it" says Dave Hopper. "And we wiped the floor with the other band that was on. Afterwards I was talking to Eileen and I said it'd be great to get back together. She said 'Ask him. I'm fed up of trying'."

Hopper did ask Joe but he was still unsure, despite the reception the band had enjoyed at the University. Eventually he gave his former Big Blues guitarist a call and they got together for a few rehearsals, along with Vernon Nash and Freddy Guite, the drummer who Joe had recruited in the Stone House. Needing only a bass player, Joe rang John Fleet. "He said 'I'm getting bored—do you fancy putting a band together and doing a few gigs?' It struck me as a nice idea but I was not long married and looking for a proper job, so in my wisdom I said 'No—can you find somebody else.' He did—he found Chris Stainton."

* * *

Chris Stainton, who Joe would later describe as "God—the best musician in the world", had been around the Sheffield music scene since his schooldays. For years he played with a local pop group known variously as The Cadillacs, Knives & Forks and Texans, co-writing their one-and-only single 'Being With You' which was released on Columbia in 1964, at the same time Joe was recording 'I'll Cry Instead' for Decca. In the intervening years his career had also hit the doldrums, but when he heard Joe might be looking for a bass player he got in touch. Christmas was approaching and there were gigs to be had. The contact could not have been better timed.

"We soon realised that Stainton was no ordinary person," says Vernon Nash. "His bass playing was immaculate and he'd got a kink for music and ideas for arrangements. Then we discovered he also played piano . . . and guitar . . . and drums . . . and anything else. I took a week's holiday and Chris got on my piano and played exactly, note for note, what I'd been playing—no rehearsal, he knew every note. Musically he was head and shoulders above anybody Joe had ever had in the band."

Stainton provided the spark that Joe needed to throw himself back into music, and The Grease Band was formed. Joe decided on the name after reading a magazine interview with Jimmy Smith, in which the soul/jazz organist described a player he knew as "having a lot of grease." Besides Stainton, there were other new faces in the line-up, which initially had only Vernon Nash from Big Blues. Frank Miles, formerly with Dave Berry, took over lead guitar from Dave Hopper, who had found a better paid gig with a local Elvis Presley imitator, but The Grease Band did not have a permanent drummer for some months. Various people helped out until Dave Memmott finally succumbed to Joe's pleas to join him in his comeback.

The Grease Band's early repertoire was subtly different from the strict R & B of Big Blues. "There was much more positive effort on material," says Bill Carr, who fervently supported the band in the same way he had Joe's earlier groups. "A lot of the material was not quite what you would have expected from Joe . . ." Soul had taken over from the blues and, for the first time since his early Vance Arnold days, Joe was making concessions to what audiences wanted to hear—opening with Four Tops' 'Same Old Song', closing the first spot with 'Can't Help Myself' and playing a stock of Tamla Motown numbers, although there were still a few from Ray Charles, and the odd blues.

It was not only in the material that concessions were made. The height of fashion—a flower-power shirt—was in order when Joe appeared at

Sheffield's Mojo Club in June 1967. The occasion was the live recording of a charity E.P. for Sheffield University Rag Week, with Joe and the band—billed as Joe Cocker's Blues Band—performing two numbers, and three other local bands one number each.

Joe's contribution opens with him introducing his first number 'I've Been Trying', adding "folks—believe me too." The old Impressions song is given a slow treatment with Frank Miles' guitar and Dave Memmott's drums to the fore, while the band also provide falsetto vocal backing. The second number, Leiber and Stoller's 'Saved' features Joe's adapted lyrics, including his popular line of the day "I used to smell and drink and tiddle down my sink," while the band rocks along.

Joe, described as 'Sheffield's veritable King of Soul' on the record, sounds powerful but does not display any real vocal quality on what was an enthusiastic but rough-and-ready session. Now a much sought-after item among Cocker fans, the E P failed to sell, despite being only half the usual price, and the organisers ended up giving copies away.

* * *

Joe's old following flocked back as The Grease Band began to establish themselves with regular weekly venues. One of the favourites was the Barrow Hill Hotel, near Chesterfield, an unusual place for rock bands to play since there was no direct electricity supply—it came via the local works and had to be converted in the pub to normal voltage. Although their amplifiers might develop a blue glow, and problems at the works meant the sound faded or even disappeared, Joe and The Grease Band played to capacity crowds every Wednesday at the Barrow Hill. Invariably they spent more than they earned from the gig drinking after hours with the landlord.

Most of The Grease Band's gigs were in pubs and their support soon reached the levels of earlier Big Blues days. Joe: "It was a good time period for me . . . it was great . . . got a little pissed, went and did half an hour—8 to 8.30 . . . had half an hour break . . . did 9 to 9.30, then 10 to 10.30 and goodnight. By that time they were just perfect . . . it was always my ideal conditions to sing in."

The occasional lunch-time gigs did not always run so smoothly. "We were doing the Shirecliffe Hotel . . . noon and night—and Chris didn't show up. So I had to pull out all the stops—I remember I did a thing then . . . I was singing like 'OH! Weell Laaaaaaawdy . . . that great Park Drive Machine up in the sky!' And I had everyone going nuts . . . 'Has he arrived yet?' No 'OH Laaaaaaaaawdy . . .' Just going nuts. Cause I was talking like going to heaven . . . and my idea of heaven was twenty Park Drive and two pints of beer—which everyone found hilarious. But I was furious . . . where is he?

Wheeeere is he? And then he showed up for the night session—he'd been to Cleethorpes for the day with his brothers!"

* * *

A preference for the seaside, rather than the Shirecliffe Hotel on a Sunday lunchtime, was just one of Chris Stainton's surprises. "There was something weird going on all the time with Chris. He was a very strange, eccentric fellow- what you might call laid back," says Vernon Nash. "When he first joined he was a TV repair man . . . drove around in an old Ford car. One day he was driving to the Barrow Hill Hotel and a wheel dropped off. He said 'We'll have to walk', got out of the car and he never mentioned it again. Just left it and that was that."

A natural musician, Stainton had a talent for arrangements and a perfect feel for both the blues and pop idioms. Joe carried on choosing the songs, just as he had always done, and Chris put in the extra detail. The band got better, but they were still playing pubs and it soon became clear that the only way forward was to play original material.

Vernon Nash: "They started smoking dope and composing together. Joe had certain ideas—he didn't know anything about chords so he used to sing it and Chris arranged it. Chris knew that he was onto something with Joe and that they could sell it. He was ambitious and without that pull from him Joe would never have made it."

The Grease Band's guitarist, Frank Miles, was also interested in song-writing. Together with a friend, Tom Rattigan, Miles was already in touch with a London music industry man, Len Black, who had loaned them a tape recorder on which they could put down their compositions. One of their numbers was an instrumental, with which Chris Stainton had assisted. Entitled 'March Of The Mysterons' it was intended as a puppet show tune, but when they played it to Joe he quickly came up with some lyrics and the result was 'Marjorine'. Other numbers were worked out and Joe began to tentatively test them out on stage.

One man who was greatly heartened by this development was David McPhie, a Chesterfield disc jockey and an acquaintance of Joe's since the Vance Arnold days. He had been concerned for a long time that no-one seemed to recognise the potential in Joe, who he felt was over-exposing himself for peanuts in local pubs: "People took him for granted. They didn't realize that he was completely unique." McPhie was impressed when he heard The Grease Band performing original material. "I thought it came across well, although he'd not much confidence in doing it. I kept pushing him—'What are you going to do?' 'When are you going to do something with it?' Nothing seemed to be happening and I eventually said 'Come over to our house and tape something and I'll take it down to London'."

In December 1967 Joe and Chris Stainton travelled to David McPhie's flat in Chesterfield, taking with them Frank Miles' and Tom Rattigan's borrowed tape recorder. Alone, they recorded 'Marjorine' and two other Cocker/Stainton compositions, 'Sandpaper Cadillac' and 'New Age of The Lily', Chris playing all the instruments. A few days later, McPhie rose before dawn and set off for London.

A far-sighted music fan who crusaded throughout the 60s to get good music across in the Chesterfield area, McPhie had earlier written an article about Joe and his music for a coal industry magazine. In it he had expressed the opinion that Joe had the ability to be much bigger in America than he was at home. Nobody took his words seriously—hardly surprising since Joe did not even have a record contract—but now, as he drove down to London, David McPhie was about to make his prophecy happen.

His target was Tony Hall, a radio D.J., who had a show on which he invited new bands to send in tapes of their music. There was also another reason for approaching him. "I'd admired him as a D.J. because he was responsible for breaking people like Otis Redding in this country. He was the only person who was regularly playing black music. So I got hold of his address and took the demo to his house. It was early morning. I gave him the tape and he was knocked out—he saw the potential in it straight away."

Tony Hall passed the tape on to music publisher David Platz, with whom he had a percentage agreement in respect of material sent to him via the radio show. Platz was in partnership with a young independent record producer in a company, Straight Ahead Productions. The producer was Denny Cordell, already responsible for hits by The Moody Blues, The Move, Georgie Fame and Procol Harum, for whom he had produced the classic 'Whiter Shade of Pale'. Cordell heard the Cocker/Stainton tape and was immediately impressed by 'Marjorine', but ironically more by the production than Joe's voice. "Whoever had produced the record had some great little ideas . . . that's what caught my attention—the structure rather than the singing, which was echoey and varied. Obviously the singing worked but I had no idea that this was a Great Voice. None at all."

Denny Cordell was sufficiently interested to summon Cocker and Stainton to his London office. Joe: "There we were . . . barrelling down Oxford Street—late for this very important meeting . . . Three o'clock and it was like three ten. I remember Chris had this outrageous suit on . . . it had fur cuffs! We charged into the office and it was all very official. I remember the girl, Janice, saying 'Mr Cordell will see you in ten minutes' and we just sat there, screwing our knuckles. Then Denny came out and he looked at Chris and said 'I expected you' and he turned to me and said 'But I didn't expect him!' To this day I've never understood what he meant."

Twenty years on Denny Cordell smiles at the memory of his first meeting with Joe Cocker and Chris Stainton. "I can quite see myself saying that. Chris sort of fitted in with the image of what was happening—his suit was made of curtain material or something you'd cover a sofa in. With tassles—the sort you'd see around the bottom of furniture—down the sleeves and round the cuffs. And it was pink! I mean, hippies were hippies and there was a lot of outrageous expression, sartorially. But this was obviously one made up on a shoestring budget. And he looked great! Just carried it off—outlandish clothes, longish hair, pencil thin—another soldier on the pop front.

"But Joe . . . He didn't look like any part of the pop scene at all. He was right chubby and he was wearing a donkey jacket . . . totally nondescript. Not someone who was making any effort at all to slot into the visuals of what was going down at the time. He could have been doing anything in life . . . a blacksmith's assistant . . . roadsweeper . . . anything. He just looked a real old scruff!"

After only a few minutes in each other's company it became clear to Denny Cordell that he was going to get on fine with this unlikely pair from Sheffield, so he agreed to travel up to see a Grease Band gig one Saturday soon afterwards. After visiting Tasker Road, where he met Harold and Madge and had tea, he went along to that evening's pub gig. "And when Joe started singing! I was with an old mate of mine, Simon Miller Mundy, who's a great music connoisseur . . . I remember we just sort of looked round at each other—mind blown! We thought we'd gone up to see a little pop band and we were seeing a really good blues band—with Joe singing."

Having seen Joe in action Cordell had no doubts that he wanted to record him, so the next stop was to get his business people interested, to secure a record deal. A gig was arranged at the Speakeasy in London, on an all-nighter, supporting Traffic. "It was a huge success," says Cordell, "but somewhere along the line I came to the conclusion, rightly or wrongly, that we couldn't record this band. So we went and recorded 'Marjorine' with Chris and session people."

For the remaining members of The Grease Band, Vernon Nash, Frank Miles and Dave Memmott, the writing was on the wall, although Memmott had already decided to leave because he felt the band were not getting anywhere. He told the others as he drove them back to Sheffield from the Speakeasy gig, which had left the band out of pocket as it was an audition rather than a paid gig.

Memmott stayed on for the next few weeks, a period when the atmosphere within the band became increasingly strained. Vernon Nash: "After 'Marjorine' was recorded we were excluded. It became a Joe/Chris sort of thing—they were writing and recording, we were playing the gigs. It wa like an incestuous relationship—they would go into huddles, or record and we wouldn't be told about it. It was never nasty, but towards the end it got rather sly and secretive. Joe was listening to everything that Chris said. He was right—Chris was sticking him in the right direction."

* * *

On March 22, 1968, 'Marjorine' was released on the Regal Zonophone label. Joe has always dismissed speculation that the song was written about, or for, his mother. "The fact that my mother's name is Marjorie was maybe self-conscious," he told a radio interviewer in 1982, "but it was never meant to be anything. It was originally an instrumental—I just came up with some words for it."

A quirky song about a girl he misses, the record opens with Joe's falsetto 'Marjorine, where have you been? Did you see the Queen?' before he comes down to his recognisable soul voice, with a male choir effect behind him. Centred on Stainton's piano, it features then-session man Jimmy Page's distinctive guitar and some tight drumming from Clem Cattini. Reviewing the single in *Disc & Music Echo* Penny Valentine wrote, "Some records are just definite hits. This is."

'Marjorine', with another Cocker/Stainton composition, 'New Age Of The Lily', as the B-side, sneaked into the British Top Fifty for just one week in May, reaching number 48 before dropping out again. Denny Cordell was disappointed: "I thought it was a hit. I still think it's a charming record to this day. I did hear a funny story about it at the time . . . saying that whoever was doing the promotion had got the hype too heavy and so the BBC dropped the record. Anyway that's as far as it got and it wasn't a hit."

By the time 'Marjorine' was released the band knew that their services would not be required for much longer. They were told about three weeks earlier at a discotheque gig in Sheffield. "We were at the Penny Farthing and Joe came late," says Vernon Nash. "We started without him, did the first spot instrumentally, and then he arrived and as he walked through the door he just said 'Sorry—it's off.' That was it. I played the rest of the outstanding bookings with him but I wouldn't play 'Marjorine'. I was more disappointed than anyone but in retrospect there were a hell of a lot of people who were a lot better than us. There's another aspect to it too—if you look and see how many other musicians he's sacked in subsequent years—we'd all have got the sack in the end."

For Frank Miles, the Grease Band guitarist, getting the sack was not to be the only reason for disappointment. He was credited on the record, along with Cocker, Stainton and his songwriting partner Tom Rattigan, as co-writer of 'Marjorine'. Interviewed in 1987 he said that neither he nor Rattigan have ever received any royalties, despite the song being included in numerous compilation albums. Leaving a group as fame and fortune loomed was not a new experience for Frank Miles—he had been one of The Cruisers who parted from Dave Berry, shortly after his first hit four years earlier. Looking back on his enforced departure from Joe, Miles says "I've no recriminations. I didn't want to move to London."

The original Grease Band played their last gig together at the Arbour-thorne Hotel in Sheffield on March 24, 1968, two days after the release of 'Marjorine'. The following day Joe told *Top Stars Special*—"It had been coming for three weeks and things were a bit tense. Finally last night we split up."

* * *

In April 1968 Joe, along with Chris Stainton, moved to London, intent on at last making their mark on the rock business. They took with them an eighteen year old keyboard player, Tommy Eyre, who Joe had been trying to persuade to join him for weeks. The son of a noted pub pianist, Tommy Eyre began playing in pubs and workingmen's clubs as an infant, sitting on his father's knee. By his early teens he was doing regular gigs with Sheffield groups and on leaving school he spent a year in Europe, playing American bases in a band that included Joe's earliest musical partner, Phil Crookes. His return to Sheffield coincided with the decision to make changes in The Grease Band and Joe, long impressed by his talents, invited him to join the new band he and Chris Stainton were about to form in London. Joe was too late—the young keyboard wizard had fallen straight into a job with The Candies, a group fronted by ex-Fortune Glen Dale. They had plenty of work and Tommy was earning up to £30 a week, most of which he was saving towards a deposit on his dream—a £700 Hammond organ.

In spite of Joe's efforts to lure him away, Tommy Eyre was reluctant to give up his lucrative gig with the Candies. "They'd come to the gigs . . . we're gonna go to London and make a fortune. I knew Joe—we'd go to London for a week and we'd be back up doing the Dog & Partridge for £4 each, so I took it with a pinch of salt and I kept turning him down. And then one day my old man came home with the *Daily Mirror* and he says 'Tom—look at this'. Don Short's column—and there's a big picture of Joe and how he's got this deal, big London producer and all that. So next time he called me it was 'Look Joe, I've been having second thoughts about this'."

Joe, Chris Stainton and Tommy Eyre moved into one room of a bed and breakfast hotel in Sussex Gardens. They began rehearsing in a converted cinema in Westbourne Grove, provided by Chris Blackwell of Island Music. Blackwell and Denny Cordell had proposed to merge their respective recording, management and agency interests into one company, but although this failed to materialize, Joe ended up represented by Island Management.

Still without a guitarist and drummer for his new band, Joe placed an advert in the *Melody Maker*. Over two hundred people replied and in one day he listened to forty-two drummers playing the same number before deciding on Welshman Tommy Reilly. Mickey Gee, like Reilly a former member of Tom Jones' backing group, got the guitarist's job. Both moved in to the hotel, so there were now five sharing one room, and rehearsals got well under way.

Joe had already recorded several songs which would later appear as B-sides of singles and tracks on his first album. These included 'Bye Bye Blackbird', 'Sandpaper Cadillac' and 'Something's Coming On', as well as 'Marjorine' and 'New Age Of The Lily'. Chris Stainton and various session men had played on these numbers, which the newcomers had to learn. Efforts then went into putting together a set to do live gigs. "We'd listen to albums and steal other people's songs," says Tommy Eyre. "We did 'Let's Get Stoned', Moby Grape's 'Can't Be So Bad' and all the songs that were on the album. We worked out a set where we'd open with a couple of instrumentals—'Walk On The Wild Side' and 'Swedening', the Brother Jack McDuff number, and then I'd introduce Joe. We rehearsed for a long time because a lot of it was new—all new equipment—and then when we were ready we decided to start off in Sheffield. We did that pub at Firth Park and everybody was there. We played a blinder, one of the best nights of my life. The band sounded so good, Cocker was singing brilliant and we were doing original songs."

From there on Joe and The Grease Band embarked on the standard college and club circuit, but after only a few weeks on the road the new drummer and guitarist seemed to be flagging, musically. Doing gigs alongside bands like Traffic, Spooky Tooth and Family—tight outfits with brilliant musicians—it was felt that Mickey Gee and Tommy Reilly were not really up to par. When they took a few days' holiday and went home to Wales the others went into the studio to record 'With A Little Help From My Friends'. On their return Gee and Reilly found themselves redundant.

* * *

'With A Little Help From My Friends' is the song most associated with Joe Cocker. His first chart-topper, it is instantly recognisable from the opening notes and it is a very rare Cocker show that does not include the song, even after twenty years. Originally a jolly little rocker sung by Ringo Starr on the Beatles' 'Sgt. Pepper' album, Joe transformed it into a classic pop record, a heartfelt cry of anguish that builds to a climax of screaming triumph.

Joe first got the idea to do 'With A Little Help' while sitting on the outside toilet, down the yard at Tasker Road. "For some reason it just flashed in my mind," he says. For a while he had been keen on doing numbers in 3/4 time and one night during the period when he was still trying to recruit Tommy Eyre, he had heard Glen Dale and The Candies do 'With A Little Help' as a straight copy of The Beatles' version. Later, as the new band rehearsed, he mentioned the idea he had to the band. Tommy Eyre: "He'd become obsessed with 3/4 but it's a weird tempo to be able to play comfortably. . . . for it to swing as good as a 4/4 thing. So when he said 'Hey, you know that Beatles song you did with Glen, I wonder what that'd sound like as a waltz?', everybody went 'Urgh. Not another effing waltz!' But I said 'No—hang on a bit, it could work'. It wasn't that long after 'Whiter Shade Of Pale' and everybody loved that pretend Bach thing. So Joe said 'Can you like give us a Bach intro and then change the chords in the verse so that it sounds more classical?'"

Tommy Eyre had studied classical piano from early childhood, and once he joined The Grease Band and got a Hammond organ he spent every spare moment practising Bach preludes and fugues. He worked out the intro to 'With A Little Help', the one which appeared on the record being one of eighteen that he had improvised in the old cinema on Westbourne Grove. "So I did the opening and then I had to re-work the chord line in the verse because Joe said 'Let's make it heavier . . .' . . . and Chris came in with a bass line, which he suggested would also work nice on guitar. And all the drum fills—they just sort of happened."

Joe and The Grease Band played 'With A Little Help' on their live gigs before going into the studio to record it. Although it had already been decided that Mickey Gee and Tommy Reilly had to go, no replacements were lined up. Anxious to get a new Cocker single out, Denny Cordell overcame the problem by booking Steve Winwood and Jim Capaldi, from Traffic, whom Joe had supported a number of times since the old Grease Band's Speakeasy gig a few months earlier.

One June evening they all went into Olympic Studios—but the session did not work out. "Capaldi was a brilliant drummer," says Tommy Eyre, "but he wasn't getting the hang of this 3/4 time. He was sounding like he was counting, which is crackers. It's just an ordinary waltz."

Hours passed, take after take—thirty five is a figure recalled—with Joe, unable to fake it even if he tried, giving his all on every one. His voice—so powerful that, even with sandbags piled up the closed door of the vocal booth, it still escaped on to the drum mike—ended up exhausted. Finally, at about three in the morning, Denny Cordell aborted the session.

"I went home and burst into tears," the producer recalls. "I knew this was a monstrous piece of work and I could not get it right . . . and the musicians were wrong. So my wife at the time said 'Well—you'll just have to do it again won't you!'" The following day he did just that. This time Jimmy Page was on guitar and B.J. Wilson on drums. The Procol Harum man had a perfect waltz feel and the song was quickly put down. Joe: "Take 13 on the second day. We just knew that was the one. I'll always remember it. You just know when you go into the control room—it doesn't matter who's on the mixing desk—it's like God's taken over."

With the next single in the bag, priority became finding a new guitarist and drummer. There was little enthusiasm for another round of auditions. So an Irish guitarist, Henry McCullough, whom the band had met in London was invited along to a rehearsal. The speed with which he picked up the test piece, 'Swedening', impressed and he was enlisted. Kenny Slade, the new drummer, was chosen mainly through the influence of Tommy Eyre, with whom he had been friendly for years back in Sheffield. An exuberant, magnetic character, much older than the rest of The Grease Band, Slade had toured Britain with visiting Americans like Del Shannon and Bobby Hebb, before going into semi-retirement in a big band at Doncaster Top Rank. Slade was seen as one man who could keep up with the high class opposition the band frequently came up against on gigs.

* * *

Throughout the summer of 1968 Joe and The Grease Band were on the road up and down the country, besides playing regular gigs at London clubs like Blaises, Revolution, Scotch of St. James and The Marquee. Reaching an ever increasing audience they faced their biggest crowd to date at the Windsor Festival, held at Kempton Park racecourse, on a bill which included Deep Purple, Jeff Beck, Jethro Tull, and one of Joe's early heroes—Jerry Lee Lewis. Tommy Eyre: "It was a lovely day . . . lovely setting—a huge expanse where all the kids were sat and then it rose up about fifteen feet to like a natural stage. It was all hippy, lots of dope, peace and love and all that. We go on to play . . . to do our instrumental . . . but before we go Joe's dropped some acid and we've all gone 'Oh no! Don't blow it!' We're just about at the end of 'Walk On The Wild Side' and it starts to rain. We finish the number . . . 'Ladies and Gentlemen . . . JOE COCKER!' Eight times round the intro to 'Let's Get Stoned' while Joe walks on—but between him coming from the tent and getting on the stage, suddenly the heavens open. And all these hippies do a runner from where they are . . . up the back and on to the stage which is covered. So there's Joe—on acid—he sees these punters coming for him. He'd only sung two words and he thought he'd offended 'em and they wanted to come up and kill him! I'm playing the organ and there's about twenty five people between me and Sladey, fifty between him and Chris. We could just see Henry . . . and Cocker's in the middle going 'No! No!'"

* * *

In September Denny Cordell made a business trip to Los Angeles. He had just arranged for A & M Records to handle all his Straight Ahead recording interests in America. Impressed by the A & M set-up, based on Charlie Chaplin's old Hollywood film lot, and by the people who worked there, he invited Joe to accompany him to have a look round. Cocker needed no persuading—it had long been his ambition to visit America.

Jerry Moss, head of A & M, was reminded very recently of the first time he heard Joe Cocker. "We've just put out a 25th Anniversary book here and there's a quote from a guy in the art department . . . He remembered me coming in with a tape of 'Marjorine' and just playing it to people, saying to everybody 'We're going to sell millions of records'. That to him was quite interesting and he remembered it vividly. What it means to me is obviously we were into Joe from the very beginning—we really liked him. You know some artists come in and they are hard to speak with, or to get to, but he was really relaxed . . . we were able to have a conversation right away . . . it was an immediate rapport. Everybody embraced . . . we had a great time."

While in Los Angeles Cordell heard the newly released Traffic album, and was immediately taken by one track, 'Feelin' Alright', which he felt would be suitable Cocker material. Joe, when he heard it, was equally impressed and they decided there and then to record it at A & M.

The line-up for the session included star studio musicians like pianist Artie Butler and drummer Paul Humphries, plus the Raelettes—Merry Clayton, Patrice Holloway and Brenda Holloway on backing vocals. "Denny had always said he could get any musician in the world, and I could never believe that," says Joe. 'Feelin' Alright' dispelled all doubts. The session was completed by a Brazilian percussionist, borrowed by Cordell, who was himself brought up in Brazil, from a nearby Herb Alpert session. Thus the final touches were added.

The L.A. session produced just the one song. They tried another but ran out of time. "In those days," says Denny Cordell, "my style of things was to book the studio and the musicians for three hours and try to cut two tunes. No messing. And Joe was great because he was a live performer." On this occasion, although only one tune was cut, no one was disappointed. Like 'With A Little Help', 'Feelin' Alright' has become a Cocker standard over the years.

* * *

On their return from Los Angeles, Cocker and Cordell found 'With A Little Help From My Friends' was starting to happen. Released on

October 2, it swiftly rose in the British charts, reaching the Top Ten three weeks later. 'COCKER'S SHOCKER' was the *Melody Maker* front page headline on October 26, with a large photo of Joe alongside the story of the record's phenomenal rise. Inside there was a Chris Welch interview with Joe, who discussed his music—"soul—but not in the gotta gotta vein", the origins of his windmill arm movements, the pretentiousness of showbusiness, and how he no longer drank ten pints of beer a night "because you can't get Sheffield beer anywhere else."

The same week Joe flew to Paris to appear on three television shows, as well as giving a press conference in a boutique owned by film star Elizabeth Taylor. He made a number of British TV appearances, on *Dee Time*, *How It Is* and *Top Of The Pops*. On October 30, he and The Grease Band appeared, along with Bonzo Dog Doo Dah Band and Tiny Tim, at the Royal Albert Hall, receiving a tremendous reception.

Only one thing marred the excitement as Joe began to at last achieve the success he had worked towards for years. On October 11, as he was about to depart from Heathrow Airport for a promotional trip to Amsterdam, he was stopped and searched by Customs Officers who found a miniscule amount of cannabis resin on him. Three days later Joe appeared at Uxbridge Magistrates Court where the court was told he had been completely frank with the police and was a man "on the threshold of what may well be a very promising career." Said to earn £30 per week, Joe was fined £55.

*　　*　　*

On November 9, Joe Cocker—described in one national newspaper as "the most refreshingly straightforward young man to ride into London on a record for many a long year"—rode all the way to number one in the British Hit Parade. He had achieved what even his closest friends had thought impossible. He had done it with a record to be proud of, through determination, total conviction and sheer talent.

Back in Sheffield *Top Stars Special* celebrated the city's first chart topper by devoting much of the December '68 edition to Joe and his success. Old friends and contemporaries like Dave Berry, Ray Stuart and David McPhie, were quoted, and even Harold Cocker made a rare public utterance, telling the paper, "I'm glad he's got to the top. He's tried hard and long enough. He really feels his music."

Joe's long-time girlfriend, Eileen Webster, was interviewed, speaking of how they had met in the Youth Club days and how she had kept on persuading Joe not to give up during the dark days of two years earlier. Eileen had only recently joined Joe in London, having spent the summer working in Cornwall. Asked about marriage she said "I suppose we'll get round to it someday."

In his time of triumph Joe did not forget those who had supported and encouraged him during the hard times. To the landlord and regulars of the Barrow Hill Hotel, where he had played every Wednesday for over a year, he sent a telegram of thanks, and to *Top Stars Special*, in which he had his very first mention in 1962, he issued the following statement:

"I would like to thank everyone who came along and saw our performances at any time during the last six years. Those days were really great and I'll never forget them.

"All that I ask is that if you see a new group or artist around that you dig locally, stick with them because it can work wonders.

"Many people said I would never make anything but I stuck at it.

"The only reason I did was because of the people who dug us. Thank you, it's amazing what can be done with a little help from your friends."

The title of Joe's chart topper caused several people in Sheffield to think back to an afternoon several years earlier in the Esquire Club. At the time he was doing little work and hopes of making the big time seemed to have disappeared. Ray Stuart: "We were just sitting in there—Joe, myself, Dave Memmott and Terry Thornton. Just messing about with Terry's Ouija board. Dave Berry had just had another hit and I remember we asked the Ouija board 'When will Joe Cocker have a hit record?' . . . You know with the glass . . . And the answer came—'When he gets a little help from his friends.'" Joe remembers the incident well. "Yeah, we got well hung up on that. It actually spelled out the letters of 'With A Little Help From My Friends'—which we didn't know at the time. Yeah . . . there's truth to that . . ."

*   *   *

Still at number one, Joe and The Grease Band took off on a major tour with The Who, Crazy World of Arthur Brown and Small Faces. "An amazing tour, that," says Tommy Eyre. "Keith Moon and Sladey were just waiting to meet each other. Such a like mind! And when they did meet that was it—blood brothers! Mooney got some dynamite from somewhere and him and Sladey blew up the shithouse at the hotel in Newcastle!"

Kenny Slade had actually first met Moon in a London music shop, before The Who even formed. "He was a real shy little lad. Completely the reverse of what he ended up. That's what rock and roll does to people." Slade has vivid memories of the tour, including himself and Moon being locked up by the police in Glasgow. "One time he caught me—he was distraught! 'Come here . . . come to my room . . .' He takes me in the bathroom and there's this bird laid in the bath—just feet and head showing in semi-darkness. I said 'What the fucking hell have you done?' So he switches the light on and it's a blow-up doll, all covered in tomato ketchup!"

The Who tour ended in Liverpool but there was no respite for Joe and the Grease Band, who continued a relentless schedule, playing seven nights a week, all over the country. They played to a totally stoned audience at the Magic Village, Manchester, a rapturous reception at Cambridge University Union and in Paisley, Scotland, on a stage thirty feet high in the air. When Kenny Slade asked the promoter why they had to perform at such a height he was told "if you don't you'll be cut to pieces with bottles and tins."

But the most triumphant night of all was November 13, at the Black Swan pub in Sheffield. Hours before the show was due to begin crowds gathered outside the pub, causing such an obstruction that the police instructed landlord, Terry Steeples, to move them or be prosecuted. "I said 'In that case I'll move 'em'. So I did—straight into the concert room. Officially it held 226 but we managed to cram in 540 at ten shillings a piece." Joe did two spots, sang 'Georgia On My Mind' as a special request, and finished on 'With A Little Help From My Friends', during which his mother, Madge, presented him with a cake!

Hardly surprisingly Joe and the band—only Henry McCullough was a non-Sheffielder—went down a storm, but the pub landlord had great difficulty finding out how much they wanted for their night's work. There had been no contract—Joe had simply said he'd like to play at the Swan and when Terry Steeples asked him "What sort of money do you want?" he told him not to worry about that. Steeples: "After the show I said 'How much do I owe you?' He said 'Oh come to this party'—I went, and when I got home I had to have eighteen cups of coffee to recover. The following day I cornered him—I'd taken 270 quid. He said 'Give me two hundred—I'm happy'. I ask you—how many men, number one in the Hit Parade would first of all want to play the Black Swan—and if they did they'd say 'I want five hundred quid'. How many men? And what d'you think he did after that? He sent me a telegram, thanking me for having him!"

* * *

'With A Little Help From My Friends' stayed in the British charts thirteen weeks and was a hit all over Europe. As it started to descend the charts, far from being disappointed, Joe exhibited feelings akin to relief. "The big thrill was when the record came into the top thirty," he told one interviewer, at the end of November. "Now it's slipping it puts everything into perspective. We're relieved of the pressure—before we didn't have a

Vance Arnold at the Sheffield Fleur De Lys, 1962. *Courtesy of Harold Cocker*

The cast of Prince Ju Ju, Lydgate Lane Junior School, 1955. Joe is on extreme left, holding ukelele. *Courtesy of Harold Cocker*

The Cavaliers in Joe's living room, 1959. Left to right: John Mitchell, Phil Crookes, Joe, Bob Everson. *Courtesy of Harold Cocker*

Joe Cocker's Big Blues, 1965. Left to right: Dave Green, Dave Memmott, Vernon Nash, Dave Hopper, Joe – with harmonica. *Courtesy of Dave Memmott*

The Star

top stars
SPECIAL

24.325 FEBRUARY EDITION 1965 4d

OVER **100 RECORDS** TO BE **WON**

Hello, Joe!

SEE PAGE 9

SEE PAGE 9

P.J. PROBY

Joins CILLA BLACK

ON TOUR
SEE PAGE 5

SEE PAGE 5

*

PAUL

JONES
SEE PAGE 1

SEE PAGE 1

On the Local Scene

TOP STARS BALL

Sheffield Newspapers Ltd

Joe with the first award for The Grease Band, 1967. *Sheffield Newspapers Ltd*

Joe makes his triumphant return to the Black Swan, Sheffield, on November 13, 1968. Joe's mother, Madge, sits in the front row facing the audience. *Courtesy Dave Hopper*

day to name our own. Now we have more time to rise artistically." He told the *Daily Mail* "When you watch your name going up the charts it makes life pretty strange. But you can't change because you're high one day and low the next." Looking back now at how it felt to be top of the Hit Parade, Joe says "It was strange. I remember being in Glasgow and thinking 'Is this it then?' I didn't feel anything at all."

* * *

At Christmas Joe and the band took a deserved, but short, rest in Sheffield. They returned to London to play New Year's Eve at Alexandra Palace, followed by a set at Annabel's in Berkeley Square. Tommy Eyre: "It was about thirty five quid to get in—in those days. Full of Hooray Henrys and chicks that looked good enough to eat! And they're all getting the hots for Cocker and Sladey—both of 'em in horrible, ripped T shirts, covered in sweat and hair all over the place—we'd come straight from this other gig . . . So we did a twenty minute set and one of the roadies comes up and says 'Look—the geezer says will you do a couple of encores—the punters really love it. He hasn't got any money but will a crate of champagne do?' So we go back on and do a couple of Chuck Berry songs. And then they said 'Peter Sellers is downstairs and he wants to meet you'. So there's a big rush for the door, and we're sitting there chatting to Peter Sellers and he's doing all the Goons voices. Next thing Princess Margaret comes up and he introduces us to her. She says 'I thought the band was marvellous Mr Cocker, how are you?' And Joe's there in his scruffy old T-shirt—'Oh 'ello luv!'

* * *

It had been an eventful year for Joe Cocker. On the first day of January he signed a recording contract with Denny Cordell's Straight Ahead Productions, and a song publishing contract with Essex Music. He had broken away from the limitations of Sheffield by moving to London, visited America, topped the charts and had been acclaimed by audiences throughout Britain. With his first album almost completed and a tour of the States lined up for the Spring the future looked bright. The years of effort were at last coming to fruition.

Chapter Six

1969

Woodstock

THE NEW YEAR had hardly begun before there was a major shake-up within The Grease Band. Out went Kenny Slade and Tommy Eyre. In came Alan Spenner and Bruce Rowland. From bass to keyboards went Chris Stainton. Only Henry McCullough stayed put. The changes had been planned since before Christmas, when Joe and Stainton invited bass player Spenner and drummer Rowland—both from a London band, Wynder K. Frogg—to an audition cum-rehearsal at the Pied Bull, Islington.

Slade and Eyre had no inkling of their impending exit. They had enjoyed a merry Christmas and thought they had every reason to look forward to a prosperous New Year. It was not to be, as Tommy Eyre found out the first week in January. "Kenny called me up—he'd phoned the office. He said 'Can you believe what the bastards have done! They've fired us!' That's the first I knew—to this day nobody's called me. They pulled the rug from under us. Cocker never said a word."

Over two decades later during which he has earned a fine reputation, working with everyone from Mark Almond to Wham! and Andy Summers, Tommy Eyre still cannot erase the painful memory of how he felt on being sacked. "I was in a daze. I just didn't know why. I still don't really know—we were too jazzy, that was the excuse. But I knew it had been partly engineered by Stainton—because he wanted to play piano. And our faces didn't fit . . . you see Joe had been elevated into that super hip society and me and Sladey weren't hip—we didn't say 'vibe' or 'far out' or smoke a lot of ganja, which made me throw up. Joe had all the super-exotic pseuds around him and I got the impression that he got wound up into that. I've seen him since and he's just like the Joe I remembered, but at the time it was very upsetting."

Kenny Slade, older and more experienced in the devious politics of rock and roll, did not let the matter depress him for too long. "I wasn't right happy about it but I wasn't right bothered either. Joe I admired tremendously—loved his singing—but the music didn't turn me on. We used to drink together but then we went different ways—I sorta went the wild side and he went the cooler side. Joe wasn't really into being a crackpot."

Joe, putting the departure of the Sheffield pair purely down to musical considerations, suggests that the decision was far from his alone. "Their leanings were towards jazz. They were always saying 'Why don't we get into more jazzy stuff? That's where it's at'—but me and Chris, we were rockers. It all came to a head at a gig down south . . . Chris burst into tears and said 'I just can't play with them anymore'. So that was it."

*　*　*

The re-formed Grease Band rehearsed for a couple of weeks, the new bassplayer and drummer getting familiar with the material, while Chris concentrated on his new role. Alan Spenner: "Chris was amazing—a thoroughbred original. Five days without sleep was normal for him. When he decided to really get into keyboards he just sorta took a hundred black bombers and went off and practised. And he came back a beautiful piano player. He used to copy people, note for note, getting all the inflections—and then gradually over a few months he'd develop his own style."

After a few settling-in gigs at small out of the way venues, Joe and The Grease Band spent most of February and March on a package tour of Britain with Gene Pitney and Marmalade. It was not easy playing to someone else's audience every night but they survived unscathed and the last week in April they flew the Atlantic ready and eager to begin their first American tour.

*　*　*

Joe's arrival in the States was not totally unheralded. The single 'With A Little Help From My Friends' had caught the attention of underground radio stations, making Number 68 in the U.S. charts. It also paved the way for his début album of the same title, released shortly after his arrival in America.

The album, produced by Denny Cordell, took a year to complete. Very representative of Joe Cocker in 1968/69 it opens with 'Feelin' Alright', the one song cut in L.A. the previous September. 'Bye Bye Blackbird' follows featuring Jimmy Page and the same backing vocalists who sang on 'With A Little Help'—Madeleine Bell, Sunny Weetman and Rosetta Hightower. 'Change In Louise', a Cocker/Stainton composition with Spooky Tooth's Mike Kellie on drums, is followed by 'Marjorine', while Bob Dylan's 'Just Like A Woman' recorded, says Denny Cordell "literally running out of the studio" on the 'With A Little Help' session, has Procol Harum's Matthew Fisher on organ, with Tommy Eyre playing piano.

Stevie Winwood's distinctive organ on 'Do I Still Figure In Your Life' opens side two. Then comes 'Sandpaper Cadillac', from one of the earliest sessions, and 'Don't Let Me Be Misunderstood'—the only recording ever released which features the late '68 Grease Band: Stainton, McCullough, Eyre and Slade. The title track follows and the album ends with another Dylan song—'I Shall Be Released'—which features Winwood and Kellie, in preference to other takes of the same song on which Al Kooper and Aynsley Dunbar had played.

It was a superb début album—fine vocal performances from Joe backed up by top-notch musicianship. The record received good reviews and, while it had no impact on the British charts, it reached Number 35 in America, by which time Joe's reputation was generally on the up-and-up.

* * *

The American public's first glimpse of Joe Cocker was in late April on the *Ed Sullivan Show*, where he and the Grease Band mimed to 'Feelin' Alright', a second single off the album, released only in the States. The show's producer, seemingly startled by Joe's physical performance and fearful of offending viewers, tried to hide him behind a large contingent of dancing girls. He failed and the television appearance was a great success. "It caused quite a stir," recalls Alan Spenner. "The older generation thought he was a lunatic and should be sent home and the youngsters thought he was the bees knees. It was the perfect start."

From there Joe and the band went on the road, playing gigs organised by Bandana Management, a New York company run by Dee Anthony, who had first heard Joe sing at the Marquee in London the previous Autumn. Anthony had an agreement with Island's Chris Blackwell to take care of his bands' interests in America. It was a situation with which Denny Cordell, Joe's producer and mentor, was unhappy. "By then the Island/Straight Ahead thing wasn't going to happen and while Chris Blackwell wasn't personally managing Joe, his organisation was. So I was in a rather tricky position regarding my man. His career was not being launched in the way I would have liked it to have been." Three weeks after arriving in America Joe signed a contract with Bandana Management—a contract that would end two years later amidst acrimony and litigation.

Joe and The Grease Band played to rapturous receptions from the earliest gigs—opening at New York's Fillmore East where Jeff Beck—with Rod Stewart—topped the bill, moving on to Boston and Detroit where they supported The Who at a skating rink for several nights. They played New York clubs like The Scene and Ungaro's, the Rahway Theatre in New Jersey, the Mid West, up and down the East Coast and, one June night, at the Fillmore West in San Francisco. Half the audience had left after The Byrds had played their top of the bill spot—the half that remained were captivated. "Five hundred people discovering something truly incredible" wrote Ben Fong-Torres in *Rolling Stone*. "Fillmore West never felt so good."

The Press was quick to seize upon the visual aspects of the "ugly-fat-boy-with-a-soul-of-gold-mystique", as termed by John Mendelsohn in the *L.A. Times*. "On stage Cocker is a marvel as he jerks around spastically, throwing his arms around his head and grimacing as if in awful pain." Albert Goldman, in *Life*, went much further. "You had heard about the strange mannerisms," he wrote, "but you never expected he'd look like a bad case of muscular dystrophy exacerbated by Parkinson's disease and St Vitus Dance." As for the effect that Joe was having on America's females—*Rolling Stone* reported a gig at the Whisky A Go Go in Los Angeles: "As they went into their explosive version of 'With A Little Help From My Friends' a nubile young admirer, apparently driven wild by Cocker's amazing voice and insane spastic contortions, stationed herself on her back between Cocker's legs and, reaching up, began to work with considerable fervour. Moments later Joe delivered the scream of his career." The article, accompanied by a photograph of the event, later appeared as an advertisement with the caption 'JOE COCKER WAILS ON A & M RECORDS'.

Not the sort of occurrence that would have happened back in the Sheffield pubs! But, as Joe wrote home to his pal, Stuart Moseley: "This tour really has been a fantastic experience. Such strange things have been happening on the road . . . You feel so free here, although there's lots of guns about there's quite a bit of love in the air . . ." The letter went on to tell how "the band has suddenly really got together, both personally and musically" and how Joe and Chris Stainton had started writing songs again, which he describes as "a blessing—I thought it had all gone." He signs off on a philosophical note—"Remember 'what the soul wants the spirit shall attain.' I think God said that, or somebody nearly as hip."

* * *

The Summer of 1969 witnessed one of the greatest chapters in rock history. All across the U.S.A., in Canada and England, fans flocked to rock festivals organised on a scale hitherto unimaginable. The first major outing was the Newport Rock Festival on 20–22 June, held outside Northridge, California.

Thirty three acts were on the bill, including Jimi Hendrix, Janis Joplin, Jethro Tull, Steppenwolf, The Byrds and Joe Cocker and The Grease Band, playing before an audience of 150,000 people. The following weekend Joe played the Denver Pop Festival, where police riot squads fought with clubs and tear gas against would-be gatecrashers. A week later it was Atlanta, with Janis Joplin, Delaney and Bonnie, Led Zeppelin, Creedence Clearwater Revival and 140,000 spectators. Joe: "They were great days out—it was pretty mind-blowing. We tended to get the bell-end of the stick because we were pretty new on the scene—like at Atlanta Stadium we were supposed to go on at eight o'clock at night then they gradually put us back for the star bands and we didn't get on until about six the day after."

Mind-blowing too was the variety of stimulants and other substances available in America. Alan Spenner: "By the time we got to the big festivals it was all a bit blurred. You have to appreciate that we were relatively young lads—not so much in years, more in that the most daring we'd been had been smoking a bit of hash . . . and suddenly we're confronted by all kinds of weird things. At that time all these young chemists, just out of university, were inventing new things. We met one in Seattle—he'd been experimenting with rhinoceros tranquillizer . . . He'd come up with this stuff which he'd christened THC . . . in a brown jelly form. We called it Heavy Jelly. He said 'This is pretty good you know . . .' You washed a bit off the end of your fingernail, down with Coca Cola. After about three quarters of an hour nothing had happened—and then your whole world turned into technicolour cotton wool! That was you for about thirty-six hours—your head appeared to have been detached from your body and was up there, looking down at you from a great height."

While such a condition raised few eyebrows in the rock business, it could lead to awkward situations with those not so directly involved—like the occasion Joe and the band were invited to dinner at the home of Dee Anthony. Bruce Rowland: "Dee's hospitality was lavish—and highly conditional. The company that night was Frank Barsalona (an associate of Anthony's), Dee's wife, who was English, her mother, who sat with a coterie of blue-rinse type ladies in one corner, and Ten Years After—Alvin Lee's band.

"Chris Stainton had been pretty well out of it for about a week and had gone to bed for four days. He got up the day of the dinner party, not wanting to eat, but rather wanting to go to the Village with his little paper bag, to see what he could fill it with.

"So after we've eaten we have to watch home movies, made by Alvin and Co. The projector was set up in the middle of this enormous sitting room, the cable as tight as a violin string over to the plug at knee height. The lights went out and the film started to roll—when Chris arrived. Like mindless and unable to stand! As he came through he took the projector and everything—total chaos. Then he sat on the floor and went to sleep.

"So the whole movie thing gets going again and it's unbelievable—consisting of Ten Years After playing cowboys and Indians with real shooters and all the gear in a Holiday Inn hotel room . . . interspersed with shots of Alvin's wife, this extremely beautiful model, slightly out of focus, through railings . . . all very moody and pretty. Suddenly there she is in full close up—a real pose—and somebody trod on Chris, who woke up, didn't know where he was, looked at the screen and said 'Who the fuck's that!' There was this most awful silence, and the only sound I could hear was Cocker trying to hold his laughter. Those poor old dears in the corner—they shot off the sofa, I promise you!"

In early August it was Alan Spenner and Bruce Rowland's turn to be shocked—as they slept in a New Jersey hotel following the Atlantic City Pop Festival. Spenner: "Six o'clock in the morning and the door just disintegrated. Me and old Bruce are lying there in twin beds and we find ourselves confronted by police issue 38s. I'm staring down the nose of this gun and a real podgy geezer in purple polka dot Bermuda shorts, with a great big gut and shades, is going 'O.K. buddy, time's up'."

When the Grease Band men were taken to the police station they found it full of people arrested at the rock festival. Spenner: "All the kids are shouting to us . . . 'YEAH!' and the police are yelling at them to shut up. It never went to court because we didn't have anything, but we were in jail a day and a night."

The main event of 1969 took place over four days in mid-August on a 600 acre dairy farm at Bethel in New York State. Woodstock—the 'Aquarian Exposition'—has been the subject of a film, a triple album, several books and hundreds of articles. It has been called 'the ultimate pop experience', 'a major planetary event' and—in *Time* magazine—'history's biggest happening'. And Joe Cocker got to play there through a case of mistaken identity in a Bahamian casino.

Denny Cordell: "I'd gone down to Nassau and after lunch, for want of something better to do, went to the casino, to check it out. And there was this hippy . . . long hair and a fringed leather jacket . . . on a fantastic roll. He'd got a massive pile of chips that was growing bigger and bigger and bigger—about $20,000, which in those days was a hell of a lot. And he scooped up all these chips into his jacket and came up and said to me 'Hey. I know you . . . how you doin'?' I'd never seen this guy before in my life . . . I said 'Fine' . . . it was one of those. We got chatting and he introduced himself—Artie Kornfield—and told me about Woodstock. I said 'You've got to have Cocker—he is a great thing'. So we went round to Chris Blackwell's house, where I was staying, and I played him the album."

Kornfield, mightily impressed, returned to New York where he passed on news of his discovery to his partner in the Woodstock promotion, Michael

Lang, who today recalls the first time he heard Joe Cocker. "I was blown away. The idea of booking was to have all the people that you thought you HAD to have—and then I realized that it would be good to have a lot of new talent. Joe was just incredible so we said 'Sure'."

Joe and The Grease Band were booked to open on the Sunday, on a bill which included The Band and Sly and The Family Stone. The fee, according to *Variety* magazine was $1375. They drove overnight from their previous gig in New England, checked into their hotel, about twenty miles from the festival site, and woke up next morning to hear that all roads for miles and miles were blocked.

Army helicopters were commandeered and the bands flown in, Joe and The Grease Band following Ten Years After. Once in the air all that could be seen was the mass of cars and people below. For weeks there had been a buzz that Woodstock was going to be the big one, but nobody in the band gave it much thought—they had already played some big festivals that summer. "It was when we got plonked on the site we realised the enormity of it all," says Alan Spenner. "I felt like I was tripping . . . naturally . . . just the vibes that you seemed to be getting. Everyone was so happy and good natured—if someone in the crowd happened to see you it was 'HEY MAN—GREASE BAND . . . YEAH!' Two or three hundred people would look round and all wave . . . it was fantastic . . . magical. When we got on stage nobody really felt nervous—just incredibly exhilarated. We had a few minutes to kill, being first on, while they were setting up . . . You stood on the stage and looked out—it was like standing on the edge of Southend Pier, only it wasn't sea it was people. Everyone in such a good mood . . . the same mood. The occasion was bigger than anything else, that was the great thing."

Joe and The Grease Band opened the Sunday show at around 2pm. They went through the same programme that they had played all summer, including, Spenner recalls, a shortened version of Joe's improvised blues rap about the Queen of England. When he arrived in America people had told him to leave it out of the show, that it would not go down, but he kept doing it and the novelty appealed to the young rock fans. "As I was walking down the street . . . YEAH! Mindin' ma own business, not lookin' to left nor right . . . YEAH! Then this greeeat big Rolls Royce comes down the street and screeches to a halt. And it's the Queen. 'Hey Joe baby, how ya doin'? You wanna come back to the Palace for a while?' Joe goes back to Buckingham Palace . . . And she said to me 'Hey Joe . . . ROLLLL this up!'".

Denny Cordell flew in to the festival by helicopter, along with A & M's top brass. "I watched it with Pete Townshend who I think introduced Joe . . . and he gave him one of the great old English 'Wake up you lot of unwashed buggers and listen to this—you'll not hear anything better all week-end.' And Joe came on—he was scintillating . . . absolutely scintillating . . . phenomenal!"

Joe was coming to the end of a rip-roaring—ultimate—seven minute "With A Little Help From My Friends" when thunder struck. He grabbed the bottle of beer at his feet and raced for safety, the band close on his heels. "No rain. No rain. No rain. No rain," the crowd chanted, but communal commitment was not enough. The rains came and Woodstock turned into a mudbath—but not before Joe Cocker had achieved a major triumph, revealed to the world when the film of the festival was released a few months later. For ever after, wherever he went, Joe would be asked about Woodstock by fans and interviewers alike. Today he says simply "It was like the eclipse. It was a very special day."

* * *

A fortnight after Woodstock Joe and The Grease Band returned home to England for an appearance at the Isle of Wight festival, the focus of world-wide attention since it marked the first official performance by Bob Dylan since his motor cycle accident three years earlier. For Joe, after his tremendous experiences in America, the homecoming was an anti-climax. "While The Grease Band swung beautifully and sounded great . . . Joe himself did not quite make contact with the audience" said *Melody Maker*. "He sang well but soul seemed a trifle out of date, or at least out of place, and his stage movements were irritating." The very same people who had lauded his arrival on the London scene only the year before were now writing him off.

Before flying back to America to continue touring, Joe headlined a show in Amsterdam, with Spooky Tooth and Free, and took a few days rest at Chris Blackwell's Berkshire home. He travelled up to Sheffield to see his parents and one afternoon drifted into the Black Swan pub, where he had last played while topping the chart eleven months earlier. Landlord Terry Steeples: "We were closed when he walked in. He looked like a ghost . . . I said 'Bloody hell, sit down. You look like death warmed up!' and he said 'Do you want me to do a show?' I just laughed—you must be joking! And he did it—an incredible man!"

* * *

Joe arrived back in America in mid-October to find his new album 'Joe Cocker!' ascending the charts. Recorded during breaks from touring in late Spring and early Summer the album had a unique touch in that it contained two unreleased Beatles songs—George Harrison's 'Something' and Lennon & McCartney's 'She Came In Through The Bathroom Window'. Denny Cordell was acquainted with The Beatles and when, one day, George Harrison commented on how knocked out he was with Joe's treatment of 'With A Little Help', Cordell, ever shrewd, asked Harrison "How about a song from you for the next album?" Harrison agreed and shortly before Joe left for America in April the call came to go to Apple. Denny Cordell: "George played us a song but we didn't like it. Then he played 'Something'—'Oh we'll take that one George, that's a killer!' So we all went downstairs into the little studio at the bottom of Apple for him to put it on a cassette. And Paul's down there and he said 'How come you haven't asked me for a song?' I said 'We're asking you now Paul'."

Joe recalls the visit to Apple as "like going to the clinic. I sat there just like a little schoolboy and Paul played me 'Golden Slumbers'. I was delighted—I thought I can't wait to put this down and then he said 'But you're not having that' and he played 'She Came In Through The Bathroom Window'." There was no argument about this one and Joe and Denny left Apple with the two songs, which they recorded soon afterwards in the States.

'Joe Cocker!' marked the arrival of a man who would figure prominently in the career of the English blues singer during the coming months—Leon Russell, who, in his ten years as a Los Angeles session musician had played on many hits without achieving fame and fortune on his own account.

Leon Russell came to the attention of Joe, Denny Cordell and the Grease Band through his piano work on the Delaney and Bonnie album, 'Accept No Substitute', which they first heard at their New York hotel. A couple of weeks later they were booked into Sunset Sound in Los Angeles to record the 'Joe Cocker!' album. It was known that Russell lived in L.A., so Cordell asked an A & M employee, Michael Vossey "Who is this Leon Russell guy? Any chance of him playing on a couple of tracks?"

Cordell: "About two or three days into the session the unmistakable figure of Leon—grey hair right down his back and completely dressed in white—appears, with Rita Coolidge on his arm. And she was stunningly beautiful—the Cherokee Indian deal. It was all terribly low-key . . . did the platitudes . . . 'Like a cup of coffee?' . . . And they sat on a sofa in front of the speakers underneath the desk—they didn't move . . . didn't say anything to anybody for three hours. Then about two o'clock in the morning they got up, said 'Thank you very much, very nice . . .' and left. So we thought 'Oh well, that was a bit strange, wasn't it . . .' A bit weird . . . And then the next day we got a message from Michael Vossey saying Leon really liked what you guys were doing last night and he's got a tune that he thinks Joe might like."

* * *

Denny, Joe and Chris Stainton went to meet Leon Russell at his house, where he had converted the garage into an eight track recording studio. They were bowled over by Russell, who played them four tunes, including 'Delta Lady' and 'Hello Little Friend', which soon afterwards were recorded for the album, with Russell playing piano. But before 'Delta Lady' was finished they ran out of studio time. Denny Cordell: "We took the sixteen tracks and went up to Leon's pad, to his funky little studio. Clapton came up there that night and then we had Rita Coolidge, Merry Clayton and Bonnie Bramlett. Leon finished it off by putting the guitar down on it and I always remember Eric saying 'Oh man, this is a hit, this is a real hit.'"

The real life 'Delta Lady' was Rita Coolidge who first encountered Leon Russell in Memphis, where she had gone to live with her parents after graduating from college. She met Russell, whose reputation had preceded him, through a friend, Don Nix, a horn player with the Bar Kays. "When Leon came to town it was something of an event. And when he left to go back to California a couple of months later, he and I had been seeing each other, so he asked if I would drive back to L.A. with him—he had bought a Thunderbird. We were together for probably about eight months and we were in the process of putting together a band when our relationship fell apart. Leon wrote 'Delta Lady' at about the time we split up."

Soon after 'Delta Lady' was recorded Joe, the band and Cordell departed for England and the Isle of Wight Festival. All the songs for the album were cut with The Grease Band supplemented by Leon Russell and guests including Clarence White of The Byrds, who played guitar on 'Dear Landlord', and Sneeky Pete Kleinow who overdubbed guitar on 'She Came In Through The Bathroom Window'. These guest appearances were necessary, explains Cordell, because of Grease Band guitarist Henry McCullough's unpredictability: "When he played well he was a genius—but he could only play in one certain bag and you had to get him just right. Otherwise he was very mercurial—he'd just fall off it."

Leon Russell accompanied Denny Cordell to London, where he stayed at the producer's home and helped out as Glyn Johns mixed the tracks. While in London Russell cut some of the tracks for his own début album, produced by Cordell with an all-star line-up of backing musicians. Chris Stainton played on a lot of sessions and Joe recalls "putting the odd scream in here and there."

Now well integrated into Cocker's circle, Russell returned to the States and awaited the release of his album. In the meantime Joe and The Grease Band were well into their second tour as 'Joe Cocker!'—with Russell credited as co-producer—rose to Number 11 in the U.S. album charts. This time they were second instead of third on the bill at most shows, headlining a few, including New York's Fillmore East in November.

In England 'Delta Lady', a single from the album, was just sliding out of the charts, where it had peaked at Number 8, when Joe and The Grease Band returned home for Christmas. The British pop press, who had dubbed Cocker a one-hit wonder when he failed to release a follow-up to 'With A Little Help' for over twelve months, were puzzled as to why it had taken so long. "Everybody asks me that," was Joe's response when the question was put to him by *New Musical Express*. "I think I got slightly bogged down by everything that had happened. I'd been in Sheffield all those years and in just half a year a lot of violent changes came about."

* * *

After a break for Christmas and New Year, Joe did a few gigs in England and in late January played the Midem Festival in Cannes, a music industry trade showcase. It was obvious to the band that a rest was needed. Nine months on the road in America had left everybody exhausted and there was an urgent need to introduce new material. But across the Atlantic Dee Anthony was lining up a new tour, with Joe headlining everywhere. For weeks prior to returning home Joe had been saying he did not want to go out again so soon, but the American manager was insistent.

The Grease Band stood aside and observed. Alan Spenner: "The more Joe said 'No' the more Dee was becoming ominous. The rest of us, we more or less caved in and said 'Well it looks like we're doing it anyway' but Joe stuck to his guns and it built up. Dee Anthony was coming over but by this time it had turned into something more—I think he could see that his life was just being taken over by people."

Dee Anthony was adamant that the tour must go ahead. Although Joe had worked almost continuously through 1969 he had been down bill most of the time and had not earned big money. The festivals had brought him valuable exposure but little cash up to that point—viz the $1375 fee for Woodstock. Now the time was right—the 'Joe Cocker!' album was doing well in the States and Joe's career was hot. Dee Anthony wanted to capitalize.

Joe, however, had different ideas. Never a man to compromise, he broke up The Grease Band. Without a band, he reasoned, there could be no question of a tour.

Chapter Seven

1970

Mad Dogs & Englishmen

DENNY CORDELL was in Hollywood when he got the call from Dee Anthony. Cordell had left England to set up Shelter Records, in partnership with Leon Russell. But the New York impresario was not interested in the new venture—he wanted to know, had Cordell seen Joe Cocker? Cocker had not turned up for an appointment with Anthony in New York the week before. "You know he goes on tour in six days' time?" Anthony asked. Cordell knew a tour was looming but not exactly when. Anthony went on to tell him that Joe had fired The Grease Band, but Cordell could only reply that he had not heard from Cocker in maybe six weeks.

The following day Cordell got a call from Joe. "He was in New Orleans or somewhere. I said 'Joe! . . . Dee Anthony! . . . Tour! . . . There's a three bar panic going on here!'" Joe was not too concerned about that, but agreed to fly to Los Angeles where he explained to Denny that he had indeed sacked The Grease Band, he was having problems with his girlfriend, Eileen, and the last thing he was interested in was a tour of the States. Cordell listened sympathetically, told Joe not to worry, then he phoned Dee Anthony and told him that in view of the situation there was no alternative but to cancel the tour. Even Denny Cordell, one of the coolest of operators, was taken aback by what happened next.

"I put the phone down. Eight hours later there's a pounding on the door. I open the door of the motel—it's Dee Anthony. We're in Hollywood and Dee's flown across from New York—and he's getting really heavy! I knew that Joe was trying to get across that there was no way he could do the tour—but Dee got extremely heavy and came across with a lot of jazz about 'Well you know if you don't do this tour Joe—you'll never work in America again. Every promoter . . . posters have been printed . . . the halls have been booked. They're gonna sue me . . . I'm gonna sue you . . . NO ONE will ever book you again! Frank Barsalona . . . he's the KING agent—if you don't work for him you don't work for nobody. Your career is FINISHED'."

For Cordell, the situation he was witnessing was one he had long feared. Mistrustful of Dee Anthony from the outset, the previous twelve months had done nothing to alter his opinion. "I hated him. I never approved of him handling Joe, as his management, because as far as I was concerned he did not really know where Joe was coming from. He'd been handling Tony Bennett. That was a very ethnic circuit—and they all came from Italy. They were all heavy duty eyeties.

"I had tried to get Joe away. I went to see Dee and I spelled it out to him one day. He completely disarmed me—he said 'Yeah . . . I love Joe . . . anything, whatever you think is right . . . we'll do it. I don't mind—I'll step down'. He said 'Let me think about it' and then a few days later he had me up to his office and there was a lot of poking of the finger in the chest . . . saying 'If you don't want to end up in the Hudson River with cement shoes . . . It doesn't matter where you go—I got a friend in every town in America'. It was very very weird and we were much younger then and slightly less worldly. It had its effect!"

* * *

Joe was in a dilemma. On one hand he had no band and had never felt less like touring. On the other he was facing very serious threats to his career in America, with potential Musicians Union and Immigration Department problems looming. He and Denny Cordell went to see the only person they knew who might be able to come up with a solution, at least on the band front: Leon Russell. Would he be interested in going out on the road? Maybe a small outfit could be put together . . . Leon on piano, Chris Stainton on bass . . . pick up a guitarist and drummer? Joe: "We really weren't going for the big band that it turned out to be . . . it was my intention of just making it a small group. But Leon said the only way he would do it was if he could put the band together." Joe had no alternative but to agree, whereupon Russell picked up his telephone.

The first calls Leon Russell made were to star percussionists, Jim Keltner and Chuck Blackwell. Then he heard that Delaney and Bonnie's band—all friends of his—were splitting due to financial problems, so he invited them along. With the tour now looking a possibility, Denny Cordell rang Jerry

Moss, head of A & M and arranged to use the record company's studios to rehearse, day and night if need be, before flying to Detroit for the opening show in five days time.

Having resigned himself to the fact that a tour was inevitable, Joe's idea had been to form a quartet, perhaps a quintet at most. It was clear from the enthusiasm with which Leon Russell had phoned around that the band was going to be bigger than that, but neither Joe nor Denny Cordell envisaged the scene that awaited them as they arrived for the first rehearsal. Cordell: "We go down there and Leon has contacted every man jack he knows who can play good! There's three drummers—Jim Gordon, Jim Keltner and Chuck Blackwell—each with their own drum kit. There's guitar players, horn players—Bobby Keys and Jim Price. We decided we needed three girl singers—at least a dozen show up. There's tambourine players . . . you name it!

So we start off and after about an hour Joe's actually having a good time. Relief's set in—and the band's sounding great. By half way through the night—about ten o'clock—the buzz has gone round that something extraordinary is happening on soundstage number one. The band is swelling and swelling and there's a full flight jam session in progress. We were mesmerised—we'd never seen anyone take the whip-hand like Leon did in organising and conducting the musicians."

Russell also brought ideas for material. Joe liked the recent Rolling Stones' hit, 'Honky Tonk Women', so they decided that would open the show. Russell suggested 'Cry Me A River', Julie London's old torch number, which he visualised in a gospel vein. A Box Tops song 'The Letter' was rehearsed—and recorded during rehearsals, along with 'Space Captain', written by Matthew Moore, one of the people who turned up at the A & M Studios and went along on the tour as a member of the Space Choir. Released as a single 'The Letter'/'Space Captain' gave Joe his first Top Ten hit in America.

The first hurdle—getting a band together—was out of the way, but Denny Cordell became increasingly concerned as the band continued to grow. He told Leon Russell "This is great . . . it's going to work . . . we've pulled it out of the frying pan. But Leon—we can't have three drummers!" Russell said "Well which one are we gonna have?" Cordell said any one—either Jim Gordon, Jim Keltner or Chuck Blackwell—would do, but Russell countered in his Oklahoma drawl "Well who's gonna tell the other two they can't come?"

All three drummers made the tour—plus two other percussionists, Bobby Torres and Sandy Konikoff. Bobby Keys and Jim Price comprised the brass section—later supplemented by Jim Horn; Carl Radle—like Keys and Price, from Delaney and Bonnie—played bass; Don Preston, guitar; Chris Stainton, piano and organ, and Leon Russell piano and guitar. There were originally ten backing singers in the Space Choir, most notably Rita Coolidge and Claudia Lennear. Lennear, a former Ikette, was featured on the Beatles' 'Let It Be', while Coolidge took the spotlight for 'Superstar', a song credited to Leon Russell—wrongly in his former 'Delta Lady's' opinion. "That was mine and Bonnie's song. If you listen, lyrically it's a girl singing about a guy. Leon and Delaney finished it and put their name on it. It was taken flat from us!"

Rehearsals for the tour went on twelve hours a day for the next four days, with an audience of several hundred turning up at A & M Studios to observe. Despite his earlier reluctance to go out on the road, Joe was reasonably happy—relieved that the threat to his career had been averted and exhilarated by the calibre of musicians he had around him. Denny Cordell came up with the title Mad Dogs and Englishmen (Joe: "It's from Noel Coward, you know. Denny's a bit like that.") and then he and Jerry Moss hit upon the idea of filming the tour.

With a band, a choir, roadies, soundmen, managers, wives, girlfriends, children—and now a film crew, a fresh problem arose. How would such an entourage be transported around America? Jerry Moss solved that one—a Super Constellation plane was hired, 'Cocker Power' was painted on its nose, and Mad Dogs and Englishmen were ready to go. In all forty-three people and a black-and-white spotted dog boarded the Super Constellation on March 19, 1970, and flew to Detroit where the tour opened the following day.

Mad Dogs and Englishmen were a sensation in Detroit. A week and four shows later they hit New York's Fillmore East, where much of the later live double album and movie were recorded over two nights, the majority from the Good Friday show. Here the film crew hit a snag. Bill Graham, the owner, had never before allowed a film crew into the Fillmore, as he feared it would distract the audience. He was disinclined to change his policy to allow Pierre Adidge and his crew to film Joe Cocker. Finally, after much persuasion, just before the show was due to begin, Graham conceded. The cameras rolled, the band laid into 'Honky Tonk Women' and 2,600 people went crazy.

A writer from *Time* magazine was amazed by what he saw. "Out there on stage is the largest—and most piebald—rock band in captivity. At stage left stands the chorus—13 girls and boys dressed in everything from shawls to what look like tablecloths. A little black-and-white dog curls up happily near the footlights. Two children romp around, just as happily . . .

"To see Joe for the first time is to wonder why no-one has yet made a star out of a camel with the staggers." But *Time* readers were left in no doubt about Cocker's vocal ability, or his success—"He knows just when to shout, just when to pout, just when to let a phrase die with a low, sad whimper. In just eight months he has become the most popular white male blues singer in the U.S."

The two small children who romped on stage were Denny Cordell's sons. Mad Dogs and Englishmen may have been sensational, Joe Cocker could well have been one of the hottest properties in rock music, but Tarka and Barney Cordell, then aged four and five, had other, more pressing matters to attend to. "I was always very fond of them," Joe told Denny years later. "But it's the closest I've ever come to beating a kid up. I was in the middle of this ballad one night and I just opened my eyes and looked down and there was Barney and Tarka on their hands and knees at my feet . . . with Dinky toys, going brrrrr . . . brrrrr."

* * *

Joe Cocker was the star of Mad Dogs and Englishmen, but it was Leon Russell to whom most of the band looked as leader—and more. Joe would later say "Leon—he was the father figure. We would all have a ceremonial dinner before we went on stage . . . till I stopped eating—they carried on of course. He would say a little prayer ahead of it all. There were like forty people on stage at times and when something becomes so communal you all get into the spirit of things. It was the whole bunch of us trying to get over the fact that life is like a stage."

The communal lifestyle was Leon Russell's ideal. "Leon was very gung-ho on the whole thing," says Denny Cordell. "He was very community minded—his community—in which he was the major figure. There was Joe, Chris and me. The rest of it was his crowd and he was very much the leader of the commune. They looked to him for everything."

A number of the Mad Dogs troupe originated, like Russell, from Oklahoma. One was Jim Keltner, who, in 1965, had joined Gary Lewis and the Playboys, a chart-topping group produced by Russell. "Leon was always real helpful to me," says Keltner. "He encouraged me and I got on real good with him. He was always in my corner, always encouraging me because he knew that I didn't really know if I was a rock and roll drummer. You see, I was basically a jazz guy." Of the atmosphere on the Mad Dogs tour Keltner says "The communal thing was real heavy at the beginning . . . everybody sticking together and doing everything together. It was 1970 and we were still in the Love period . . . flowers and love and free sex and all that. I've really got to say that the whole Mad Dogs thing was definitely one big long party. There was no indication that it was gonna be great, or any big deal. It didn't seem important, it just seemed like a big, wild party. And we were playing for the party."

But after a couple of weeks on tour the party spirit began to crumble for some, an inevitability with such a large and mixed group of people. There were emotional problems, ego problems, and before long tensions crept in that would be extremely debilitating—especially to Joe—as the tour wore on.

The relationship between Joe and Leon Russell began to deteriorate as the band looked to the piano player for every cue. The gigs were tremendous—everywhere Mad Dogs and Englishmen went there were wildly enthusiastic crowds, but to Joe the tour was turning into a monster. Cordell: "He was now just the vocalist in this big, runaway band. There was no finesse about it—and Joe is a man of great finesse. He had to go up there and roar his guts out every night with this huge, egocentric, pulsating, out-of-control big band behind him. He wasn't doing what he wanted to do, while Leon was enjoying it—because he was being the major domo."

Although over the years many interviewers have asked Joe about Mad Dogs, and in particular about his subsequent feelings towards Leon Russell, he has rarely, if ever, been forthcoming. The early 70s is a period of his life that holds too many bad memories, too much pain that he has no desire to recall. Today, however, he does say of Leon Russell: "We fell out pretty badly . . . a big ego clash. I'd revered the man but he'd make it obvious on stage. I'd be singing and he'd go 'Alright! Come on . . . come on.' He'd make it look to the audience as if he was pulling the strings—as if it was just . . . everyone was saying he was upstaging me all the time and it got to me after a bit."

Jim Keltner did not feel that his fellow Oklahoman was upstaging Joe. "The last thing on my mind was that anybody was being upstaged. But I did hear that and on reflection you could see where Leon was strong during that time. He was the musical director—but I don't think he overshadowed Joe at any time. I don't think there was ANYBODY could have upstaged Joe."

The role Russell assumed on the tour came as no surprise to Rita Coolidge. "Prior to the Joe Cocker tour Leon had become a total recluse, he wasn't seeing anybody in the old group. Then one day we were at A & M, before we went into rehearsals, this is after Leon had kept a very low profile for a while—and he came strutting across the parking lot in what looked like an Uncle Sam suit with a top hat, these outrageous clothes. And I just went 'I think I know whose tour this could be!' There was just no doubt about it—he came in and he was laughing and cracking jokes and being real aggressive and outgoing, which is not his nature. He's really a grump. But then he would come out and be such an extrovert—such a peacock! It was amazing!"

But on a free night on the tour Russell found he could not be the centre of attention. Joe: "We heard Chuck Berry was on at a club so Leon and I went along. We tried to creep in but the manager noticed us and we were led to this table right at the front. Chuck spotted me and invited me up on stage, but he didn't recognise Leon. So Leon's sitting there—right at the front—doing his nervous cough and looking put out, while Chuck's tuning up for ages. He's known for not bothering with tuning—give him a guitar and he'll just play it, but he went to a big effort that night. We did one of his rockers . . . I improvised the words as I went along. But Leon had gone—he'd slid out of the club when Chuck didn't call him up!"

There were other stand-out moments, especially involving Bobby Keys, the high-energy, hard-knocking sax player from Lubbock, Texas. "He always clowned around . . . He came up to me . . . said 'Joe, come here—I want to show you something . . . look at this.' He opened this case and Selmer had custom-made him a brand new sax—where they're usually gold this one was black. He'd got it in his mouth and he said 'What d'ya think of that?' and I poured a pint of beer in it! I ran out of the room before he could catch me . . . He hit the roof! 'You motherfucker! These things are delicate instruments'!'"

Drugs too led to some bizarre events. Jim Keltner recalls an early one, backstage at Fillmore East. "We all got into a big huddle and there we were, swaying back and forth, getting ready to go on. Everybody was psyching themselves up. This big, massive huddle—togetherness kinda thing! The whole band! And somehow, somebody had slipped us some Angel Dust into something and all I remember is that I came to on the floor, in the hallway—among all kinda crap and garbage and cigarette butts. And somebody was tapping me on the shoulder . . . Jim . . . come on, we gotta play . . . time to go on. And I came to and went downstairs and played!"

On another night, in Seattle, the effects were more profound. "I was always very reluctant to take acid and then play, but this time Jimmy Gordon talked me into doing it. The acid started coming on just before we went on stage. By the time I sat down at the drums I was peaking and in front of me was a huge wall of red and blue, blurry lights—and Joe in a sort of mist, with his fingers running down through his hair, the way he used to do it. It seemed such a weird thing—my mind was so confused I couldn't figure out why this guy was standing there, tugging at his hair in this red and blue fog. And then I looked over to my left, and Jim Gordon who was sitting there at his drums, right next to me—he looked like he was two blocks away. I just remember him playing and looking at me, going 'Play! Play!' I had a stick in my hand and I put the stick up to the cymbal and my mind immediately started to think 'What is rhythm?' Typical dumb-ass trip! Typical reason why you would never recommend acid to anyone . . . It scared me, scared me to death, so I got off the drums and turned to Chuck Blackwell . . . I grabbed him by the arms and sat him on the kit. And he's saying 'I don't play on this . . .' I said 'You're gonna play, sit down!' And I just left the stage and I went back and I sat down on the stairs. I remember sitting there, listening . . . I was crying . . . sobbing . . . and I heard Joe singing 'Bird On A Wire'. That song sticks in my mind forever. Everytime I hear it. That was a very poignant moment."

As Mad Dogs and Englishmen rolled around America, from the East Coast to California, via Chicago, Minneapolis, Tulsa, San Antonio and forty-odd stops in between, Joe was becoming increasingly drained by a tour which he had been forced into in the first place. Night after night he went on stage in front of crowds who had bought tickets to see Joe Cocker, but who were then confronted by the exotic, limelight-hogging presence of Leon Russell, strutting the stage in his top hat, rattling off machine-gun riffs from his Gibson guitar, stopping dead the band—and Joe—with one sweep of his arm. "All this star business—it's rubbish," Joe told a pressman in Pennsylvania. "Sometimes I think I would like to go back to things just as they were, like in the old days in Sheffield pubs—with people enjoying themselves. You can make better music that way."

In the meantime he had to get through the tour—and stopping eating did not help. "He was doing a lot of dope and he was drinking," says Denny Cordell. "He probably drank more to take the edge off it, when he'd got to go through it night after night. And then somehow . . . some con of Dee Anthony's—the tour had got into debt and therefore more dates were added. It was supposed to be a smallish tour—something like thirty dates over six weeks—but it went on a lot longer than it should have done. And there's no doubt in my mind that at the end Joe was pretty despondent with the whole thing."

Rita Coolidge recalls Joe's despondency setting in long before the end of the tour. Her own feelings had changed, from an initial excitement at setting out on the biggest rock tour that had ever taken place, to frustration and unhappiness. After breaking up with Leon Russell prior to the tour she had formed a relationship with Jim Gordon but this broke down after a short time on the road. "I felt so desperate to leave the tour because there was just a lot of shit going on, I was just so sad a lot of the time. I sat with Joe a lot on the plane, he and I were real close friends. I would sit there, after the shows, flying into the next city, and I would try to explain to him why I couldn't go on, why I had to go back home. And he would sorta turn round and look at me with that face sweeter than Jesus Christ and say 'You can't leave me, you cannot leave this tour—you're the only friend I've got.' And I couldn't leave. I'm telling you—his heart was the only thing that kept him going."

Finally the tour came to an end—in California on May 16. It had been eight weeks and two days since Mad Dogs and Englishmen left Los Angeles for the first show in Detroit and now, forty-eight cities later they were in San Bernadino in front of a Saturday night crowd of 5,000 people. Looking tired and deathly pale as he walked on stage, when the band struck up Joe did what he had done every show for the past two months, in every major city in America. Such a performance inspired Albert Goldman in his *Life* article *Sound Of Superscapegoat* to declare Cocker the voice of "all those blind criers and crazy beggars and maimed men who summon up a strength we'll never know to bawl out their souls in the streets. To a generation that has turned everything upside down in order to locate reality in poverty, filth, affliction and holy idiocy, Cocker is Original Man."

The Original Man himself would say much later of Mad Dogs and Englishmen—"It was an experience . . . it was something else. We all thought we were off to Venus, heading for outer space . . . next stop after that . . . but it didn't evolve that way. I ended up in a heap in Los Angeles, very disillusioned with the whole rock business."

* * *

Joe remained in L.A. for many months. Rita Coolidge: "He was sleeping on a doormat in the foyer of Denny Cordell's house. It just broke my heart after what he'd been through on that tour, to be sleeping on a mat like a dog—and taking drugs. At the time I was living with my sister, Priscilla, and Booker T. and I'd take Joe over. He'd stay with us for two or three days—he would sober up, dry out, and I would cook soul food, which he liked. I'd get him sober and straight and then the next thing I knew he would be back on the floor again."

He had been working almost continuously for two solid years, since leaving Sheffield for London in May '68. The intervening period had seen him transformed from local pub singer to international rock artist and all he wanted to do now was rest and give some thought to his experiences. Just once he ventured into a recording studio, with Leon Russell: "A sad re-union—we put down one track which will never be released—'Wake Up Little Susie', the Everly Brothers song. We went in and only did the one song. I dunno—our friendship and everything fizzled. That was the last we ever did."

While Joe lay exhausted, Leon Russell lost no time in seizing the opportunity to make fame and fortune his own. With a small band, including former Mad Dogs, Chuck Blackwell, Don Preston and Claudia Lennear, he began his solo career in front of a reported 30,000 people at the Anaheim Stadium in California, before entering into eighteen months of frantic activity that saw him do sell-out tours of America and Britain, write and record with the likes of Eric Clapton and Bob Dylan, and, in August 1971, star in the mammoth Bangla Desh concert at Madison Square Garden. His supreme moment was to play bass alongside George Harrison and Ringo Starr in the trio that backed Bob Dylan at this concert.

Not surprisingly there were many accusations that Russell's solo success had been achieved at the expense of Joe Cocker, although Cocker, incommunicado for months, was not making the complaint himself. Denny Cordell, Russell's producer and partner in Shelter Records, and a man who to this day holds Joe Cocker in great esteem and affection, was perhaps better placed than anyone to judge. "Yes, you can see why a charge like that was made—but in Leon's defence, that's how the cat behaved anyway. That was him—he was by nature a guy who hogged the limelight."

As to Leon Russell's opinion of Joe, Cordell: "He always said Joe was 'The Voice of the Common Man'. He said that's how everybody, when they've finished a day's work, would like to be able to get up and sing."

In the summer of 1970 Russell was interviewed in England by Pete Frame, for *Zig Zag* magazine. He said "I'm a Joe Cocker fan . . . If he doesn't feel it he doesn't sing it. I mean, he can take ridiculous songs and make them work." However, in 1988 Leon Russell said he did not wish to discuss Joe Cocker, as he had only negative things to say about him. From Nashville, via his manager, Brad Davis, he said, "If I don't have anything good to say I'd rather not say anything at all."

In September Joe did briefly emerge to speak to the rock press, who were eager and very curious as to his future plans—but he could not tell them. When he spoke to a *Melody Maker* correspondent there was no mention of Leon Russell and only a slight indication of the deep disillusionment that he was to later feel. "The trip was great, tough and tiring, and I reckon I picked up around 10,000 dollars at the end of it," he said. "I was physically and mentally exhausted—I've spent a lot of time thinking about what I wanted to do . . . I don't really have much respect for my career. All I do is sing. I just take time as it goes by. I've got no big ideas. Money is handy, there's a lot you can do with it, but I've got no great ambitions. I'm just waiting to see how it comes out."

Meanwhile A & M set about capitalizing on a tour which, for all its sellout shows and vast media coverage, had made little net profit. Expenses had been high due to the large number of people and the travelling involved, while venues were mostly in the 2,500—5,000 capacity range, rather than the 20,000+ stadium shows that became *de rigueur* for big rock acts as the seventies progressed.

It was intended from the outset that a live album should come out of the tour and several shows besides Fillmore East were recorded. On hearing the tapes, however, Denny Cordell and Leon Russell, who by now had a greater involvement in such matters than Joe, were disappointed. They did not feel that the tapes reflected the true quality of the live shows. A & M, refusing to let such a potential money-spinner slip through their hands, asked Glyn Johns to become involved. Johns had worked for Cordell on the first two Cocker albums and on Leon Russell's solo album and had the highest regard for Joe, whom he later described as "one of the finest—if not the finest rock 'n' roll singers ever to breathe."

Glyn Johns listened to the tapes, discarded all but those recorded at Fillmore East, and concluded that the only real problem was an out-of-tune choir. This was not surprising since on many nights the Space Choir had included all kinds of hangers-on, many of whom could not sing. Johns re-recorded the basis of the original choir in the studio, mixed the album and saved the day for A & M.

The Mad Dogs and Englishmen double album reached number 2 in the U.S. album charts and number 16 in Britain. Critically it was not so well received. "Probably indispensable to die-hard Cocker fans," wrote *Sounds*, warning "anyone else should proceed at his own risk." "An impressive document," said American writer Robert Christgau, "but the same overkill that was so exhilarating live wears a little thick over a double L.P." At least back in Sheffield the record got an unequivocal review. "One of the most exciting releases in a long time," said *Top Stars Special*. "It will be a big seller."

"We sold over a million albums in America, and the figures for the rest of the world were impressive," says Jerry Moss. "It was a big success for us that soundtrack album . . . You see we never had Joe Cocker worldwide, originally, we only had him in the U.S. and Canada . . . but David Platz did allow us to have that album because it was a soundtrack. It's an extraordinary record . . . one of the greatest records we've ever put out—and we've had some nice live albums."

Speaking of the album to *Zig Zag*, Leon Russell said "It is a weird album for me to listen to because I can't help but compare it to the nights when we didn't have the tape machine there—it was better on those nights. I guess if you don't have that frame of reference then it sounds good. But there were so many film men and other extraneous people walking around the stage that it was very difficult to concentrate on playing."

The film *Joe Cocker/Mad Dogs And Englishmen* was released in America in the Spring of 1971. Made at a cost of half a million dollars by an A & M subsidiary, J & H Films, it was directed by Pierre Adidge, who told *Circus* magazine "There is a great deal of interest, I think, on the part of the record buying public. They're really interested in what's going on behind the scenes . . . seeing the ups and downs and the end results . . . the feelings of the people involved, that's really what the approach is. Basically this was no ordinary tour. The film is music. We've tried to capture what they tried to capture on their journey, what their hopes and dreams were."

The two hour movie, out from seventy hours of film, falls short of these aims. It contains some excellent music from two concerts—Fillmore East and Santa Monica Civic—and in between follows the troupe to recording studios, rehearsal rooms, dressing rooms, hotel rooms, buses, aeroplanes, cafeterias, even a picnic. However, the feelings of the people involved, their hopes and dreams—which Adidge hoped to capture—are none too evident. There is stoned philosophy aplenty and no lack of cosmic mumbling but the film reveals little insight into the characters and no inkling at all of the tensions and traumas which pervaded the actual tour once the initial euphoria had faded.

Joe, looking thinner than he has ever done before or since, begins the film cheerful and chatty, becoming inexplicably withdrawn, almost a man apart, as it progresses, while Leon Russell surveys the entire scene with glacial cool, onstage and off. The two are never seen in conversation with each other during the entire film.

Jerry Moss, who was on the early part of the tour, speaks of the relationship between Joe and Leon Russell at that time. "From where I was sitting it felt OK to me. I think they had such a great respect for each other musically . . . Then I saw the tour when they came to California—and in a way Leon was upstaging him. But still Joe had a tremendous power and everybody felt that he could take it over anytime he wanted to. He was sort of letting this thing happen . . .

"There were a lot of drugs on that tour and Joe was just starting to become very evasive and not very communicative. Joe was a guy that, especially during that tour, would never say no to anybody—about anything. This was apparent during the filming—and we had to make a decision on that film whether we wanted to shoot a film that was documentarily very interesting but somewhat damaging to our artist. I guess you might say we ended up a bit on the boring side, but we just didn't want to make him look bad."

Overall, Cocker personally received a better critical reception than did the film, which suffered from adverse comparisons to *Woodstock*. "He does hold the screen and you submit to his weird, mesmerising power when he's singing," said the *Toronto Globe & Mail* in a piece that condemned the movie as "unrelieved tedium". *Time* described Joe as a "holy man seized by a vision, sweating, growling, rolling his eyes and moving in great bursts of spastic energy." A little more generous than most, *Time*'s reviewer concluded "If 'Joe Cocker' cannot compete with the best, it has enough talent and energy, and an abundance of sensational sounds, for its audience to sit back and, like the old song says, let the good times roll."

Joe, in no mood to heed such advice, found the financial aspects of the film only added to his disillusionment. "I signed a contract where I got something like 95% of the gross, which I thought was fantastic . . . I didn't realize I had to pay for every expense imaginable. I still have a deficit for making it," he said in 1982. Even now, with the movie available as a video, Joe says he has still not received any payment in respect of the film.

Nor did his anticipated earnings from the actual tour come up to expectations—the $10,000 he mentioned to *Melody Maker* in September 1970 was reduced to $862 after unforeseen expenses had been deducted. Fortunately the success of the double album provided substantial royalties.

* * *

Still lying low in Los Angeles, Joe Cocker was the subject of much press interest as 1970 rolled on without any sign of his return to live appearances. When a proposed autumn tour was cancelled the rock pundits shook their heads sadly and speculated as to what had gone wrong.

Cocker was frustrated by his inability to play an instrument, they said, hence his "wandering fingers"; he was hung up because he couldn't write songs; depressed because the old time rockers like Chuck Berry and Jerry Lee Lewis looked years younger than they had ten years earlier, while he looked older than he had only a year ago. The finger was pointed at A & M who, it was supposed, could not handle their first real rock star; at Joe's background in the North of England; at his naïvety in the cruel, hard world of rock and roll. Joe had neglected his mind, the story went, he was afraid that he could not repeat the fantastic success of Mad Dogs, and he had succumbed to every intoxicant known to man.

There may have been some truth in some of these assertions but the plain fact was that Joe Cocker, a sensitive man of total musical integrity, was not going to resume his career until he saw fit. Mad Dogs had been a profound and devastating experience, forced upon him. The realization of how little control he had over his own destiny had left a scar which would take many years to heal.

* * *

In November Joe was persuaded by Denny Cordell to travel to Muscle Shoals in Alabama, where, together with Chris Stainton, he recorded 'High Time We Went' and 'Black-Eyed Blues', both joint compositions, which comprised the next single. Since his first Top Ten hit, 'The Letter', Joe's single success in the States had declined, 'Cry Me A River' making number 11 and 'She Came In Through The Bathroom Window' reaching only number 30. 'High Time We Went' did only marginally better, reaching number 22. Also in November, Joe was seen on British television, where he duetted with Tom Jones in the latter's show, recorded the previous February, before the Mad Dogs tour. Then, as Christmas approached, he returned to England.

Arriving at Heathrow Airport, Joe made for the nearby home of Bruce Rowland, former Grease Band drummer. The band had never been formally sacked—in classic rock business style they discovered they were no longer required when their £30 per week wages stopped, and they learned Joe was in L.A. rehearsing for a tour he had sworn he would not do. They had seen his disbanding the group as a token gesture, a ploy in his protracted argument with Dee Anthony, and were amazed to find that he was going through with the tour.

Despite the unsatisfactory manner of their dismissal, however, there was no bad feeling towards Joe from his former band. Indeed Bruce Rowland says "I was relieved. I'd had enough of those people . . . Dee Anthony, A & M, Premier Talent—it all seems pretty sick looking back." But Rowland and Alan Spenner, pleased to see Joe again, were shocked by the state he was in. Spenner: "He was like a different person . . . talking to himself . . . he could be talking about something and then in a second he'd change subjects and be talking about something completely different. He seemed very depressed, very unhappy, very alone and it looked to me as if he'd suffered a lot. I know he did the tour under protest and I think he just downed as many anaesthetics as he could . . . The damage had been done, because he was not the same guy that we'd waved goodbye to. He didn't want to know about music—he was adamant about not doing anymore. He was totally shattered and disillusioned by the whole business."

Joe's brother, Vic, was in London on a course relating to his work as a Water Board economist when he got a call from Eileen Webster, who had split up with Joe prior to the Mad Dogs tour. "Eileen got hold of me and suggested that I ought to contact Joe. She was living with some guy who Joe had known previously but she'd heard stories about drugs and she told me to get in touch with him and make sure he was all right. I met him and he came up to our house and stayed a couple of nights. He chatted, but it was difficult to know what was going on."

From his brother's house near Birmingham, Joe headed home—to Tasker Road, Sheffield, where he would remain, apart from occasional wanderings, for the next year. His parents, who had not seen him since well before the Mad Dogs tour, were deeply concerned by his physical and mental condition. Harold Cocker: "He was like a zombie. He just sat here all day, staring into space. He never said anything—he just ate his meals and sat here. He seemed played out entirely."

* * *

In the aftermath of Mad Dogs and Englishmen it was not only Leon Russell who carved out a successful solo career. Bobby Keys, Jim Price, Matthew Moore, Claudia Lennear, Chris Stainton and Rita Coolidge all subsequently released albums under their own names. Although Russell made the biggest impression at the time, Rita Coolidge's career has been the most consistent—with nearly two decades of Top Ten singles, Gold and Platinum albums, and a Grammy. Mad Dogs and Englishmen holds many unhappy memories for her—all of which fade when she recalls the excitement of the actual shows. "I've said it time and time again—no matter how horrible and depressing and how insane the life on the airplane and in the hotels . . . the second that the music started and Joe hit the stage I was the happiest girl in the world. And there would be nights when I would have sworn that the man could not make it to the stage, much less do a show—yet every time Joe walked on the stage and began to sing—the show was his. He never missed a lyric. At that time he was still able to drink and do the drugs without falling down. He would walk on a stage and he would be a hundred per cent there. There was no doubt about who the people came to see, and who was controlling the magic moments . . . Just seeing the power, the incredible power that he had with music. When the music was over he was almost like a helpless child, but when he was singing there was nobody could touch him. It was an amazing thing to be able to share that."

Jim Keltner, still one of rock's most sought-after drummers, remembers his disappointment when he learned it was all over. "Playing in that band was absolutely fabulous—some nights we were ten feet off the ground. It was just an incredible experience and I've never had an experience like that since . . . I didn't see the parting but I remember being annoyed with both of them, with Leon and with Joe. After the whole thing was over and we got *Time* magazine— hey this was a big deal! and I remembered all the fun that we'd had. That was one of my first big disappointments about rock and roll people. You know, they've all got egos and they've all got problems. It just seemed like a big shame."

However, in Denny Cordell's mind, there is no doubt that, for Joe, Mad Dogs was a mistake. "The only point of the tour was to try and salvage what Dee Anthony had told us, which was the ability to work again. It was a strange court, Mad Dogs and Englishmen, a very strange court, and as great as a lot of it was, ideally I wish that it had never happened. Because ideally we would have gone out with a quartet or a quintet and done a different show—rather than a circus. I'm not saying Joe's subsequent career would have been any better or any worse—but I'd like to think that if he hadn't done Mad Dogs and had gone out and played with a quartet and a tenor sax, or a quartet and three girls, that he would have finished an exhausting tour having gone through another stage in his development and come out of it feeling that he'd achieved something. One of the most bitter things for Joe probably was that at the end of the Mad Dogs and Englishmen tour he was being acclaimed for something he knew was pretty hokey. I always thought Joe was on a par with the Greats."

The last word on the tour which "set out to Venus, heading for Outer Space" must go to Joe Cocker. In the spring of 1988 he said, "At the time I was left feeling exhausted and with no ambition for the future—that was the horror of it. I remember being in the hotel, the Sunset Marquee, and I'd lost so much weight—for me I was like down to the bone, and I felt real bad. You're asking me how I feel about it now? It left its scars on me—but so have many other tours and stuff. When I look back—there were a few girls on that tour, in the background, I know a couple of them died . . . and then the drummer, Jim Gordon, he killed his mother. It left its scars on me but . . . it was just one of life's little ventures."

79

Chapter Eight

1971

Alive And Well
And Feelin' Alright

THE BRITISH MEDIA could not comprehend why Joe Cocker was back home in Sheffield. They were especially puzzled when he said he had no plans to return to America, nor indeed any plans at all, other than perhaps buying a house in the countryside around Sheffield. In 1970 he had sold three million dollars worth of records in America and, with the Mad Dogs album high in the charts, he was well on the way to a third Gold Disc. American *Playboy* had recently voted him number one vocalist in their annual jazz and rock poll—above Paul McCartney, Tom Jones and Frank Sinatra—and promoters in the States were reported to be clamouring for his return, offering up to $50,000 a night. None of which appeared to interest him in the slightest.

To the outside world the only sign of success was a new blue Rover car, which stood out among the older models parked on Tasker Road. Occasionally Joe would venture out in it but most of the time his only excursion from the home was to walk round the corner to the local pub, the Mason's Arms. "I tried to get him to go out or to go and listen to music, but he wouldn't," says his brother, Vic. "He didn't want to know about music. I couldn't understand it but he just wouldn't communicate."

Communication was a problem when a Yorkshire Television crew unexpectedly arrived one day, as Joe was eating his breakfast. "They burst in the door with like nine cameramen as I'm eating my Weetabix. I said 'What are you guys doing here?' and they're giving me the old bit 'Why have you come back to Sheffield?' Then they took me down town and started to film me walking past the Gas Board Showrooms. There was a pub on the corner and this fitter who I knew came past and said 'How tha' goin' on?' So I went in the pub with him and forgot all about the television crew."

Ray Stuart, at that time a freelance broadcaster, interviewed Joe for BBC Radio's *Scene And Heard*. "He was very disappointed with what had happened on the Mad Dogs tour. He said 'It started out as love and peace man, and ended up . . . chaotic! He was disillusioned. He seemed to be thinking 'That's it—I've done it now and I don't want to do it anymore.' He just wasn't bothered about rock and roll music—I don't think he wanted to be mixed with music people."

Joe's original guitarist, Phil Crookes, had not seen him in a long time when they met by chance one day. Phil was saddened by the change in personality. "The humour had gone. One of the things I always loved about Joe was that spontaneity . . . that humour. He just got into sitting around and umming and arring. Joe is a very deep feeling feller—you've got to realize that. Everything comes out through his music—he's got that much soul. He's like a painter who paints from within . . .

"Going over to the States . . . working with someone like Leon Russell—it had all made a profound impression on him. Going through all that—it would have given any normal person a lifetime to think about it. And afterwards it was a funny time—a lot of people smoking dope and just sitting around. It seemed to be the thing to do—sit there in ethereal silence . . . You see Joe was the sort of person who liked to chatter . . . to communicate . . . and that had all gone."

Another of his former musicians, Dave Memmott, got in touch. "I rang the house one Sunday lunchtime and we went for a drink. He'd got wellies on—God knows why, it wasn't raining. He didn't say much but I remember him saying that he wished he could trust somebody . . . he felt he'd lost control and was just being used."

After weeks when he rarely moved from Tasker Road, doing hardly anything within except eat, breathe and sleep, Joe slowly began to stir. During his schooldays he had shown some inclination towards drawing, illustrating his school exercise books with pictures of rock stars—now he briefly took his interest a little further. "He painted a portrait of Ray Charles in oils," recalls Harold Cocker. "It was on a piece of hardboard . . . head and shoulders . . . I don't know where it went."

Joe also made some vague moves towards buying a house out of the large royalties cheque he carried about in his jeans pocket for many months. He recalls visiting Sheffield estate agents. "I'd be there in big wellingtons and hair down here. . .
'I'm looking for a house. . .'
'Oh yes. What sort of price range are we talking about?'

'Weell. Hundred thousand pounds?'

'Ohhhh. . . Very good'

Then it would be 'Will somebody get him outa here? What kind of loony is this?' No one would take me seriously so I ended up leaving the cheque in my jeans and putting my jeans through the washing machine—and the cheque just faded away."

Kenny Slade, who had put his earlier sacking from The Grease Band behind him, began making regular calls to Tasker Road, and when Joe did emerge, the diminutive, highly-charged drummer was usually in attendance. "We went all over together" recalls Slade. "He once came to my house . . . I was in the flat—little maisonette with the wife and child—skint as usual—and I hear this really loud rock and roll. I open the door and Joe's stood there in his Afghan coat. He's got a Roller outside—new Roller with a driver, tinted windows and stereo blaring—all the neighbours are coming out, to see what's going off. He says 'Come on, does tha want to go for a drink? So I made an excuse to the wife—didn't even bother getting changed. I think I was away about five days. We went all over the place . . . down the Smoke, all over . . . getting drunk and just being outrageous . . . chauffeur driving us everywhere. Plenty of pills, plenty of acid and plenty of booze."

Kenny Slade has difficulty recalling much of the time he spent with Joe in the post Mad Dogs period. "We were usually stoned. He used to do all the paying, I'll give him his due. He never talked about Mad Dogs but I know he didn't like Leon Russell at all, I do know. Hated him."

On Saturday February 27, 1971, Leon Russell and his band played Sheffield University. "Glad to be in Joe Cocker's home town," Russell told the crowd that packed the Students' Union. "We phoned Joe at his home this afternoon and we're hoping he's gonna show tonight." The audience, electrified by Russell's presence from the moment he walked on stage, applauded wildly, unaware of the animosity between the two men. Joe was in Sheffield that night, at the home of a friend who tried to persuade him to go to the show. "I'd dropped a bunch of acid . . . I said 'no'. We'd fallen out pretty badly."

Nearly three months later Joe did appear on stage with a former member of the Mad Dogs troupe. Rita Coolidge, who, like Russell, had embarked on a solo career, played Sheffield City Hall as support on The Byrds tour. She was halfway through her spot, backed by her band, The Dixie Flyers, when Joe suddenly appeared from the wings, announcing that he was "sorry to break into someone else's show, but this is such a great band that I just had to sing." He improvised two rambling 12 bar blues before duetting with Coolidge on Bonnie Bramlett's 'When The Battle Is Over'. Rita Coolidge: "I called him when we got in, just said I wanted to see him. So Joe showed up that night, he came backstage and we decided that he'd come out and sing with me. I remember he was on stage and we were having the time of our lives—and Roger McGuinn was on the side of the stage, pacing back and forth and pointing to his watch, screaming 'Get him off . . . GET HIM OFF!' Cos there was no way he was gonna be able to follow that. He was as livid as a snake! I know that Joe had taken a lot of acid that night. I said 'Joe—how can you do that? How can you take ten tabs of acid and function at all?' 'Rita' he said 'The only difference in one tab of acid and ten tabs of acid is the pain in the back of me neck!'"

The following month saw Joe at Island Studios in London, where, in the course of a week, he recorded nine songs. Most of the numbers were composed in the studio, Joe putting words to Chris Stainton's musical ideas. B.J. Wilson played drums on most of the sessions, apart from one day when Ringo Starr turned up. Steve Winwood played bass and some organ, and Mick Wayne, from a little-known band, Junior's Eyes, played guitar. Joe, revealed Denny Cordell in a *Melody Maker* interview, played drums on a few tracks—"straightforward stuff, very basic, no frills at all."

The initiative to return to the studio, said Cordell, had come from Joe, who "just fancied a toot". They needed two more tracks for an album, which it was hoped would be out in the autumn, by which time Cordell expected Joe and Chris Stainton to have formed a band for the road. Meanwhile, he said, Joe was looking for a house in the North of England, somewhere he could install a recording studio.

"We went all over looking at houses," says Kenny Slade. "We looked at Stoke Hall . . . Bakewell Manor House. I remember that—we were both on acid, stoned out and wearing wellingtons and old jumpers. We turned up in a Daimler Sovereign Joe was driving at the time—he was a brilliant driver when he was stoned, but he tapped a few motors when he was sober. We parked it in this big courtyard. It was a beautiful place—millions of windows and big, high ceilings. Three brothers owned it and they'd fallen out with each other. They were a bit baffled by us—I was so bombed out on acid but I was completely aware . . . I was all over the house—bit of damp here, bit of rot over there . . . while Joe's just wandering about. I explained that it was him who was interested but they hadn't a clue who he was. They said 'Well where's he got his money from?' I said 'Singing'. It was good but he ended up buying nothing."

* * *

The proposed new album did not materialize in the autumn and the nine tracks recorded at Island were later considered to be below par and discarded. Despite Chris Stainton's best efforts, the band hinted at by Denny Cordell did not happen either, and Joe spent the second half of 1971 as he had spent the first—"trying to get himself together" in the words of an Island spokesman. His disillusionment and lack of motivation was not helped by disagreements behind the scenes between his business representatives.

Denny Cordell, whom Joe regarded as his mentor, had fallen out with his partner in Straight Ahead Productions—David Platz, also head of Essex Music—and they no longer communicated with each other. Cordell was also at loggerheads with A & M Records over his entitlement to a production royalty for the Mad Dogs album, and also because A & M were treating the record as a single, rather than a double, album for royalty purposes.

Cordell was now concentrating his attention on Shelter Records, with the emphasis on Leon Russell's career which was flourishing in the wake of the Mad Dogs And Englishmen tour. This was a situation not likely to give much comfort to Joe Cocker. Nor was Joe happy with the publishing deal he had signed with Essex Music. Since signing contracts with Straight Ahead Productions and Essex on January 1, 1968, he had been mulling over the ramifications of the deals, and his period of inactivity had given him plenty of time for thought. Out of character though it was for him, Joe decided to settle the matter himself.

Joe found that royalties were falling off, and suddenly thought... "Jesus, that means I have to sell loads of records before I make any real money. So I set up a meeting with Essex... and sorted it out. The thing is... when you're young and hungry you'll sign anything just to get a record out. Everything's groovy... we've got a deal... you don't care about the small print."

As a result of his own efforts Joe was able to increase his royalty income substantially.

While these events were taking place, Chris Blackwell, who had previously played a significant role in Joe's business affairs, retreated from the arena. But Dee Anthony, who had become Joe's American manager through his arrangement with Blackwell, was not so reticent. Anxious to get Joe back to the States and working again, he made a number of visits to England in 1971—seven, he later claimed—without managing to meet Joe once. This time there was nothing Anthony could do to force the situation—threats would be meaningless to a man showing such total disregard for his own career. "I think that hurt 'em a bit," muses Joe today.

Puzzling as Joe's attitude might have been to Dee Anthony and others who could not understand his reluctance to work, it came as no surprise to his brother or father.

Vic Cocker: "You see, my father is stubborn and Joe's the same. When he's taken a decision he doesn't go back on it. All the 1971 business—he couldn't make up his mind what he wanted to do, but he knew what he was not going to do."

Harold Cocker: "It seemed that they'd all just used him for their own ends and then washed their hands of him. If he decided that he was being exploited in any way then he'd set against it—and money or anything wouldn't influence him.''

*　*　*

In September, with the Mad Dogs and Englishmen film due for release in England, London's *Evening Standard* reported that MGM were scouring the country for Joe. A spokesman for the film company said, "We want him to attend the premier of the film at the Ritz Cinema, Leicester Square on September 23, but the last time his agents heard of him he was driving a lorry.''

Driving a lorry, broke and back working as a gas fitter—myths abounded as to Joe's whereabouts and activities. In fact he had become re-united with Eileen Webster and the two of them took off on a haphazard tour of the British Isles in a Ford Transit van with a drum kit in the back. "I just decided to truck around. I drove up to the Lake District and to John O' Groats . . . And back down to the bottom—called in at Wales—and just slept in the van. I ended up leaving the drum kit at Chris's house.''

His low profile served to fuel the belief that Joe was finished with music for good—a prospect which caused quite a number of American fans to cross the Atlantic and make their way to Tasker Road to discover the truth for themselves. "The house was like a railway station in those days," recalls Harold Cocker. "They used to come from all over the place. Madge used to take them under her wing—she'd sit them down in the front room and give them a cup of tea and talk to them. Sometimes she took them round to the Mason's Arms.''

One who made the pilgrimage in September 1971 was Carolyn Shaw from New Jersey. She had seen many of Joe's shows on the East Coast, from his first appearance at Fillmore East through to Mad Dogs and Englishmen. "I read somewhere that Joe was not going to ever tour again. I went up to the house with a friend . . . we must have walked past about a hundred times before we got the nerve to knock on the door and as we walked past we saw a woman in the house—it was Madge. What a nice person! She invited us in and made us some cookies and called Joe to get up. I was so nervous that he would come down and say 'Who are you?' but he didn't—we talked and listened to some records. I was so happy to hear that Joe was not quitting the business and that he just needed some time to unwind.''

In the same calm way that they had coped with the Cavaliers' nightly practice sessions, Joe's parents never complained about the invasions of fans and other visitors into their home. On occasions, though, Harold was grateful to be able to escape to his allotment, as he did the day a team of journalists and photographers arrived from *Life* magazine. Intent on including Joe and his mother and father in a large colour feature on rock stars and their parents, they soon found that while Madge was most co-operative, making tea as well as being photographed with Joe, Harold, in the magazine's words, "preferred gardening to posing." He remembers the visit, in the autumn of 1971, well. "It was a Saturday . . . they turned up with a big van, full of people and set lights up in the front room. As soon as I saw that I cleared off! I came back later and they were still here so I went off again. It was about eight o'clock at night before they went. They'd been taking photographs of our John and his mother. That wasn't for me—I'm a bit of a loner."

* * *

As 1971 came to a close it looked as though Joe Cocker's career was in ruins. He had not done a gig in nineteen months, had not had a fruitful recording session in over a year and there were no indications that the situation might improve. He had left it too long, said the pundits; the public had forgotten him; he would never come back now. But three weeks into the New Year, the man who many predicted a prime candidate to go the same way as Jimi Hendrix, Janis Joplin and Jim Morrison, surprised everyone by flying to Westport, Connecticut, where Chris Stainton was rehearsing with his own recently formed band.

* * *

After Mad Dogs and Englishmen Chris Stainton returned to England with his American wife, Gail, whom he had met on the tour, and bought a house in Buckinghamshire. Later in 1970 The Grease Band reformed and the following Spring Stainton played keyboards with them on an American tour. Back in England again he spent the rest of 1971 trying to interest Joe in a return to work and when all efforts failed he decided to put together a band of his own.

Stainton recruited steel guitarist Glen Fernando Campbell, from Juicy Lucy, Alan Spenner and Neil Hubbard who had both been in the re-incarnated Grease Band, and drummer Conrad Isadore. There were complex contractual problems but these were eventually resolved by the new band's manager, Nigel Thomas, a young Englishman who had previously managed Juicy Lucy, and in early January the band flew to Connecticut to rehearse.

Having got his musicians together, Chris Stainton needed a singer. Auditions were held and various people came along but no one impressed, and then one night Stainton telephoned Joe Cocker back in England. "We're getting this band together. Why don't you come over and have a sing," he said. The following day Joe was on his way to America.

With Cocker about, the Stainton band took on a different complexion. Word soon travelled around Westport and beyond and several hundred people turned up at the town's movie house each night, hoping to catch rehearsals. "Joe's just a singer in the band," Nigel Thomas told the press. "It's not meant to be the Joe Cocker show."

A tour was announced, to begin in mid-March and take in New York, Canada, California and Hawaii. Advertisements were placed, support acts were booked and rehearsals rolled on—and then one cold winter's evening, as Joe returned to the band's rented house from a King Crimson concert, he got a surprise. There waiting for him was a man who said he had been hanging about all day, hoping for an interview. Joe hesitantly agreed and, with the interview completed, found himself holding an injunction, restraining him from taking part in the forthcoming tour.

A spokesman for Dee Anthony's Bandana Management, who had obtained the injunction on what they called "Joe's Illegal Tour", said "We did this for Joe and in the end he'll realise it was for his own good . . . Either Cocker functions under Bandana or he buys himself out of his contract."

Joe's contract, it was claimed, had another two years to run. Nigel Thomas, at that point only the Stainton band's manager, but now representing Joe's interests in the Bandana dispute, saw the situation differently. "The whole thing was a matter of some substantial litigation and one of the terms of settlement was that no one was to give the details. However, it appeared to be the case that Chris Blackwell had originally managed Joe. He had made an arrangement to take care of the American management—as to whether Joe was under contract to Dee Anthony, or not, was what the subject of the litigation was about."

While Nigel Thomas and Dee Anthony briefed their lawyers, there were, as Alan Spenner recalls, "Some heavy scenes . . . black limos at the end of the street . . . various threats. There was pressure on the band, the road crew . . . the lot. It got to the stage where Nigel Thomas hired a security company who put an armed guard on the two houses where we were staying and the place where we rehearsed."

Prior to all this Dee Anthony had expressed strong words regarding Joe's situation, in an interview with *Phonograph Record Magazine* of Los Angeles. "Joe's gullible and he's clumped himself with people that have just poisoned his mind," he railed. "I can tell you this—if you look at the totals to see who made the most money on Joe Cocker, I would be the last in line."

Claiming that Joe had been misled into blaming management and agency in America (Bandana and Frank Barsalona's Premier Talent Inc.) for his current predicament, Anthony said, "I fought to break him in America. I mean, agents and promoters were telling me that Joe Cocker was a figment of my imagination . . . if only Joe can look back at that and really see the people who were there and who believed in him. Instead he believes those Johnny-come-latelys. It's these lecherous parasites he should get rid of. He doesn't need four headshrinkers and all that jazz. They destroyed Joe, they made a mushroom out of him. This whole situation is probably the sickest thing that has happened in the business."

Two weeks before the tour was due to begin, at Madison Square Garden on March 15, the dispute was settled. Nigel Thomas: "There was an amount of money paid to Dee Anthony. That money was paid partly by A & M, partly by me, partly by Joe and partly by the band's proceeds of the first tour." The settlement was reputed to be in the region of $250,000, in return for all managerial rights—a considerable sum for a contract which Joe claimed he had never signed. Bandana issued a press release: "In announcing the settlement Cocker expressed his appreciation and admiration of Dee Anthony for the success Bandana has helped him to achieve, but stated that he was interested in new projects . . . and that Nigel Thomas would assume the management role at this stage of Cocker's career."

A full-page advertisement in *Billboard* announced to the world that Joe was "alive and well and feelin' alright." To reinforce the point A & M re-released the 'Feelin' Alright' single. Joe Cocker might have been "just the singer in the band" but his return to rock and roll was a cause for considerable celebration.

* * *

"It came at exactly the right time, this band," Joe later told *Sounds*, "because I was beginning to feel vaguely ill-at-ease—you know, the guilt feeling you get . . .? I just let my mind drift too far away from music . . . I was always thinking of some future project, but you can think too long."

It was not easy to come in from the cold. "He was coming to all the rehearsals, but not doing much," recalls Neil Hubbard, the new band's guitarist. "He was mainly just listening. He used to sit by the drum kit, listening." Slowly Joe began to shake off his hesitancy and reticence and a programme was put together. And then about a week before Madison Square Garden he and Stainton sprang into action, deciding that girl backup singers were needed. Off they flew to Dallas, held auditions, and returned with three girls who called themselves The Dips. Alan Spenner: "They were pretty awful—they couldn't really sing. They weren't so keen about playing with whiteys either. At the audition Joe said to Chris 'Well what do you think of them?' And Chris said 'I think they're pretty terrible actually'. 'Great—we'll hire 'em'. Typical Joe anti-thing!"

With the first date fast approaching it was decided to hold a proper rehearsal on a stage, vivid in the memory of Neil Hubbard. "We hired the village hall in Westport . . . a theatre. . . . and somebody had the idea of throwing the doors open to the local people—and any musicians who wanted to come. And that's where Rick Alphonso and Fred Scerbo came in . . . trumpet and sax. They just came down for a night out and ended up in the band. Trouble was the gig was only a couple of days away so they didn't have a lot of time to rehearse. There was a third guy who also came down—he wasn't very good but he insisted on going to Madison Square Garden and 'having a blow' . . . and they were having to physically restrain him from getting on stage!"

*   *   *

Twenty thousand people filled New York's Madison Square Garden for Joe's comeback. His first show since Mad Dogs and Englishmen nearly two years earlier, it caught the attention of the media, even making the main TV news. But the show did not live up to the expectations of those who hoped for a re-run of Mad Dogs, a rootin' tootin' backtrack of the Joe Cocker catalogue.

'Love The One You're With', 'St. James Infirmary', 'Midnight Rider', 'Black-Eyed Blues', 'Woman To Woman'—a song Joe and Chris had put together only a few days before—the audience was faced with a set comprising almost all new numbers. "His biggest mistake," said reviewer Lillian Roxon, "was to choose to perform unfamiliar material when the audience was nostalgically dying to hear old favourites."

The old favourites never came—not even 'With A Little Help From My Friends'—but, just as certain cynics from press and music business began to mumble that Joe was putting the audience to sleep, he brought them to their feet with a rousing 'High Time We Went' and ended his set with the crowd screaming for more.

"It never got off the boil," Joe told the press afterwards. "I've just been out of action for so long. I didn't hit very many exciting notes but I thought we played well. I just didn't want to dwell—I didn't want to go back into the past too far."

In the aftermath questions were asked as to the wisdom of doing the first gig of a comeback tour in such a major venue. "To open in New York is to try to pick up dead weight at the center of the earth," wrote Alfred G. Aronowitz. Today, Nigel Thomas, who took the decision to open there, says: "It's always easy in hindsight and in that particular instance hindsight came a bit smartish. It was a mistake to play Madison Square Garden. We shouldn't have done it."

From New York the tour moved up to Montreal, where reviews were better, then back down to the Deep South. Crowds flocked to the shows, but no one could predict what would happen. Alan Spenner: "Looking back,

Joe was definitely not ready for it. He'd have good days . . . remember the words, and then the following day he'd just not be up to it. And he refused point blank to do any of the songs he'd done in Mad Dogs—or any of the old songs. I think if we'd known better we'd have said 'We can't do this at the moment . . . let's leave it for a few months'."

The problem was not just Joe's health, or his reluctance to perform old material; it went much deeper than that. Since his last live show, San Bernadino, in May 1970, he had been seen to dynamic effect in two major rock films, *Woodstock* and *Mad Dogs And Englishmen*. Says Nigel Thomas: "Joe Cocker had come to mean . . . to fans and to people in the rock and roll industry . . . something that was thirty feet high on a screen. He realised that he's not thirty feet high—and he could never compete with that . . . But since he'd become an icon, he'd become an icon to every bit of low life on the fringes of the rock and roll business. When you arrived in town for a show with Joe Cocker you'd have to seal the floor off to stop the dealers getting to him. We did that. We had security people on the whole hotel floor—and still they'd get to him. It was a nightmare—he attracted these kind of people because they knew he was an easy touch."

In Miami, just eight days after setting out, Joe was on top form. "It was like the wolfman returned," said the *Miami Herald*. "Cocker was out to wow his audience and he did, turning the evening into a revival meeting gone mad . . . Fierce as a bird, hard with energy as a thunderbolt, he is like some violent phenomenon rather than a person . . . The audience stood right up and jived to the beat . . . it's nice to have him back in action."

From Jacksonville to Albuquerque to New Orleans to Dallas and on to the West Coast the tour rolled, hitting L.A. the last week in April. Here the band underwent changes.

First to go were The Dips, replaced by the Sanctified Sisters—Viola Wills, Virginia Ayers and Beverly Gardner. Concern about lack of firepower led to veteran saxist Jim Horn coming in to bolster up the brass section—whose pre-tour experience had been only in and around Connecticut clubs. Drummer Conrad Isadore was not working out, and so Alan Spenner and Chris Stainton sounded out former Mad Dog Jim Keltner. Spenner: "To our amazement he said 'Yeah. I'll do it. Be pleased to—I've always liked Joe.' We couldn't believe it so we reported back to the manager and he got on the case."

Jim Keltner: "They called me up and took me out to dinner, my wife and I, and I really fell for old Nigel. I played the Los Angeles Forum, Las Vegas and San Diego. Then we went on to Baltimore and Pittsburgh before spending most of May recording at Sunset Sound."

Assisted by a second drummer—initially Jim Gordon and then Jimmy Karstein—Keltner played all the remaining American dates and on into Britain and Europe. He left after a wages dispute with Nigel Thomas. His recollections of the tour are of an anti-climax after his previous Cocker outing. "I think we were having a hard time—because we all remembered how great it was with Mad Dogs. I don't think it was quite as good—I missed Leon's direction. I loved Chris Stainton's playing—thought he was an amazing player—but I don't think we had a whole show together, somehow. That was my impression."

*   *   *

In May Joe arrived in England to top the bill at two open-air festivals, the Great Western—held at a farm near Lincoln—and Crystal Palace, London. Subjected to a great deal of media attention, he told the London *Times* that the million dollars taken on his recently ended U.S. tour was utterly meaningless. "O.K. I want a house. I can take some money and get a house and a couple of cars," he said, "but every time I eat a hamburger somebody wants to eat me."

Mad Dogs and Englishmen, and his ensuing hibernation, were the topics most interviewers were interested in, but the British music press did give due coverage to the new band. "It's been a good tour," Joe told *Sounds*. "When a band's playing like this band I feel I could do a 200 day tour without a day off and still not be tired. These days I am very relaxed and lay back on stage and enjoy myself much more."

But the two English festivals provided little cause for enjoyment. At Lincoln there was a one hour delay before the band went on stage, and the audience, who had been sitting in howling wind and rain for two days, failed to respond in the same way that they had to the previous band, Sha Na Na, who had done three encores. The Cocker set by now included a few of the old familiar numbers—'Cry Me A River', 'The Letter' and 'Feelin' Alright'—but the wait had been too long. It was not a happy homecoming for Joe, who was left at the end pulling his hair in frustration.

Crystal Palace, five days later, was no better. Headlining a similar bill to Lincoln, including The Beach Boys, The Faces with Rod Stewart, and Richie Havens, Joe again had to contend with diabolical weather, and an appalling sound system too. It was so cold, and the sound was so bad, that the band could only tell Joe was singing because they could see steam coming out of his mouth!

From London Joe and the band flew to Germany for one show, returning to England for two nights at the Rainbow Theatre. Then they embarked on the first ever Cocker tour of Europe, a series of shows celebrated by an official tour programme which stated "All complaints, writs etc to be delivered personally to Nigel Thomas. No legal claims will be considered unless in excess of $1,000,000." By now the second drummer was Englishman Alan White, previously with John Lennon's Plastic Ono

Band. Saxist Milton Sloane had taken over from Jim Horn and steel guitarist Glen Campbell had departed, a move hastened by his insistence on playing twice as loud as everyone else.

The European tour went very well. Joe was in good voice and was beginning to enjoy the rock and roll life once again. "Europe was best for us, that's when it really started," he later told *Melody Maker*. "You don't get a chance to do much except sleeping, getting in a few drinks, and rocking." They played France, Germany and Holland, before moving on to Italy, where, in Milan, after playing to a crowd of 32,000 people, he received a surprise back stage visit from Vernon Nash, his very first piano player.

The former Big Blues and original Grease Band man was in Italy on business for a Sheffield steel company. "I saw the show advertised, bought a ticket and went along to this great stadium. . . . there was half the Italian army out with riot control gear and guns. The show was absolutely brilliant—Stainton on the piano—impeccable. An incredible trumpet player in a wheelchair (Rick Alphonso) . . . it was a knockout. I went back to the hotel and we listened to a recording of the show. It was like Mao Tse Tung's China—every member of the band had something to say—'You were too loud there' . . . 'You shouldna played that, there' . . . They did a total post mortem on the show—stopping the tape all the time. They listened to every note that was played. I thought 'We never used to do that—God, these are real pros! Smoking dope and drinking like maniacs!'"

In mid August Joe returned from Europe and set out on a second tour of America. For trumpeter Rick Alphonso and saxist Fred Scerbo who had gone along for a jam back at Westport in March and ended up travelling America, Canada and Europe, it was journey's end. Alan Spenner: "They did improve, but only so far—so it was in for a penny in for a pound and the flavour of the month at that time was Bobby Keys and Jim Price—they'd been working with the Stones. So we phoned them up and they did the second American tour . . . We had a plane in the States—the pilot was brilliant. He had a sign outside the cockpit—'Normal cigarettes only in the cockpit please'. After the gigs he'd be partying—at the time I thought it was marvellous but looking back I think 'Christ! Was he really flying us about?' He used to pull strokes, flying back from gigs . . . 'Listen . . . we can't land at Hollywood—it's fogbound . . . we've got to go to . . . oh some really dodgy place right out in the wilds—but it'll only take three hours to get home.' Then we'd land at downtown Burbank and everybody'd be getting off, going 'Hey isn't it amazing, it all looks the same, California . . . really looks like Burbank to me!'"

* * *

On the first American tour some shows had been recorded—Tuscaloosa, New Orleans and L.A.'s Hollywood Bowl and Long Beach Arena, besides both London shows, at the Crystal Palace and Rainbow. The intention was for Joe's first record with his new band to be a live album of the previously unrecorded material that the band had been playing throughout the tour. In the end the album did contain the new numbers but only two tracks from the live shows made it, the remainder coming from studio sessions with Denny Cordell.

Confusingly titled 'Joe Cocker' in America—without the '!' of the similarly titled 1969 album—the new record made number 30 in the U.S. album charts. Released in Britain and Europe as 'Something To Say', it made no impression on the charts but received an encouraging response from the music press.

'Something To Say' is unique among Cocker albums inasmuch as Joe wrote the lyrics to six out of the ten songs. Put to tunes composed by Chris Stainton or, in the case of the title track, by roadie Pete Nicholls, they were written in hotel rooms or at rehearsals going right back to the first Grease Band tour of the States. Alan Spenner: "'High Time We Went', 'Black-Eyed Blues', 'Something To Say'—they were written back in '69 on the road in America. Joe put the lyrics on—he was a master. They just used to roll off his tongue . . . catch 'em on tape . . . write 'em down . . . they made sense."

Musically the album signalled Joe's change of direction, away from the commercial rock feel of his first two albums into a more jazzy, blues style— nowhere more evident than on 'St James Infirmary', one of the live tracks, and 'Woman To Woman'—another Cocker/Stainton number with a hypnotic beat and a seemingly impossible falsetto chorus which Joe handles magnificently. Greg Allman's 'Midnight Rider' gets the full holler treatment, while the hymn-like 'Do Right Woman', originally an Aretha Franklin B-side, has Joe sharing lead with Sanctified Sister Viola Wills.

"There's not a track on this album that's dud, not a note out of place and each track moves perfectly into the next" said *Melody Maker*. "If only every live show could have the consistency of 'Something To Say' Cocker would be right at the top for more reasons than a handful of hit singles."

The album has a subtlety and excitement that grows on the listener. The band, driven by the funky Spenner and Keltner is punctuated by the light brass arrangements and sealed by Stainton's piano riffs and beautiful single note runs, and Neil Hubbard's melodic guitar work. Uncompromising as ever, Joe's vocals just ooze feel and emotion, crying his blues, screaming from his soul in a comeback album that left no one in any doubt that he could still turn on the magic.

Chapter Nine

1972 — 1973

Locked Up Down Under

FEW ROCK ARTISTS are awarded twelve Gold Discs before they have set foot in the country awarding them. Fewer still arrive for their first sell-out tour, are twice thrown into jail, and leave the country before the Minister for Immigration can deport them. In Australia in 1972 Joe Cocker achieved both distinctions.

Joe arrived in Sydney on October 9 with an entourage of thirty people and forty tons of equipment and baggage. He came by way of New Zealand, where, three nights earlier at the Western Springs Stadium in Auckland, he made his antipodean début before a crowd of twenty thousand people.

Sipping champagne he met the Australian press who, surprised by his low-key and unassuming personality, seemed curiously bland with their questions.

"How long will you play at each concert?"

"One hour . . . one and a half hours . . . two hours . . ."

"Do you play rock and roll or rhythm and blues?"

"Yep . . . Something like that . . ."

"Do you sing many numbers from Mad Dogs and Englishmen?"

"Three."

"COCKER POWER FIZZLES OUT" declared one headline. "BUBBLY FAILS TO LOOSEN JOE'S TONGUE" said another. It did not look as if the visiting rock star was going to be too newsworthy.

The tour started well enough with four shows at the Hordern Pavilion in Sydney. The band now had Jimmy Karstein back on drums, assisted by Felix Falcon, a Cuban percussionist who had been around on the States and European tours. Bobby Keys and Jim Price never made it to Australia—they arrived in New Zealand with the band but left after the Auckland show following a wages dispute with Nigel Thomas. Without horns, the Chris Stainton Band was now supplemented by an extra guitarist, Ollie Halsall, from support band Patto, which also provided second drummer, John Halsey.

The Sydney shows went well and the tour moved on to Adelaide. At this point events off-stage thrust Joe Cocker's name onto the front page of every Australian newspaper, where it would remain for the next week. From being indifferent to the reticent rocker, who insisted "I'm really just excessively ordinary", the Australian media soon became avidly interested in him. His continuing presence in Australia was the focus of radio and television bulletins. His every word and action were reported and relayed to the world's press. People without the slightest interest in popular music suddenly became aware of Joe Cocker. Not through his records, or his reputation as the greatest white blues singer in the world, but through seeing newspaper headlines like "CRAZY JOE", "THE WILD MAN OF ROCK" and—inevitably—"THE MAD DOG".

* * *

Things started to go wrong shortly after 10am on Saturday, October 14 when two police drug squad officers arrived at Adelaide's Park Royal Motel. Acting either on a tip-off, or on the assumption that rock and rollers were bound to have some illegal substance in their possession, they went to Joe's room, got him out of bed and asked him if he had any Indian hemp in his possession. Joe produced a small quantity, which he told police he had bought in Sydney. Police reinforcements were called, other rooms were searched and Joe, five members of his band, and one of their wives, were arrested. They were taken to police headquarters and questioned before eventually being released on bail of $200 each.

On Monday, October 16, Joe and the others appeared at Adelaide Magistrates Court. They pleaded guilty to the charges and were remanded on bail for a further two days, when they were each fined $A300 (£140). The magistrate, passing sentence, said that he gave each of them credit for frankness and co-operation with the police, and for the fact that there was no suggestion that any of them were distributing drugs. As he left the court Joe told waiting pressmen "I think the verdict has been fair." Putting the bust behind them as an occupational hazard, an unfortunate brush with the establishment, Joe and the band immediately left on a flight to Melbourne, where they were booked to play four shows. Little did they realise that the matter had not ended in the magistrates court. Or that their troubles were only beginning.

Nigel Thomas: "When we arrived in Melbourne it was like someone had just assassinated the president . . . it was unbelievable. While we were flying from Adelaide some M.P. who no-one had ever heard of decided to make a great issue out of it—'Chuck all these corrupting poms out of our country.' In those days Australia was a terribly Victorian sort of society. It was also just before the Australian elections—I suppose M.P.s latch on to this kind of thing and he decided to get himself some press and he called for their deportation—which everybody thought was hilariously funny. The press thought it was funny—until such time as he somehow managed to inveigle the support of the Immigration Minister . . . who also decided, no doubt, that this would be good for votes—and decided to get on the bandwagon."

The Member of Parliament who raised the issue was Frank Stewart, a Labour politician of New South Wales. As the Cocker party was in flight to Melbourne he was asking the Minister for Immigration, Dr Forbes, in the Federal Parliament, if he was aware that the group members had pleaded guilty to drug charges. He went on to ask Dr Forbes if he had authority to withdraw their entry permits, and if he would exercise such authority "in the interests of the young people of Australia." The Minister replied that enquiries would be made, adding that he had various powers in relation to deportation.

Dr Forbes' inquiries did not take long. The following day, Wednesday, October 19 he signed deportation orders on Joe and the six others fined with him in Adelaide. They were told they had two days, until noon on Friday, to leave Australia, or they would be taken into custody and subsequently deported. The Minister said, "I have to do this because this government takes a very serious view of such offences, especially when committed by persons in a position to have a profound influence on many young Australians." "GET OUT" screamed Australian newspaper headlines, "POP KING WILL BE DEPORTED", "JOE COCKER PLEADS TO STAY".

Argument raged over the Minister's decision. In Perth a street quiz of young people—many of whom had tickets for Joe's forthcoming show there—voted five to one in favour of deportation. In Adelaide a Methodist clergyman protested that the order was a misuse of justice. A television pundit expressed the opinion that "any ordinary decent Australian" arrested in Joe's circumstances would be jailed. Labour's immigration spokesman publicly disagreed with his colleague who had started the ball rolling, saying that on the available evidence the Cocker party should not be deported, while the Sydney-based *Daily Mirror* pointed out "Pop star he may be but the fact is that a good 75 per cent of the people who have paid to see him in Australia were not our tender impressionable youth but consenting adults between the ages of 23 and 28."

Joe, in an interview with the *Mirror* said "We were nicked and we were fined. It's as simple as that. I'm not bitter about it. How could I be? We bought a bit of grass in Sydney and if we hadn't been nicked we'd have smoked it that night . . . but God, I wouldn't want to be deported. I wouldn't dream anything like that could happen." Sitting in his Melbourne hotel, holding the hand of Eileen Webster, with him on tour but not one of those arrested, he asked, "Why are they after me? I'm sorry for what I did . . . I was busted and fined . . . Now all I want to do is get on with my concert. That's all I came here for in the first place."

Besieged by press, radio and television reporters Joe went ahead with the first Melbourne show, as his lawyers prepared an appeal against the deportation order. Introduced by the M.C. as "Number 173567"—his newly acquired police number—to a tremendous reception from the six thousand strong audience in the Festival Hall, he began his first song with a full glass of wine in one hand and a near empty bottle in the other. "I've had crazy celestial words with the police, I just want to say I'm ready," he told the fans, putting his hands together as though hand-cuffed. Then came what one paper called 'the boomer' as Joe told the crowd "I'll take a bet with you that in five years' time marijuana will be legal in Australia . . . and that same cat who's trying to throw us out now will be smoking it himself."

The Australian press, reporting what they generally agreed was "one of the wildest pop concerts ever seen in Melbourne", enjoyed the treat. Barely mentioning the music, they gleefully recounted how Joe drank wine, whisky, beer and champagne on stage, took his sneakers off, threw drumsticks into the crowd and twice knocked the mike stand off, once hitting a reporter on the head. After an hour he staggered off, returning ten minutes later to send the audience into a frenzy with 'With A Little Help From My Friends' and, with the crowd screaming for more, he took off his T shirt, threw it to them, along with another handful of drumsticks, and left the stage for good.

Nigel Thomas: "Joe was tremendously harassed . . . there'd been the court hearing in Adelaide, we'd flown to Melbourne . . . the press were driving him crazy . . . he wasn't getting any sleep and we had to change hotels . . . and the night of the first show in Melbourne—he got drunk, basically. Then we went back to the hotel, where the Australians had yet another little number in store."

Joe: "I'd lost my shirt and I was barefoot . . . I just had a pair of jeans on. I go to get in the elevator and there were two black girls with me . . . Viola Wills and one of the other backing singers. And I'd got a six pack of beer to take up to the room. I was pushing the elevator button but it wouldn't close and all of a sudden this guy says 'Mr Cocker, we want you to leave the hotel.' I said 'All right I'll get out of here but let me go and pack my suitcase.' He said 'No—I mean right now.' I was so furious and I took one of these cans of Fosters and I was going to throw it at him—and the girls blocked him out of the way. So the elevator wouldn't go and this guy's screaming at me and the next minute plain clothes policemen came in and dragged me outa there . . . Cranked my arm up my back . . . I said to this guy 'Eh up mate, steady on—You don't have to break it, I know what you're trying to do . . . you're taking me off to jail.' Eileen Webster, my girlfriend of the time, and Neil Hubbard had a girl called Eileen—it was so funny—they were hitting these policemen with their handbags, over the head . . . saying 'Leave him alone' . . . 'Let him go' . . . with plenty of profanity. So they arrested them too. But it was so sensationalised . . . it was on the news every night—Cocker arrested. My mother saw it in the *Daily Express* and nearly had a heart attack!"

In all, Joe, the two Eileens, and a roadie, Keith Robertson, were arrested. Arriving after Joe at the hotel and unaware of what was happening, the roadie had no idea that the men who were ramming Joe head-first through the hotel doors were police officers, and he tried to rescue him. All four were taken to the police station and locked up overnight.

Joe: "So I get in this cell and the door clanks to and I'm sat there in the dark . . . I thought there was only me in there and then I hear this . . . like shuffling noise. Then suddenly a match lights up and this guy says 'Would you like a roll-up?' So I said 'That's very nice of you mate, it'll calm me down a bit.' He said 'What are you in for?' I said 'I don't know . . . creating a disturbance or something . . . how about you?' He said 'They call it murder. I killed an abo but we don't class it as murder' . . . and I was going 'Jesus! What have they done to me!' But I just talked to him and then about seven in the morning they let me go. Australia's where I got the reputation as 'The Mad Dog'. They invented sensationalism down there."

Joe limped into Melbourne Magistrates Court on Thursday, October 19, his foot injured on stage the previous evening. He was charged on ten counts—including assaulting the police, assaulting the manager of the hotel, resisting arrest, offensive behaviour, indecent language, insulting language and failing to leave licensed premises when requested. The case against him, and similar charges against the two Eileens and the roadie, were adjourned for a week, all four being granted bail.

The Immigration Minister had a stronger case for deportation now, but the order could not legally be carried out because Joe was on bail. The Australian promoter entered the argument, saying that he would lose $50,000 if the remaining shows were cancelled. Nigel Thomas tried to re-negotiate with the Immigration Ministry but they refused, declaring that they intended to carry out the deportation order regardless of Joe being on bail and would arrest him and the others in the hotel. At this point, besieged on all fronts by the world's press, and suspicious that the police had infiltrated the hotel staff—"There were always four or five room service waiters to bring up a cup of tea," recalls Neil Hubbard—the Cocker party struck back.

A hired furniture van was ordered to wait in the hotel basement, its engine revving. A sympathetic hotel employee fixed the lift so that it went straight down to the basement, without stopping at the lobby where the press lurked. Joe and the band then went down in the lift, into the back of the furniture van and were driven out of the basement to the countryside, where they enjoyed the hospitality of a friend of the promoter's. Meantime, support band Patto descended in another lift to the lobby, emerged with coats over their heads, to be rushed out of the front door and whisked off to the airport at high speed, with the press in hot pursuit.

"By this stage they were about to deport—but there was no one to deport," says Nigel Thomas. "And everything everyone did was on T.V. 24 hours a day . . . There was a marvellous moment with Viola Wills, singing to a news crew at the airport . . . We were still maintaining our position with the Ministry that it was all very silly, but they were getting maximum press out of it. So we played the show that night and they didn't attempt to arrest them, and then we played a midnight show."

These two concerts took place—without incident—on the Friday night— the deadline for leaving Australia having passed at noon while Joe was taking his furniture van ride to the Melbourne countryside and the Immigration Minister was attending a luncheon in Victoria. Shortly after noon Dr Forbes hastily left the luncheon, brushing past reporters with the words, "I have to leave because I have got a small problem called Joe Cocker. If I don't go now we'll have a national crisis." Later that afternoon Forbes, whose eighteen year old daughter had attended Joe's Adelaide show and, according to the press "loved every minute of it", announced that he had agreed to let the Cocker party leave by the first available flight the following day, at their own expense, instead of having them deported at a cost to the public. Thus the two Melbourne concerts were squeezed in, but the two in Brisbane—where the Police Minister had declared, "I will take every step in my power to ensure that young Queenslanders are not contaminated by such people"—were cancelled, as was an open-air show in Perth. All the shows were sell-outs.

*   *   *

Angry at the Minister's decision to force them out of the country, Nigel Thomas held a press conference where he expressed the doubt that any pop groups would want to visit Australia in the future. "There are a lot of political shenanigans going on," he said. "Dr Forbes has seen fit to ignore all the courses of legal justice. If this is Australian justice it smells. It smells if they are prepared to drop eighteen counts against so-called criminals the day after they are laid. We wish to contest those charges and have said so in court. Joe Cocker's reputation is something that nobody in the government cares about. He is not even being given the right to deny the charges brought against him."

The following day, Saturday, October 22, Joe and his party arrived at Melbourne airport in a fleet of cars. Hundreds of fans and a large contingent of T.V. and press reporters descended upon him as he stepped from his car. "I believe I was given a raw deal," he told them. Asked about the wild scenes at his first Melbourne show he said, "I got angry—it was a couple of your bottles of cream sherry. I don't do it every night."

He boarded a London-bound BOAC plane and flew to Sydney, where during a one-hour stopover he was kept in tight security, unable to leave the plane. It had been announced that he was travelling to London, but when the plane made its next stopover, in Los Angeles, he disembarked, thus fooling the hordes of pressmen waiting at London Airport.

In Australia it was time for the press post-mortem. "Cocker won't be the last", said the *Sydney Daily Telegraph*, reporting the Minister for Immigration's comments that all visiting drug offenders in future would "receive the same treatment as Joe Cocker." The *National Times*, in an article headed "GIVING THE JOE COCKERS THE RIGHT TO BE HEARD", criticised the Minister's wide powers in respect of deportation, saying "The Joe Cocker affair had undertones of haste and arbitrariness," although it was suggested, "No doubt Joe Cocker and his group have sufficient resilience to weather this nation's disapproval."

The most vociferous Cocker supporter was Craig McGregor in *The Australian*: "So they busted Joe Cocker. They even decided to deport him. It's a wonder they didn't crucify him as well.

"And for why? . . . Why was he raided at all? What possible threat could he pose to the Australian nation by turning on in his hotel room? He's here for a few days only, touring a country where marijuana grows wild like grass . . . and he's raided in the hope he has some on him!

"Who ordered the bust anyhow?"

Haranguing the police and politicians, whom he accused of "jumping in", McGregor commented: "Deportation. As I remember it, that's how Australia was started . . . by people who had run foul of a vindictive establishment. Now the wheel has turned full circle, and a purer than thou Australian establishment is re-enacting the past in reverse."

* * *

After a week in Los Angeles Joe flew to England, telling reporters who met him at Heathrow Airport, "I'm not in a hurry to get back to Australia." A few days later he talked to the *Daily Mirror*: "We walked into it, just like an ambush. Australia is so far away from here. It's like being on the moon."

Back home in Sheffield with girlfriend Eileen, Joe took his mother to see Buddy Rich at the Fiesta nightclub, where John Fleet, his old bass player, was in the resident band. Interviewed for the club magazine, he spoke briefly of the horrors of Australia. "We were hounded day and night. At virtually every gig there was a bomb scare. Everything was done to disrupt the tour. They stopped at nothing to get us out."

*   *   *

Over Christmas and the New Year he lay low, avoiding interviewers and spending his time either in Sheffield or at Eileen Webster's flat in London. In January he was in the audience at the Rainbow for Eric Clapton's comeback concert but what he wanted to do most of all was get back on the road himself. The previous year had brought its ups and downs but as it rolled on Joe had got increasingly into performing again, the nucleus of the band became tighter and tighter and, by Australia, he was singing better than ever. Unfortunately, progress had been hindered by off-stage events, but now he wanted only to get back to singing, with two Rainbow shows scheduled for early March, followed by a tour of Scandinavia.

The Rainbow shows were sold out soon after being announced and everything was set. Then, with a month to go, Chris Stainton dropped a bombshell. He had decided to retire from the road to devote time to building and running his own recording studio. Nigel Thomas tried to persuade him to change his mind, to no avail. It was a severe blow to Joe—one from which he would take a long, long time to recover.

Stainton was Joe's friend, his right-hand man, his arranger and the communicator of his musical ideas, as well as the leader of his band. For more than six years each had inspired the other and together they had made an impression on rock and roll that neither could have dreamed of, and almost everyone else had considered impossible. But now the partnership one former Grease Band man describes as "like a marriage—consummated in blood, sweat, soul—and in the end printers' ink"—was over. Nigel Thomas: "It was a great shame . . . one of those impossible things. Gail Stainton said that she wasn't allowing her husband back on the road and Chris said OK, if that's the way she wanted it then he wasn't going on the road anymore . . . If that hadn't happened I don't think a lot of things subsequently would have happened." Fifteen years later, speaking of Chris Stainton, Joe said "I miss him. We just had . . . a rapport."

101

Replacing Stainton was a different matter from replacing any other musician, and it soon became clear that the Rainbow shows and the Scandinavian tour would have to be cancelled. The British music press were not slow to comment that Joe Cocker's career was now in jeopardy—but there was more to come. With his right-hand man departed and his band dispersed, Joe now decided to part company with Nigel Thomas, barely twelve months since he signed a management agreement after the litigation with Dee Anthony.

Nigel Thomas: "When the thing with Chris fell apart he went into a depressive downturn and during that time we re-negotiated his recording agreement with A & M. That was the cause of my falling out with Joe because we re-negotiated on what were very favourable terms. David Platz, who was paying Joe a very low royalty, fell away and Joe became signed directly to A & M with a greatly increased royalty. But as part of the deal we committed with A & M that we would go into the studio very quickly—and we set up three basic formulae for recording."

The plan, recalls Nigel Thomas, was for Joe to spend six weeks recording in Nashville with Bob Johnston, who had produced The Byrds, Aretha Franklin, Leonard Cohen and Bob Dylan, among many others. From there he would go to Memphis and record an album with the Staple Singers, produced by Al Bell. As a failsafe, studio time was also booked at Muscle Shoals, using the famous rhythm section with Denny Cordell producing. One can only imagine what the outcome of these sessions would have been, not least an album with the Staple Singers, because the sessions never materialised.

"Literally the day before Joe and I were due to go to Nashville," says Nigel Thomas, "Eileen refused to let him go. For some reason, she said, they wanted another week. That was OK—I called Bob Johnston and put the studio time back. And then when I went round the following week to pick him up there was a furious row going on between Eileen and Joe . . . things were being flung across the room and she said 'He's not going'. So there's this huge row going on and then I have a row with both of them and say that it's grossly unfair to sign a deal with a record company—and after all they've paid a substantial advance to Joe—and then to just not go into the studio . . . completely unreasonable. They didn't think so and so they said 'OK, if you don't think that way . . . well then . . . do you want to not manage him anymore?'"

For a man who lived to sing, and who had been keen to get back to live work, Joe's refusal to go to America and record with such luminaries as Bob Johnston, Al Bell and Denny Cordell, not to mention the Staple Singers, was difficult to understand, as was his apparent eagerness to get out of his management contract, which he knew from previous experience would be costly. But at the time, depressed and disillusioned after the unexpected blow of Chris Stainton's departure, followed by the band's dispersal, Joe had sunk into a state of mind where reason and logic had little influence.

Joe: "What had happened—I'd started taking smack. I was living in this flat in London, that Eileen owned . . . and like anybody who's ever been involved in that stuff—you tend to think that nothing else really matters. I was in one of those states. I always remember Bernard Pendry, my English accountant, shaking his head in disbelief . . . because I went to this meeting and I said to Nigel Thomas 'I just want to get rid of you!' I just wanted him out of my life. And he said 'Well it's gonna cost you' . . . I gave him the whole lot . . . something like 400 grand. Jerry Moss was livid."

Says the A & M head: "That was the 400 we gave him to re-sign. We made a new deal . . . negotiated it with Nigel . . . and part of the deal—it was unwritten, but we felt that Nigel at least was getting Joe to go on the road and perform . . . It looked like they were getting along from where we were. Imagine how I felt when I heard that he'd just turned round and given the 400 to Nigel? I thought I was giving the money for the guy to get a house or something for his future. Cos it didn't look like he had a whole lot of money left, you know. The whole gesture . . . even though we all knew Cocker was a tremendous artist, at that time his stock had gone down a bit. He was disengaged from record producers . . . and it looked like he wasn't really together."

Nigel Thomas: "I'll tell you exactly what the circumstances of the split were. I don't think it's in anybody's interests to go into the precise details—but it's very easy to calculate. There were roughly two years left to run on his management agreement. During the course of 1972 Joe Cocker and associates—the band were partners in the live appearances—had grossed upward of $2\frac{1}{2}$ million. The A & M records deal that we had negotiated in the early part of '73 called for advances to be made to Joe in the sum of $2.4 million—which was a very substantial sum of money in those days—obviously not all payable up front, but over the course of albums to be delivered. We calculated the amount of money based on essentially the A & M Records deal—because that was something finite. The goodwill aspect of the further two years to run did not come into the negotiations. We said the thing which is obviously going to run over the period is the deal which I had negotiated with A & M. So we calculated the management commission payable on that deal alone—and that was the settlement."

Bernard Pendry, initially Nigel Thomas's accountant, had begun to also act for Joe and was thus in an awkward situation. A cheerful, down-to-earth Londoner who immediately hit it off with Joe when they first met in Jacksonville on the '72 U.S. tour, he studied both sides and tried to get the disenchanted singer and his manager back together—to no avail. No longer acting for Nigel Thomas, but still a great friend of Joe's, he offers his view of the situation at that time. "Joe had disappeared off the scene—he must have gone on a bender somewhere . . . nobody knew where he was—he'd disappeared off the face of the earth—no contact. Sometime in May '73 he wandered into the office, obviously wanted to split with Nigel Thomas, come what may. He was in a terrible state. He'd stewed up to it, you could tell. The reason that Joe split is that he got mind-wise that he couldn't stand Nigel Thomas. Joe always thought he spoke down to him and he had no rapport with him . . .

"It was lined up that we'd have a meeting and Joe turned up and offered to give him a million pounds or something . . . totally out of his head. It even shocked Nigel Thomas! Joe was so crazy he would have given away anything. Now the additional advance that Nigel Thomas had negotiated was $400,000—he had already had his 25% so it was down to $300,000—and Joe didn't have it—it had already been used for different things. But he said 'You can have all the advance.'

"I got Joe outside . . . tried to talk sense into him but he was beyond it . . . I think it's fair to say he was on heroin at the time. So we said 'Right—this is crazy—go away—we'll get the documents drawn up'. We advised him he must go and see a solicitor—got to have independent advice. He wandered off with the papers, never saw a solicitor, turned up the next day to sign everything—and promptly fell asleep at the meeting. The solicitor acting for Nigel Thomas said 'This is no good, you can't do this', so the meeting finished. He said 'We'll not be a party to it'. The next day Joe turned up—not legally represented—and signed everything. He was just like a steam train going towards a cliff—which you just could not stop. Unless you put Joe in a strait-jacket there was nothing you could do with him in '73. Nothing."

* * *

Befuddled by heroin, Joe disappeared again, not to be heard of for months. The financial settlement with Nigel Thomas was paid over a period of time for, although he had earned a lot of money, there was not much left. Out of the gross take of $2 million from the 1972 tours there were substantial expenses for the large entourage. Certain musicians had been on high wages and the net profit was split between the Chris Stainton Band that had started out in Westport. Thus, despite being the person most people paid to see, Joe received a share equal to Stainton, Neil Hubbard, Alan Spenner and—until they left—Glen Campbell and Conrad Isadore.

He did have royalties from earlier records and there had been the additional advance from A & M, which, as Bernard Pendry has said, was already used up before the split from Nigel Thomas. As to where Joe's money did go around this time, one can only speculate, given his uncaring attitude towards material things and his quite staggering generosity.

Joe Cocker has always been vulnerable to the tappers, spongers and freeloaders who proliferate within the world of rock and roll. "Money used to seem to be easily taken from him," says Harold Cocker, while Bernard Pendry says "He gave money—large amounts of money—to people I wouldn't give the time of day." There are stories of £30,000 to a man who wanted to open a record shop in Australia, £50,000 to another for a recording studio in Fiji—plus numerous lesser sums over and over again to the so-called friends and hangers-on who existed in abundance.

Today, looking back without any bitterness, Joe says "I went through the business of renouncing earthly things. And when you want to give away your money there's always somebody eager to take it off you!"

Chapter Ten

1974 – 1976

"Got Some Whisky From the Barman, Got Some Cocaine From a Friend"

NOT FOR THE first time in his career it looked like looked like Joe Cocker might have disappeared from the rock scene for good. There was no news of another manager taking over from Nigel Thomas, no news of recording, despite his re-negotiated A & M contract. There was no news of his activities, his future plans, even his whereabouts. For months there was no news of Joe Cocker at all.

Sitting in Eileen Webster's flat in Shepherd's Bush Joe was, in his own words, "In a drug mode . . . I was hanging round doing nothing at all." Blotting out of his mind the recent problems of his career, he had begun sniffing heroin and, just like many before him and many more since, he had quickly found himself gripped by the power of its euphoric effects. Although he was never reduced to injecting the drug, Joe looks back . . . "It had got a hold of me. I felt paranoid . . . if I was sitting in a bar I thought everyone was looking at me . . . wanting to kill me."

Jerry Moss tried hard to contact him: "I made several trips to England in those days and I always tried to reach Joe. I tried to call him . . . leave a message . . . I just had to get another record from the guy." On one occasion when they did meet, for dinner at the Dorchester Hotel, the turmoil in Joe's life was all too apparent. "We'd invited Joe up to the suite to have dinner and he and Eileen showed up . . . nice girl. It started out as a very convivial dinner and then at one point either Joe or Eileen excused themselves and went to the bathroom or something . . . and then one called the other and they were in one of the other rooms. Abe Somer (A & M's attorney) and I were listening to some music and we heard these sounds coming from the room . . . Then we heard some glass shattering and pretty soon we walked in there . . .

"There was blood coming down Joe's head and it looked like it was coming out at a pretty pace you know . . . There was blood on the carpet and the mirror was busted and the lamp was torn. I said 'Joe, I gotta call somebody . . . you may be hurt' but he said 'No—we're just gonna go home now.' I said 'You can't go home, you've gotta get fixed up' . . . 'No, no—we can go' and at this point Eileen ran out and I believe we were on the top floor of the Dorchester . . . We were in the hallway now . . . and she ran up the staircase, towards the roof. I said 'Oh shit—you can't go to the roof! Don't go to the roof!' I was starting to get just a tiny bit scared at this point . . . It was horrendous, but finally the two of them worked it out and they left."

Joe knew he had to kick the heroin habit, to pull himself back from the brink of a doom that many who knew him thought inevitable. "I had to . . . like, the dealers I met in London—they always play a game with you . . . They start off and there's plenty around and then—all of a sudden it's a hundred quid for a little taste . . . And I realised the game they were playing—so I went through what's commonly called cold turkey . . . which was dreadful . . . such pain . . ." Unlike other rock stars with drug problems, there was no expensive therapy or private clinic. Joe did it the hard way—alone.

In June he and Eileen travelled to Cornwall, intending to stay for a fortnight but remaining nine weeks in a remote, sparsely furnished cottage on Bodmin Moor. Afterwards they headed for Sheffield, where, sitting on the front room floor at his parents' home, Joe talked to Frank Heath of *Sounds*, the first interview he had given since before the parting from Nigel Thomas. "I'm on my own now" he said "And I'm not looking for a manager. Not right away anyway. I have a record contract to fulfil and I want to start on a new album. I can't wait to start again. I want to get a band together but now that Chris has gone it's difficult—we'd worked together for a long time."

He spoke of being temporarily banned from returning to the States—following the drug bust in Australia, of writing songs and of possibly finding a band of unknown musicians. The article gave hope to Cocker fans, even the most optimistic of whom had begun to fear the worst during this lay-off. "I'll head to London to get things moving on the album as soon as I can," he said. "I'm looking forward to it—it's been a long time."

It had certainly been a long time since Joe had got together with Denny Cordell, who had guided all his albums up to that point. And now, distanced from his former protégé, Cordell was no longer available. "I was running

Shelter, my own company—and Joe wasn't on Shelter. He was on A & M and was an A & M act. There was a bit of rivalry on the A & M front."

There was another, sadder reason for the break-up of what had been a productive and enjoyable relationship. Denny Cordell: "Joe and I had been absolutely tight. . . until a music biz lawyer put a spoke in our relationship by suggesting to Joe that I was ripping him off. He said to him—'You think he's getting 3% for his producer's royalty but in fact he's getting 4%.' And I could never get Joe to understand that I'd owned this record company in England and I'd sold my interest to Essex Music International—all the artistes I'd had in England—T.Rex, Procol Harum, The Move, Joe—in return for an ongoing interest in the company. Which amounted to a royalty over-ride of all records of the artistes out of the production company's end.

"So I said to Joe—'If I didn't get it then Essex Music International would get it—it's not as if it's coming out your part of the royalties' and he said 'Yeah luv, but you're a producer and you should only get 3%—and you're getting 4%. It's not right—producers don't get 4%.' That was it—he's a stubborn cat and the attorney had got it fixed in Joe's mind that I was ripping him off. And so there was a sort of lull in our relationship and we didn't see each other for a while .. . also, he'd gone into a pretty negative frame of mind."

* * *

It was Jim Price, who had first played with Joe in Mad Dogs and Englishmen, who got him back into the studio. Since that tour Price, together with his sidekick, Bobby Keys, had become one of the most in-demand horn players around, but it was as would-be producer, not a backing musician, that he came to Joe in 1973.

Joe: "That was the oddest thing, that got me back into it. I was doing nothing at all and Jim Price came round to the flat in London and played 'You Are So Beautiful', a Billy Preston tune . . . It sort of re-kindled my imagination a bit and he said 'I'd like to make a record with you'—so we set about it."

The ballad, 'You Are So Beautiful', would become an anthem to Joe Cocker fans the world over. His mother's favourite song, Joe would say many years later "Yeah, I still get a feeling . . . it's one of those songs. It doesn't matter if it's Japan, Spain . . . Italy—all over the world—the fact that it's so basic . . . simple words. It still moves me to sing it."

The first sessions for what was to lead to two albums—'I Can Stand A Little Rain' and 'Jamaica Say You Will'—took place in November, with Henry McCullough, who had recently left Wings, playing guitar. Joe had been pondering on the idea of working with his old Grease Band pal for a while, mentioning it in the *Sounds* interview three months earlier. Also on the sessions were bassist Chris Stewart and drummer Jimmy Karstein, with Jim Price playing piano and organ, besides producing.

"The first half of the tracks we went all round England," recalls Joe. "We recorded in tons of different places . . . Woburn Abbey . . . then down in South Wales—we stayed in this huge castle down there. I think Jim wanted to make a double album but then we got . . . confused. That 'Jamaica' stuff laid on the shelf for about six or seven months."

Eventually they ended up at Village Recorders in West Los Angeles, where, among the musicians who came along were star soul men—Richard Tee, Cornell Dupree, Chuck Rainey and Bernard 'Pretty' Purdie, the self-styled 'World's Greatest Drummer'. Joe: "I'd asked Jim about them—they were the top Atlantic session men at that time. I'd listened to them on record, with Aretha and such . . . So he said 'Would you like me to get them?'—and I said 'Yeah'. Fair blew me away but I remember Richard Tee coming in to the studio—he didn't know what to make of me cos I was drinking beer and I was very in awe of all those guys. He just sat at the piano and started playing all this funky stuff—and I went under the piano in ecstasy and fell asleep. He was most offended—'Hey this is not very nice—I come all this way and the guy falls asleep! 'But it was like . . . just a relief to hear such playing. He'd do all the church runs . . . flowing runs . . . and it was just so soothing to me."

The 'I Can Stand A Little Rain' album was released in America in the summer of 1974. As much a change in direction from 'Joe Cocker' (or 'Something To Say' in Europe) as that album had been from its predecessor, 'Mad Dogs and Englishmen', it revealed Joe's ability to choose and enhance other people's songs at its best. The title track was written by producer Jim Price, while Jimmy Webb provided 'It's A Sin When You Love Somebody' and 'The Moon Is A Harsh Mistress', endorsing Joe's treatment of his song by backing him on piano. Henry McCullough came up with 'Sing Me A Song', while ex'Mad Dog' Daniel Moore contributed the rousing opener, 'Put Out The Light'. Harry Nillson's 'Don't Forget Me' precedes the haunting 'You Are So Beautiful' with the two most dramatic and emotional tracks—Allen Toussaint's 'Performance' and Randy Newman's 'Guilty' saved to the end.

The Atlantic session men, Richard Tee and co., only appeared on one track—a frenetic Cocker/Price composition 'I Get Mad', their major contribution coming on the follow-up album. But 'I Can Stand A Little Rain' was not short on musicianship. Some of the finest of West Coast studio players are on the record, together with Randy Newman, whose rolling piano is heard on 'Guilty', backing vocalists Merry Clayton and Clydie King, and much-sought-after pianist Nicky Hopkins, who provided piano accompaniment for 'You Are So Beautiful'. A former Jeff Beck sideman and a contemporary of producer Jim Price in the Rolling Stones touring band, the list of notables with whom Nicky Hopkins has worked since he began in the mid 60s reads like a Who's Who of Rock. But Joe Cocker he describes as "one of my heroes", and 'You Are So Beautiful' as an all time favourite out of the thousands of songs he has played on: "If I've got three or four records that I'm really proud of, that's one of them. What a wonderful record."

The album was well-received by the rock press. *Billboard*: "After almost a two year lay-off Joe Cocker is back with what may well be his most consistently excellent singing since his heyday nearly five years back and perhaps the most entertaining variety of songs he has ever come up with. The powerful, bluesy vocals of Cocker stand better than ever and he can still belt with the best, but he has also picked up the ability to control his vocals on the softer side."

Music Week commented "He makes an emphatic re-statement of his capacity to penetrate the emotions better than any other white singer," while *Sounds* predicted few radio plays in Britain: "Joe Cocker is strong stuff for those fed since birth on milk and thin toast—but his agonized voice is always worth hearing. He sings 'Somebody reached up and put out the light', yet he can still sing the arses off most other singers even in the dark."

It was *Rolling Stone* that observed the "painful pertinence of the material" to Joe's personal experiences: "It is a record about pain and decline which, to make its points, cruelly exposes and exploits Cocker's damaged condition . . . even the titles of the tracks reflect Cocker's meteoric rise and fall . . . the suffering in his voice is so intense that no setting could enhance or dilute it."

At A & M Records Jerry Moss marvelled at the way in which producer Jim Price came up with the goods in the face of great odds. "He was the guy . . . he made this record which was a tremendous record. When you think of all the splicing that had to be done under the most amazing set of circumstances . . . I went to the studio in L.A. . . . The musicians that Jim picked were so great that the second or third take they were there—but Joe would forget the lyrics! So I went out to see him and I put a lead sheet together—I said 'Joe, you know it would make it a lot easier on everybody, including yourself if you just read the lyrics off'. . . He said 'WE DON'T DO THAT!' 'Oh . . . Okay' . . . But when you think of a song like 'You Are So Beautiful'—without the second verse in there . . . ! He would drink tremendously during those sessions."

'I Can Stand A Little Rain' reached number 11 in the American albums chart in November 1974. A single, 'You Are So Beautiful', made number five the following March. It would be more than eight years before Joe Cocker had another hit record in America.

*   *   *

The success of 'I Can Stand A Little Rain' was achieved in the face of some rather less than successful live shows. One widely reported debacle occurred in early June '74 at the Roxy Theatre on Hollywood's Sunset Strip, when an invited audience of journalists and music business people—Diana Ross, Cher and Marc Bolan among them—gathered to see Joe preview the material off his new album. Jerry Moss: "We had lunch the week before to talk about the show. He'd been fishing for a couple of days with Dick La Palm and he looked fantastic . . . tanned, his eyes were clear . . . he was wearing a white suit . . . I'll never forget this. He was so charming at lunch, he said 'Man, we're gonna do it. It's gonna be great. Don't worry about it.'"

But when he showed up for the gig he was too drunk to perform. "I had to tell them to pull the curtain" says Jerry Moss. "It was just sad. Jim Price had put together a band that was just extraordinary . . . Jimmy Webb on piano . . . but Joe couldn't remember any words. He was stumbling around the stage . . . had that sort of naughty boy look in his eye, like he was pulling one out on everybody. I remember looking down at Diana Ross, who just had these tears streaming down her cheeks. Everybody knew what he was going through—it was just terribly sad. By the third song he was lying on the stage in the foetal position."

*   *   *

Shortly afterwards he started looking for musicians to go out on the road. His first target was Henry McCullough, at the time trying to get a band together in San Francisco. He abandoned that idea to join his old leader, bringing with him Mick Weaver, keyboards player and former leader of the London band, Wynder K.Frog. Jimmy Karstein came in on drums and the bass player was Buffalo Gelber—"a huge geezer from New York," recalls Mick Weaver, "had a huge head of hair and a big beard-looked just like a buffalo. Never heard of him before or since."

By this time Joe once again had a manager. Reg Lock had been managing Heads, Hands & Feet, an English rock band featuring ace country style guitarist Albert Lee, when he met Joe in Los Angeles. Lock, an ex-roadie, was very different from Joe's previous high-powered representatives and it was soon agreed that he would look after Joe's business. With a tour booked to promote the album, first priority was to find somewhere to rehearse the band.

Karen Lee, a real estate agent based in Southern California, was given the task. "It took a long time. They wanted to rehearse twenty four hours a day and I was very surprised how many people . . . older people who had

111

their houses for rent . . . knew who Joe Cocker was. They'd say 'Who wants to rent it?' and I'd say 'Well, a singer named Joe Cocker'. 'Oh no! He's not having our house!' I finally found this place in Buleton, which is about forty miles from Santa Barbara . . . it belonged to Hastings Harcourt. It was a stud ranch which had been sitting vacant for a while and it was perfect for them . . . lots of acres of land . . . nobody around—they could do what they wanted up there. I think Hastings Harcourt had had some sort of controversy with people in the town and liked the idea of a bunch of people in there who were gonna outrage everybody. They did—they terrorised the town!"

Mick Weaver: "We were supposed to rehearse, but to get everybody sober enough at any one time proved impossible. It was summer-time and everybody just sat out on the lawn, drinking Tequila Sunrise until the sun went down . . . and by then nobody was in a fit state to rehearse . . . We'd all get up in the morning . . . hung over from the night before . . . splash around in the pool and try to recover. The locals couldn't believe it—we all had our wives there and they used to go down to the town every day and just about half empty this supermarket of food and beer . . . endless bottles of whisky and Tequila—and every day they'd be down for more. I don't know who paid for all that—it must have cost a fortune."

There was rarely a dull moment in Buleton. One day Henry McCullough and Joe went horse-riding. Henry tried galloping, the horse fell, rolled on top of him and crushed his shoulder, while Joe fell off his mount and broke a wrist. One night Mick Weaver, tired of sitting around, took one of the rent-a-cars for a drive round the neighbourhood. Skidding on grass, he spun the wheels and a spark set the grass alight. By the time the fire brigade arrived the car was burned out and a large area of the countryside was in flames, with the night sky an orange glow. But that was not all—"Jimmy Karstein carried a gun . . . a pistol—it fired real bullets. When I burned up the car it took a couple of days before I'd got the nerve to go and look at what I'd done. And there was Jimmy—using the car as target practice. Caused a bit of a furore with the insurance man. He came to see a charred wreck and there's bullet holes in it!"

Karstein's gun almost brought about an untimely end to the career—and life—of Joe Cocker. Amidst many arguments between the band members—usually precipitated by drink—matters reached a climax between McCullough and Cocker. Joe: "He got real funny one night—tried to shoot me! He said 'Joe—you've not got it anymore'. So I said 'Well if that's how you feel then there's no point continuing together'. Then he picks up a whisky bottle and starts menacing me with it . . . so I pick up a Courvoisier bottle and the next thing he was asking Jim to lend him his gun to blow me away! We've met since—but we were incorrigible with each other . . . For getting drunk and then just getting silly."

McCullough left the ranch, to be followed soon after by Jimmy Karstein. Keener to work than the rest of the band, Karstein had kept himself apart from many of the wilder goings-on, but his departure was not the result of frustration or impatience—he broke his arm jumping off a roof into the swimming pool.

There was only a fortnight to go to the first gig and a new guitarist and drummer were needed—urgently. Reg Lock did not have to look too far. Heads, Hands & Feet had disbanded and Albert Lee and Pete Gavin were hanging about Los Angeles. Both moved into the ranch and rehearsals at last got under way. At that time Albert Lee's reputation as a guitar phenomenon was just getting into gear. In the 60s he had played with Chris Farlowe & The Thunderbirds in Britain, before going into session work and then country rock. One of his first sessions had been playing rhythm guitar on Joe's 'Marjorine' and when, shortly afterwards, Joe was looking for a guitarist for his first London Grease Band, Albert had been invited to join. He turned down the job, to his later regret, but now, six years and several bands later, he jumped at the opportunity. "I'd just done an album with Don Everly and I was waiting for him to go out on the road. The thing with Joe was a big deal . . . I was happy to be doing it—Joe was really good to the band, we all got an equal split, which was unheard of from somebody as big as him. We also incurred the debts, Pete and I, of the previous couple of months rehearsal. So we didn't start getting money until two or three weeks on the road . . . but we still did pretty good out of it."

The tour, Joe's first for two years, opened at the end of August in El Paso. The band—called the Cock 'n' Bull Band—had, with the exception of Mick Weaver, totally changed from that which began rehearsing two months earlier in Buleton. After McCullough and Karstein, Buffalo Gelber soon departed—why or where to, nobody can recall—to be replaced by Greg Brown. But it was soon decided Brown was not working out and so a New York bassist, Andy Denno, was flown in. He watched the show for a couple of nights, learning the set, and on the third he played bass while Greg Brown was on the plane home. Completing the line-up on back-up vocals were Marianne and Phyllis Lindsey.

"There were two tours," says Mick Weaver. "The first was about six weeks in the States and Canada . . . concerts, theatres. Then there was a break for two or three weeks in the Bahamas—we were supposed to rehearse but . . . you know. Then we were off again. We got slagged off on just about every gig really. There were one or two good ones . . . San Francisco was one—he came out sounding just like the old Joe Cocker. I remember we got to New York and Chris Wood (of Traffic) came stumbling into the dressing room in a terrible state. That was all Joe needed—we tried to get Chris out but I think the damage had been done."

A review of that show appeared in *Melody Maker*. "With somewhat weary fingers and a rather sad heart I must take up my typewriter to inform you that Joe Cocker is a shadow of his former self," wrote Chris Charlesworth. "The once great voice that thrilled thousands seems to have succumbed to the punishment Joe has been enjoying during his long lay-offs . . . On stage at the Academy of Music he came over as a stumbling drunk."

Albert Lee: "He could still be impressive . . . some of the songs would really bring thrills to you . . . but in general he was really nervous. We'd get to a gig early, go to the hotel and he'd start on a bottle of brandy before the gig. We'd get a call from the tour manager "Come up to Joe's room . . . he's got a bottle of brandy . . . come and help him drink it. We'd go up there and barge in on him . . . He wasn't eating and he was very nervous . . . throwing up on stage . . ."

In Toronto, where Joe and the Cock 'n' Bull Band played a fortnight after setting out, the *Globe And Mail* likened the attitude of people who attended Cocker shows to those who kept a death watch at Pablo Casals' last concerts. "Except for Cocker it's a drunk watch. Will Joe fall off the stage tonight?"

"A lot of Joe's crowd used to go to see him stumbling about," says Mick Weaver. "He'd managed to get a reputation for it. There was one line in that song he used to do . . . 'Guilty'—'got some whisky from the barman, got some cocaine from a friend'—and everytime he got to the cocaine bit the whole place used to erupt. I think if he'd stood there and had a snort on stage that would have brought the house down! Just about every night he'd try making the high notes . . . and he'd gag . . . then he'd throw up and we'd pack in . . . then carry on. I got the feeling that people were coming just to see if he'd get through the concert."

Tapes recorded at several shows on the Autumn 1974 tour do not make easy listening. At Allendale, Michigan on September 15, Joe's voice sounds hoarse and strained. The set was made up of numbers from 'Joe Cocker' and 'I Can Stand A Little Rain', plus the as-yet unreleased 'Jamaica Say You Will'. Ironically the best vocals of the show come on a song Joe has never recorded—'In A Station', from The Band's 'Big Pink' album.

Nine days later, at Niagara Falls, further deterioration had set in. Carried for much of the show by Mick Weaver's piano and Albert Lee's guitar, Joe's vocals lack any power at all and are at times inaudible. His in-between introductions are incoherent, he has problems keeping up with the band and he makes no attempt to reach many of the high notes. Towards the end he appears to be engaged in an argument with someone about how long he has been on stage, whereupon the band strike into 'High Time We Went' and it is all over. On this occasion there was no 'With A Little Help'.

On other nights it was a similar story. The press panned Joe almost everywhere he played. "No fire" . . . "lack of variety and pace" . . . "unintelligible lyrics" . . . "a voice that has suffered from ill use" . . . "a shadow of the best white soul singer he once was". But he did get through the concerts and he did complete the tours. And that was much more than many people expected him to do.

*   *   *

Joe's next album, 'Jamaica Say You Will', did not fare so well as its recent predecessors, reaching only 42 in the U.S. album charts. Released in April 1975, it had been recorded during the early part of the previous year. 'Jamaica' featured the Atlantic house band—Messrs Tee, Dupree, Rainey and Purdie, on six out of the ten tracks, with Nicky Hopkins, Jimmy Karstein, Jim Horn and Bobby Keys all putting in appearances.

Although it has at times been dismissed as merely a collection of outtakes from the previous album, 'Jamaica' has its own distinctive funky feel, with Richard Tee's piano very dominant. There are two songs by Matthew Moore—'That's What I Like In My Woman' and 'Forgive Me Now' where Tee's three-in-the-morning piano is well complemented by Sid Sharp & Co.'s strings. Daniel Moore also provides two numbers—the loose and laid-back 'If I Love You' and a folky blues 'Jack O' Diamonds' that Leadbelly might have sung. 'I Think It's Going To Rain Today' is the first of Randy Newman's two offerings, along with 'Lucinda', the sad tale of a girl who is flattened into the sand by a beach cleaning truck, while lying there in her graduation gown.

Jim Horn's alto wails strong on 'Oh Mama', a typical Cocker cry-from-the-soul, written by Jim Price. Horn shines too on the title song, Jackson Browne's 'Jamaica Say You Will'. 'Where Am I Now', a Jesse Ed Davis ballad features the veteran session man Ben Benay on guitar, while an up tempo 'It's All Over But The Shoutin'' powers along, providing some satisfaction for those who complained—as they had with the last album—that Joe had forsaken rock to be a blues and ballad singer. The track is not one of Joe's favourite recordings—"I hated it. I could never finish the song because we put the track down when I was drunk underneath the piano and I'd put it in too high a key. It was real hard work for me to get through it—I still think I made a bit of a hash of it, which I've tried not to do ever since."

The rock press who had been so critical of Joe's live shows—not without some cause—did give credit where due to Cocker on record. "The powerful bluesy vocals of Cocker sound better than ever, and he can still belt it out with the best. Cocker is still a superstar" declared *Billboard*. "He sings with more subtlety and power than I've ever heard him before," wrote Michael

Davis in the *Los Angeles Free Press*. "Cocker's ability to vocally reach out and grab your heart is unfaded," said *Record World*, while *Times-Weekend* wrote: "Cocker has reached a maturity, a wisened gentleness, that reveals a side of him we've never quite fully seen."

*   *   *

Joe enjoyed working with Richard Tee and the Atlantic session men. "We got along together. They didn't think I was just a white man, pretending to sing the blues. They took me seriously. There's something special about when you work with black musicians . . . a bit of rapport. It was just something I'd always wanted to do." And having worked with them in the studio, what Joe wanted now was to take them out on the road.

There was, however, a problem. Promoters in America and Canada were very reticent after the less than successful Autumn '74 tour. Britain and Europe were unviable—Joe's records had made little impression there since 'Mad Dogs & Englishmen'. But Australia, the country where he had so much trouble only two and a half years before, was willing to let bygones be bygones.

Soon after Joe's hasty departure from Australia in October 1972, the Liberal government had been voted out of office. The new Labour administration took a more enlightened view of the affair and, despite objections from the Australian Musicians Union who claimed Joe had brought disrepute on their profession, in January 1975 it was announced that he would be returning the following month for four concerts.

When Joe flew into Sydney on February 18 security was tight. The tour organisers, Paul Dainty Promotions, had received a series of telephone calls threatening, "If the Government is stupid enough to let Cocker into Australia then it is up to us to stop him in our own way. He may do his first concert, but I guarantee he will not do the second." As it happened Joe did all four, plus an extra one in Sydney.

At a press conference at Randwick Racecourse, venue for the Sydney shows, Joe said that he was not bitter about what had happened on his earlier visit and anticipated no problems this time. "I'll take things very cleanly and very cool," he said. Asked about drugs, he replied "I'm not that much of a drug taker," adding as he pointed at the drink in front of him, "I do tend to wallow in this a bit." He told those reporters who suggested that his visit was a last ditch attempt to rescue his career, "There's no chance the tour is a do-or-die effort. I'll sing just as long as I have the ability."

The Cock 'n'Bull Band which toured with Joe was a curious blend of musical pedigrees. Richard Tee, classically trained graduate of New York's High School of Music and Art, was on keyboards; Cornell Dupree, discovered in Texas at the age of nineteen by the legendary King Curtis, played guitar; Gordon Edwards, whose own band Encyclopedia of Soul was a New York club attraction, played bass; Albert Lee, a Londoner who had risen from skiffle origins to playing with Buddy Holly's old band, The Crickets, before joining Joe, was also on guitar; Pete Gavin, Lee's sidekick in Heads, Hands & Feet, was the drummer; and to complete the outfit, Kenny Slade, once of The Grease Band, resurfaced in the world of rock and roll, playing assorted percussion. Slade had met Joe in Sheffield at Christmas, returned to the States with him and ended up in Australia. "He was a lot of fun," Joe recalls with amusement. "He'd go out ahead of the show and you'd hear this massive roar . . . and he'd be going 'Come on . . . come on . . . you can do better than that! It's JOE INNIT!'"

The tour, with shows in Sydney, Brisbane, Melbourne and Adelaide, went well. The Australian media paid close attention, their cameras ever awaiting a slip, and the police went through the dressing room at a couple of gigs while the show was in progress, but nothing untoward occurred. Albert Lee: "Joe was great . . . he wasn't sick at all on that tour and for me it was great to be playing with Cornell. I think he thought I was a bit of an odd one—he wasn't used to playing with a country-rock guitar player, but the rest of the guys seemed to like it. The shows were really good."

From Australia they flew to Auckland, where the *New Zealand Herald*, surprised by the mellowness of Joe's repertoire, headed their review of the show, "COCKER TURNS IN HIS RAVE". There was another show in Hawaii on the way back home and then it was back to the house Joe had rented in Paradise Cove, Malibu. "It was playtime," says Kenny Slade. "We went out and about around L.A . . . got thrown out of the Troubadour and that sort of thing."

Albert Lee and his wife Karen lived at the Malibu house. A frequent visitor too was Eileen Webster, now married to a Hollywood shop owner, and the mother of a small baby. "She used to come to the house all the time," recalls Karen Lee. "She'd arrive in a cab from Hollywood and move in for a while with the baby. Joe would take her in . . . she caused him some wild times . . . she seemed very resentful of his fame—as if she should have had some of it. She was always in competition for attention . . . and pretty outrageous." Other people recall incidents like a night at the Roxy when Eileen, drunk, stripped off backstage at an Elkie Brooks gig. They speak of how she embarrassed Joe, of the feeling that she was leading him on and of how, regardless of everything, he still thought the world of her.

* * *

In mid 1975 Joe went to Kingston, Jamaica to record what would be his third album released in as many years. Producer of the album—'Stingray'—was Rob Fraboni, who had been responsible for sound on Joe's most recent tours, while most of the instrumental work came from Stuff—Richard Tee, Cornell Dupree and Gordon Edwards, plus two contemporaries from the New York Studios, Eric Gale on guitar and Steve Gadd on drums. Stuff would later achieve great success in the jazz/funk market with three Warner Bros. albums.

'Stingray', a favourite Cocker album among many musicians, did not impress Jerry Moss, head of A & M Records, when he first heard it. Joe: "He was appalled . . . he was saying 'What do I do with it?' And I said 'Wellll—do what you do with most of 'em—try and sell it!' He was saying 'But there's nothing in this . . . there's nothing in it that can work!'"

Joe later accused A & M of failing to promote the record. They apparently replied that he had not given them anything to promote! The album sold poorly, reaching number 70 in the U.S. charts—his lowest album placing up to that point. Musically though—and this was Joe's only real concern—the album marked further significant development, as he put his indelible stamp on material both new and old.

'Stingray' opens with Bobby Charles' 'The Jealous Kind', a mid-tempo number which Ray Charles—no relation—later recorded after hearing Joe's version. 'You Came Along', by the same writer, features a guitar solo from Albert Lee, one of several guests on the album. Matthew Moore wrote the upbeat 'I Broke Down', as well as two ballads—'Moondew' and 'Worrier', where Eric Clapton plays guitar and Bonnie Bramlett's backing vocals echo Joe's cry "Guess I'm a worrier". There is a Cocker/Tee composition, 'Born Thru' Indifference', George Clinton's 'She Is My Lady', and a sad look back in 'A Song For You', which Joe had first heard Leon Russell play in 1969. There were also two Bob Dylan songs—each with their own surprises.

Joe first discovered Dylan back in Sheffield in 1964. At a time when he refused to sing anything unless it was pure blues his attention was caught by Dylan's melodic 'Don't Think Twice, It's Alright', on the 'Freewheelin' ' album. He began performing Dylan's songs with The Grease Band and had recorded several before including 'The Man In Me' and 'Catfish' on 'Stingray'. 'The Man In Me', from 'New Morning', is given new life here in a bouncy reggae version arranged by Peter Tosh and Tyrone Downey. 'Catfish', which Dylan has never released, is probably the moodiest number in a collection that Joe has described as "my after-hours album".

As to how Joe came to record Dylan's eulogy to the baseball pitcher, Catfish Hunter—"I asked him . . . I was a bit nervous about even approaching him . . . I just asked him for something he hadn't recorded and he said 'Tell you what, I've got this old blues I wrote about Catfish' . . . and he gave me a demo."

The album was on the whole well-received by the critics, many of whom seemed amazed that the man whose voice all but disappeared at times during his last American tour could sound so well on record. "Cocker remains the king of interpretative singers" said the *Winnipeg Free Press*. "Cocker's voice simmers and burns" said the *Melody Maker* reviewer, "a solid, good-but-not-great album."

'Stingray' was released in May '76 and Joe went on the road with Stuff to promote it. He did over sixty dates in the coming months but, while he sounded so good on record, many of the concerts came over as lacklustre and disappointing. What good reviews there were seem to have been reserved for Stuff—"The Original Doctors of Sound" as *The Village Voice* had called them—while Joe was criticized for being in poor voice and health. "The wisest thing Cocker could do is take a year's holiday on a health farm," said *Melody Maker* of a New York show in May.

Many of Joe's memories of this period are not happy, but there were amusing incidents on the tour. He recalls Stuff's reticence with regard to stage presence. "We went up to Canada and they were pretty new to being on stage . . . they would hide. They'd sit down with sheet music—which they didn't need cos they knew all the songs—they'd just have E . . . B flat written on it . . . and the road crew used to be saying 'Joe—why don't they stand up? Why don't they put a bit of life into it?' And I was saying 'Hey man—they're musicians—they do what they want to do . . .' And I go out one night . . . I'm so used to them all sat there . . . and I turn round—what a shock! They're all stood up . . . and Gordon Edwards . . . he's about nine foot tall . . . What is it? And I came off and what I didn't know at the time, the roadies had gone and put centre-folds out of all the raunchiest magazines—in the middle of their sheet music! So when they got to 'With A Little Help From My Friends' they opened up the pages and there were these pussies and they all went HEYYY! And shot up! It did the trick!"

In early October Joe appeared on *Saturday Night Live*, a massively popular American TV comedy, to be joined during the second verse of 'Feelin' Alright' by the show's star comic John Belushi, doing a highly exaggerated Cocker impression. Belushi, who later starred in *Blues Brothers*, had performed a similar skit in an earlier show, giving a bizarre rendition of 'With A Little Help'.

The duet brought the house down, but when the idea was put to him beforehand, Joe was not so enthusiastic. "I hadn't seen the 'With A Little Help' impersonation so I didn't know what to expect," he said later. "And the band—Stuff—they didn't want to know at all. Belushi was just a piece of the woodwork as far as they were concerned. But I had a sore throat during rehearsals and he took me to see this voice specialist so I got to know him a little better, and he was telling me about when he was rehearsing it at home . . . He scared his mother to death—he'd been practising it for three months and she was getting really worried because she didn't know who he was trying to impersonate!" Ranked as one of the best *Saturday Night Live* shows ever, the clip of Joe and John Belushi duetting has been frequently repeated over the years.

*   *   *

Working with Stuff proved expensive for Joe. All triple scale musicians, he had to pay them the sort of money they could earn in the studios. Even then, if there was a gap in the schedule they would fly long distances back to New York to fit in the odd session. "I'm sure if I met any of them now we'd get along famously . . . but it was a weird time," Joe says today. By the time he parted from them in late '76 he was heavily in debt and once again his career was at a low ebb. His tour had not gone well, his latest album was a commercial failure and his partnership with manager Reg Lock was on the rocks. "Reg was a pleasant bloke," says Joe. "But some people just don't have that aggression that's necessary to get across to record companies. He tried hard but it seemed like in the business everyone thought he was not up to it."

Anxious to get a manager with enough force and credibility to help restore his fallen fortunes, Joe approached Albert Grossman. Former manager of Bob Dylan and The Band, Grossman had a reputation in the rock business as a shrewd, hard headed operator. Joe: "I asked him to manage me—and he said he wouldn't. Said he wouldn't deal with me. He said 'You guys—you make a lot of money and then you stop making records!' A strange way to say "No", even for an enigmatic character like Albert 'The Bear' Grossman!

Returning to England in December, Joe visited Alan Spenner at his home in Ladbroke Grove. At the time Spenner, along with Neil Hubbard, was a member of Kokomo. They had gigs coming up at Bristol and Brunel Universities, and a Birmingham club, Barbarella's. Joe went along and jammed with Kokomo at these gigs and the ensuing press attention led to a promoter booking him and the band to appear at Bingley Hall, Birmingham on New Year's Day.

It was not too auspicious a beginning to 1977. Only a couple of hundred tickets were sold beforehand for a hall that holds several thousand people, and before the show began it was agreed that the fee would be reduced by half. Joe was nervous but he showed that he could still do it and got a good reception from the audience. He even got reasonable write-ups in the music press for what had been his first scheduled performance in England in four and a half years. Asked by *New Musical Express* why he had agreed to do the show he replied "I need the money right now."

Seven albums—plus a couple of compilations, sell-out tours around the world, and an American top ten hit with 'You Are So Beautiful' only nine months before—and Joe Cocker was broke.

120

Chapter Eleven

1977

Luxury You Can Afford

THE FIRST TIME Michael Lang heard Joe Cocker sing was on record in 1969. In Lang's words he was "blown away" and Joe was immediately booked for the Woodstock Festival, of which Lang was the main organiser. After Woodstock Lang settled for a quieter life, forming a record label-cum-production company, Just Sunshine Inc. It was an eclectic set-up—with Billy Joel, White Elephant, Voices of East Harlem, Mississipi Fred McDowell and Stuff.

One day in the Summer of 1976 Lang received a telephone call from Michael Rosenfeld, a rock business lawyer who at that time represented Joe Cocker. Rosenfeld had heard that Lang was organising a jazz festival in the South of France, at Marseilles, and wondered if he would be interested in booking Joe. Although it was a jazz event and Joe would be the only rock act there, Lang agreed.

Joe did the show, with Stuff, and went down well before a young audience who responded to a change in tempo after hours of jazz. But for Michael Lang the pleasure of booking Joe again was almost out-weighed by his dismay at the extent of his deterioration in recent times. "He was in really bad shape . . . That tour with Stuff was a rough one for him . . . he wasn't well and they were really tough to be on the road with. Great musicians and he loved their music, but very hard guys to get along with—very greedy . . . He was drinking an awful lot . . . throwing up a lot on stage. I think that tour probably clinched his demise in terms of a career at that point. It just

121

wiped his career."

The full realisation was brought home to Michael Lang a short time later, at a Beacon Theatre show in New York. "It was awful. Joe was drunk and he introduced the band in a really insulting way . . . he didn't mean it viciously—he was just not there. And they left him on stage. It was a really sad point in his career."

A few days after the Beacon Theatre show Lang received another call from Michael Rosenfeld. This time he asked would Michael be interested in taking over Joe's management? Lang was not too keen—he had managed Billy Joel for six months on a temporary basis but he had no ambitions in the management field. He and Joe discussed the possibility and there the matter seemed to end.

Several months later, in early 1977, Joe had more talks with Michael Lang, who had given the earlier proposal a great deal of thought. "I sat down with Joe and I said 'Listen . . . if you want to do this . . . if you really want to get up and put it back together . . . and pick up the pieces that are rightfully yours—then I'll do it with you'."

It was the breakthrough Joe had begun to fear would never come. After years of management hassles, what he needed—now more than ever—was a manager who cared for him, both as an individual and an artiste. But at such a point in his career, in poor voice, poor health and with his reputation in tatters, there was little incentive for anyone of standing to become involved—as Joe had discovered when he approached Albert Grossman.

Fortunately, Michael Lang's considerations were not influenced by the potential for swift financial return. "It was just so sad for me to see him in that kind of shape . . . Joe's such a sweet guy and my memory of him was so strong. There's only one Joe Cocker—it's like a national treasure."

Lang was young, dynamic and had proved at Woodstock that he could pull off what others thought impossible. But even the challenge posed by the greatest event in rock history must have sometimes looked simple compared with the task of rescuing one of its heroes from himself. "I remember going round to his house in L.A . . . just hanging around, trying to find out what his life was like . . . It was horrendous! There were so many people living off him . . . He was still drinking really heavily and there were so many people around him whose interests it was to keep him in that condition. And of course you're always fighting that—it's a double-edged sword. You're trying to eliminate certain things and Joe's resisting it somewhat because he feels kinship there . . . and on the other side he also knows what it's about."

The house was in Nicholas Canyon, one which Joe had rented in September '76. "That place got a bit scary" he recalls. "There were about nine or ten dealers there in no time with it being so close to Hollywood. And these black folks used to come round and say 'Can we borrow your piano?' They were good players so I said 'Sure'. Then I went away and they took the whole window out and went off with the piano! I remember coming down one day and there were all these people in the living room and I thought 'Eh up—this is getting a bit weird . . .' Then when they finally got up to the top of the stairs . . . I'd be coming out of the bedroom and they'd be sat there on the landing!"

*   *   *

One of the first things Michael Land did was to check out how promoters felt about Joe, to try to assess the touring possibilities. He quickly established that there would be very few—the Stuff tour and a late '76 worse-for-wear appearance on *Saturday Night Live* were still fresh in promoters' minds. Lang decided that the best plan was to get Joe work out of America, to give him a chance to find his feet away from the pressures. But before that could be arranged, the situation with his record company, A & M, needed sorting out.

Joe had been signed to A & M, via Denny Cordell's Straight Ahead Productions, since 1968. The company had a family kind of atmosphere in which he had felt comfortable. "I always enjoyed A & M," he says today. "Denny introduced me to the lot, which was Chaplin's lot. Back in those days you'd go down there and Randy Newman would be working in a little office with a piano . . . just writing songs . . . And you'd go in and have a chat with somebody—I knew all the girls there and I could go and knock on Jerry Moss's door any day of the week, without an introduction. It was a very homely thing . . . but gradually, as the gears of life changed, all that started slipping away."

At the same time Joe's career had been slipping away and by 1977, when Michael Lang became his manager, he was $800,000 in debt to the record company. Lang: "The relationship he had with them was one, I felt, like you'd have with a parent where it's almost expected and so it's given. And Joe said 'They'll never let me go'. There were so many shadows at the time . . . he was looking at them more like a mafiosi kind of family . . . cos he felt so locked in . . .

"In any case I went up and had a talk with Jerry Moss—he thought it was over, that his voice was pretty much shot. I said 'Listen Jerry, this is how I see it . . . Joe's being here is very unhappy . . . I don't think he'll survive it frankly, if you insist on keeping him. You have this kind of relationship with him and I know emotionally you're very tied to him'—and he did, he loved Joe—'but you know, it's just not healthy'."

Jerry Moss: "Joe had become very unwieldly as an artist, to promote. It got down to—if he did two shows at the Winterland in San Francisco—the first night, when the press were there—everybody was there—he'd throw up on stage. The second night would be a fantastic concert but by then the word was already out. It was getting to be very hard as a company, trying to work his records . . . he wasn't very convivial with the disc jockeys and press. For me—I'd known him a long time and I cared about him in a big way—but to ask a young promotion man to take Joe Cocker to visit some radio stations, which was very important to do in those days, the guy would shudder. So it got very hard for us as a company to get it up for him in that sort of professional sense . . . so that's when Michael Lang came to us and said 'Look, would you let him go?' And we agreed. There was some sort of cash payment—it wasn't substantial—it wasn't anywhere near $800,000. I think we just wrote it off."

Now the new manager was in a position to begin to plan his rehabilitation programme for Joe. At the outset of their getting together Lang had made it clear that Joe would have to mend certain ways, in particular with regard to drinking. "We sat down and made an agreement that he would not go on stage drunk. I said 'I'll cancel the shows if you do . . .' And he said 'Yeah, fine. I'll do it.' And at that time there were very few moments when he was really coherent. The thing about Joe is that he'd wake up in the morning and drink a bottle of Scotch—and be out of it. But the things that happened . . . the comments that people would make . . . I'd watch them come back the next day, and so I knew that his mind was good. Anyway he said 'Yeah' and I thought there was a sort of desperation there . . . he didn't see a way out of the picture he was in, but he wanted to get out."

With the record company situation cleared, Michael Lang set up a tour in one of the few countries where Joe still had a following—Australia. He had already decided the type of band Joe needed—"a young, straight, rock and roll band who would be thrilled to be out with him, would work hard and wouldn't add to the problems." Through a business partner he heard of an outfit who might fit the bill—the American Standard Band, based in Boston and managed by a man named Dan Cole. Cole's own band, Quill, had been one of the opening acts at Woodstock.

Michael Lang took Joe to see the American Standard Band play at a nightclub, the Widow McCoy, in Frankland, Massachusetts. Lang: "They were good. There was no brilliance there but they were a good solid band. At that point he didn't need brilliance—he needed someone who was gonna work out the way he wanted it."

The five piece band had been together since their schooldays in the mid '60s, playing cover material and their own original songs in the New England clubs. They had a smooth, pop sound but Joe was nevertheless impressed—they were good musicians, capable of playing in a tougher, more soulful style. Kevin Falvey was lead vocalist and keyboards player with American Standard. He recalls the first meeting with Joe. "He came in, saw the band, and said 'We'll have a rehearsal tomorrow.' Tomorrow being a Sunday—in the afternoon—and if he liked what happened we'd continue from there . . . It was a whirlwind after that. He came, we did a rehearsal, then we were on our way to Australia. The band was just swept up in it."

*   *   *

After a week's rehearsal in Worcester, Massachusetts, Joe and American Standard moved to a rented house in Provincetown, at the end of Cape Cod. The band—Kevin Falvey; Cliff Goodwin, guitar; Howie Hersh, bass; Deric Dyer, sax and John Riley, drums—was supplemented by Bobby Keys and Nicky Hopkins—surprising choices considering the efforts being made to keep Joe on the straight, if not narrow. Michael Lang: "He needed people of his own stature around, and of course they're great players . . . with their own, at the time, drinking problems—Nicky especially. It was sort of weaning him from it—he needed that."

Rehearsal moved from Cape Cod to Frank Zappa's studio in Los Angeles and, in mid-June, the party set off for New Zealand and Australia, on a tour billed by the promoters as "The Return of the Mad Dog".

For the media Down Under, reluctant to mention Joe Cocker without detailing the disastrous events of 1972, the tour began to look very promising when the Cocker party arrived in Auckland—without Joe and Bobby Keys, who had been left behind at a stopover in Honolulu. 'MAD DOG COCKER TAKEN OFF PLANE' ran one headline. 'ROCK STAR ORDERED OFF' declared another, while the tour manager, Hobie Cook, told the crowd of waiting pressmen. "It's not exactly correct to say he was ordered off. He and Bobby felt rather sick and when you're like that you're inclined to get irritable. They were feeling a little bad so they voluntarily got off the plane."

In fact Cocker and Keys, just like old times, had tried to liven up the long flight to New Zealand by playing a Derek and Clive tape at top volume. When the steward approached them, complaining that they were terrorising other first-class passengers, Bobby Keys pulled the man's moustache, and shortly afterwards, at Honolulu, he, Nicky Hopkins and Joe became detached from the rest of the party. Joe: "I was very impressed with the steward. He said 'There are some very good gift shops here, sir. Well worth seeing. Why don't you take a look?' And when I got off the plane he shut the door and they took off!" The move was so smoothly executed that the rest of the band did not realise that anyone was missing until the plane was in the air.

*   *   *

Their first tour with Joe Cocker was an amazing experience for the relatively inexperienced members of the American Standard Band. Cliff

125

Goodwin: "Everyone was in their early 20s . . . we were thrust into it in this very strange way. I remember it well—I was in pretty much shock." Kevin Falvey says, "We were totally blown away by the fact that we had an opportunity—never mind working with Joe, which was so spectacular, but the other people in the band with such great reputations. We learned a lot in a very short amount of time."

Joe, Hopkins and Keys arrived in New Zealand in time for the first show, at Hamilton. Joe gave the crowd what they wanted to hear, playing all the old hits, plus material from his recent albums, and new numbers, like 'Wasted Years' which had not yet been recorded. "It must have been a very happy Joe Cocker that left a capacity Founders Theatre crowd drumming the floorboards and calling him back for more on Sunday night," said the *New Zealand Herald*. Four more shows—at Auckland, Christchurch, Wellington and Dunedin followed, before the party moved on to Australia. In between, however, they stopped off for a week in the idyllic paradise of Great Keppel Island, where, according to publicity, possums feed from the hand and visitors are lulled to sleep in soft moonlight by the sound of water lapping on the golden sand.

"It was a gift from the airline, TAA," recalls Cliff Goodwin. "In the middle of the tour there was a break for about a week and they put us up there on this fabulous little island. Flew us there by Piper Cub—there were no roads or anything on it, except a landing strip, a main house and a bunch of cabins. All we had to do was a show at the end of the week for the people that had sojourned out from the mainland. It's very memorable to me still because I've never been in a situation of complete paradise—no phones . . . no TVs for sure . . . totally isolated—in a good way. It was fabulous—we all spent the time drinking and sunning . . . hanging out at the beach watching the yachts go by. Joe did his usual amount, flanked by Nicky and Bobby.

"The day of the gig it was like an invasion on the beach . . . getting the gear there. They couldn't fly it in, they had to float it across on a barge, up the beach. There was just us, no other band. It was a very informal evening—I've got a tape where Joe . . . in the middle . . . he says 'Nicky will keep you entertained' and Nicky began to recite the albatross sketch."

Joe: "Nicky was a strange cat. What a genius—next to Chris . . . He used to go on and do that sketch from Monty Python—'Albatross! . . . First take a bunch of flowers . . .' he'd always be quoting Monty Python . . . everybody loved him, a raving maniac . . . He'd had terrible stomach problems all his life . . . the doctor used to give him Valium. He'd take loads of Valium before a show and then drink Triple White Russians—vodka with that cream in it. He'd be absolutely legless—you'd have to help him up on stage, but sit him down at that keyboard, man, and it was magic. Even when he was BLITZED! He didn't know the titles of any of the songs. 'What is it?

'I Can Stand A Little Rain?' 'Oh you mean G flat', or whatever it was in. He was quite amazing."

On occasions Nicky Hopkins drank Triple White Russians until he blacked out. Today, still in great demand as a session pianist, his drink problem firmly in the past, he looks back on his time with Joe: "It was a bit like the blind leading the blind . . . this is why I can't recall too much about the tour. But it was a great time . . . Jesus, he could sing!"

Resisting the temptation to join his pianist's more excessive sprees, Joe kept to the agreement he had made with Michael Lang: "He made a tremendous effort . . . and you know how hard it is for someone who's that much of an alcholic to pull himself out. He did it himself . . . he would take a couple of drinks before a show but he would never get drunk . . . and when Nicky did—as Nicky tended to—he would get on Nicky's case and it was almost like . . . you have to take sides . . . and he would feel weird about taking a side other than theirs . . . But he understood what it meant to his life . . . he was working for it."

Interviewed by the *Sydney Morning Herald* Joe revealed a little insight into the spiral into which alcohol had so often led him. "I just have to watch the drinking habit before performances," he said. "I know when I do a bad show and it hurts me—so I drink another gallon of beer to try to forget it."

But in Australia that did not happen. Joe's fourteen shows, including five in Melbourne, were a great success. The only dark moment occurred at Perth, when he disembarked from a plane and vomited on the tarmac. A press conference followed in which strong words were exchanged with several reporters, but the evening's show at the Entertainment Centre, before a crowd of 6,000, was a great success.

When he left Australia at the end of July, Joe told reporters he had been happy with the tour, although he would have liked to have played more new material. "We're going to do a brief tour of South America now," he said, "and then we'll go back to the States and put down an album."

*   *   *

"South America was like going to the Wild West," says Michael Lang. "It was unbelievable. Nobody had been there for years and it was one of the few places in the world where I could go with him, where he hadn't destroyed credibility totally. It was kinda a frontier but I was looking for status for him, where he could be Joe Cocker without having to apologise—because I don't think someone of his talent should ever have to apologise."

He may not have been at the peak of his career, but in Brazil, where he played shows in Rio, Santos and San Paulo, Joe and the band were certainly well looked after. The Brazilians were concerned about their visitors being kidnapped and each member of the band was provided with his own bodyguard who, armed with a machine gun, slept outside the hotel room each night. If anyone took a stroll down the corridor, their bodyguard followed.

It was a strange situation for a rock and roll band but they did not let it inhibit them. Kevin Falvey: "The band, because of Nicky and everything else, got totally outrageous. Someone had a Castro type hat and we would walk through the streets, following this guy who'd be smoking a Castro cigar, while we carried a boom box that had crowds screaming and cheering as we walked along . . . Everybody in the street's scratching their head as we pass . . . On the plane we were always trying to think of something to amuse ourselves—if it wasn't food fights it was the robot! We bought a robot—this thing that you wound up . . . and we cut a newspaper picture of Joe's face out and put it on the robot. We had it march up and down the aisle on the plane . . . people would just crack up as it walked by. The weirdest thing you ever saw in your life—a robot Joe!"

In Buenos Aires, Argentina, where Santana had been the most recent visiting rock band—four years earlier—the South Americans' casual approach to the shows amazed Cliff Goodwin: "That was a real peculiar gig. It was supposed to happen let's say on a Monday, a Tuesday and a Wednesday—three dates in one place, called Lunar Park, a giant arena. But that gig didn't happen until Thursday, Friday and Saturday and no one seemed surprised. It was almost as if it was built into the schedule . . . The people showed up on cue—three days late."

While in Buenos Aires Joe made a surprise telephone call to Denny Cordell, who had been brought up in the city. "The phone rang about 4 o'clock in the morning. I picked it up, said 'Hello'. He said 'Are you awake luv?' I said 'Yes'. He said 'Well I want you to know that I'm in your city and it's the arsehole of the world!' I said 'Well where's that?' He said 'Where you were born . . . Boooeyniz Airiz. It's the fucking arsehole of the world and I just had to call you up and tell you that!'"

The tour continued up to Mexico and a series of chaotically organised shows in venues ranging from a bull ring to a school gymnasium. In Juarez the party arrived late, Nicky Hopkins having been banned from travelling on the planned flight after an altercation with a promoter. With only an hour and a half to get from the airport to the gig, and back to the airport for their next flight, the situation was a little tense. Arriving by mini-bus at the gig—a basketball gym—they found a hostile crowd and considerably less equipment than the promoter was contracted to provide. Kevin Falvey: "Nicky was playing piano and I was playing organ and synthesizers. We'd ordered the equipment and we get to the show—there's one organ! That's it—for the two of us! And it doesn't work! So all through the show there's four little Mexican kids trying to make it work—while people are throwing fire crackers at us. We did about a half hour show and then ran to the bus.

Bobby Keys' mother was along with us . . . Why? Who knows—but it made it more insane. She has an umbrella she's holding over Joe's head—it's hot and we're running to the bus. She was madly in love with Joe . . . it was just something else!"

After Mexico Joe's next show was in Caracas, Venezuela. By this time conflict had broken out between Michael Lang and the tour promoters after the poor organisation of the shows. With everyone ready to leave, tour manager Hobie Cook went off to finalize ticket arrangements. Michael Lang: "He came back and I said 'Are we all set to go?' Hobie said 'Yeah. The promoter has the tickets'. I said 'What d'ya mean the promoter has the tickets?' Hobie was getting a little drifty here and there . . . I had just gone through this huge battle with these guys over money . . . and finally got them to agree to pay us . . . then Hobie gave 'em the tickets! I knew we were in trouble! He said 'No, no, no . . . it's gonna be fine—they'll be there at the airport.' So . . . we get to the airport, ready to leave—and there's no tickets. The only flight to Caracas comes . . . and goes!"

The only way to reach Caracas in time for the show was to travel via America. But Joe, still a British citizen, had no entry visa for America—arrangements had been made for him to collect one at the Embassy in Caracas. After their baggage had already been pulled apart once by Mexican customs men—even down to squeezing out tubes of toothpaste—the party arrived in San Antonio, Texas for Joe to be refused entry. No amount of persuasion by his manager could persuade the Immigration Officer to allow him through to Caracas and to make matters even worse Joe was arrested. The following day he was put on a plane back to Mexico City, where he obtained a visa to re-enter the States and flew home. Another eventful tour had come to an end.

*   *   *

The Australian and South American tours, bizarre as the latter had been, were milestones in Joe's recovery. Always nervous before shows—he remains so still, even after almost thirty years—he had avoided the temptation to rely on alcohol to get him through, something which had ruined so many shows in earlier times. His voice now was in better shape and Michael Lang had secured a new recording contract which bode well for the future.

Negotiations had begun while the Australian tour was still in progress. Armed with tapes of some of the shows, Lang flew back to America to meet with Elektra/Asylum in Hollywood. "I'll never forget this because I flew for three days from Australia into L.A. and back again in the middle of the tour. I brought the tapes with me and I sat down with Joe Smith and Steve Wax . . . played 'em the songs and made a deal . . . a really good deal. Then I flew back and finished the tour and when we came home we started to try and approach putting the album together . . . the 'Luxury You Can Afford' album."

* * *

Some time earlier, not long after Michael Lang had taken over Joe's management, there had been an attempt to re-unite him with Denny Cordell in a Los Angeles studio. Within ten minutes of arriving, Joe had laid down on the floor, gone to sleep and refused to be budged, while the musicians berated Cordell. This time it was decided to approach Allen Toussaint, famed New Orleans producer. Toussaint agreed and would say later, "I always liked the way Joe sounded. I was amazed early, I was a fan of black-eyed blues", but when recording of 'Luxury You Can Afford' began at Criteria Studios in Miami, Toussaint seemed somehow reluctant. "It was a strange time in Allen's life," recalls Michael Lang. "He was pretty moody throughout the whole thing and just wouldn't take charge. We got a great band—Richard Tee, Steve Gadd . . . Chuck Rainey . . . It cost a lot of money doing it."

After weeks of working with these musicians, during which Joe caught a cold and had difficulties with his voice for a while, the nucleus of American Standard Band were summoned to Miami. They recorded 'Fun Time'—an Allen Toussaint song, 'Boogie Baby'—one of three numbers Phil Driscoll would have on the album, and 'I Just Want To Rock And Roll Tonight', which was never released. "We did it all in one day," says Cliff Goodwin. "The Stuff guys, they'd been down there for two months and they had basically taken Allen Toussaint around the bend . . . They had really taken advantage of him. He wanted a record from Joe with some fire and these guys were just playing like a little bit of reggae and a little bit of blues . . . With 'Fun Time', Allen Toussaint said to us 'I've got this tune I want you to try' . . . He said 'I've got a version of it but I won't play it for you because it'll give you the wrong idea'. And all he did was sing it to us . . . 'It kinda goes . . .' He sang us a verse, then he left the studio. We just fooled around with it for a couple of hours . . . we were jamming with it . . . and he came back and said 'That's it!'"

The album was two-thirds completed when it was decided that something extra was needed, and sessions moved to Muscle Shoals in Alabama. With little to do there except work, the remaining tracks were soon put down, with Barry Beckett producing.

'Luxury You Can Afford' features an all-star cast of guest musicians, in addition to the basic band. Members of the famous Muscle Shoals rhythm and horn sections appear, besides former veterans of the Ray Charles band—Hank Crawford, David 'Fathead' Newman, Leroy Cooper, Marcus Belgrave and Philip Guilbeau.

Dr John appears on two songs, an atmospheric 'Southern Lady' and the upbeat 'What You Did To Me Last Night'; Donny Hathaway plays piano on the biographical 'Wasted Years' and on 'Lady Put Out The Light', a powerful anguished ballad. Billy Preston is on organ for 'A Whiter Shade Of Pale'—composer Gary Brooker later told Joe he liked the version—and also 'I Heard It Through The Grapevine', where Rick Danko of The Band plays bass. Both numbers, plus 'I Know (You Don't Want Me No More)' were late inclusions, requested by the record company who were anxious about commerciality. Allen Toussaint did not apparently mind, but Joe, turning down a suggestion to include 'In The Midnight Hour', told the Elektra/Asylum President, Steve Wax, "I must remind you, I come from a soul school élite!"

With 'Luxury You Can Afford' in the can, Joe took a short rest before going out on the road to promote the album. A little over a year earlier his career had seemed over. The roller coaster of highs and lows which he had ridden since topping the British chart in 1968 with 'With A Little Help From My Friends' appeared to have finally ground to a halt.

His record company had given up on him; he had no manager, no band and no prospects. With a great deal of help he had pulled round and the future was beginning to look a little brighter at last. But the struggle was not over yet. He was back on the ladder, but there was still a long, long way to climb.

Chapter Twelve

1978 – 1981

So Glad I'm Standing
Here Today

M U S I C A L L Y, Joe was rolling again, but in his personal life there remained much confusion. Hangers-on were at his door day and night, giving him no opportunity to rest and seriously hindering his own and others' efforts to straighten out his life. "It was continuously dragging him down," says Michael Lang. "They were horrible people back there. I would go and I would try and just be uptight enough so people would leave . . . there were some real derelicts . . . they were a problem."

Not that Joe, unlike in the old days, had money to give away. By now it was he who was being subsidised, by his lawyer, Michael Rosenfeld. "He would pay my rent. He said 'I know Joe, that some time in the future you're gonna make some money'." To get away from the house Joe moved to the more peaceful district of Woodland Hills. "The idea was to try and write. Bobby Keys and Nicky Hopkins shared a house with their wives—their's was pretty decent, with a pool. And I was with Eileen—and Daniel, from that first marriage—we'd got back together again. In this real dump! I think we lived there for about eight months altogether, and we never once got round the piano. Which was the idea—but it was just such a bad set-up. They chose the nicest house and gave me this shed to live in—so it never really worked."

Nor did the reconciliation with Eileen work for very long. Over the years they had broken up and got back together again on numerous occasions. It was a volatile relationship that was doomed to fail. Eileen left and returned

With Leon Russell, Mad Dogs & Englishmen, 1970. *MGM*

Publicity shot, 1970. *Photographer unknown*

With the album of the tour, 1971. *Sheffield Newspapers Ltd*

Chris Stainton's All-Stars, 1972. Top – Chris Stainton; middle – Conrad Isadore and Alan Spenner; bottom – Glen Campbell, Neil Hubbard, Joe. *Photographer unknown*

Bobby Keys, Joe, Nicky Hopkins 'Return of The Mad Dog tour, Australia, 1977.
Photographer unknown

Joe advises Cliff Goodwin, Australia, 1977. *Photographer unknown*

Carnegie Hall, New York City, November 3, 1978. *Ebet Roberts*

With The Crusaders, 1981. *MCA Records*

Madge arrives with The Liquorice Allsorts, Lyceum, Sheffield, 1982. *Sheffield Newspapers Ltd*

Right, Eindhoven, Holland, 1983. *Heide Woicke*

Duetting with 'The Genius' – Ray Charles – in Hanover, West Germany, 1985. *Heide Woicke*

West Berlin, 1985. *Heide Woicke*

Joe and Michael Lang, 1989. *J.P. Bean*

Chris Stainton and platinum disc for the 'One Night Of Sin' album. *J.P. Bean*

Joe and wife Pam, 1987. *Rex Features*

after months, even years; Joe, ever the soft touch, took her in. Rows and arguments would soon follow and Joe turned to the bottle to try and block out the inevitable depression. But after one such disagreement, it was not Eileen, but Joe who left. "I'm such a crazy mother sometimes but there was one time when something dawned on me, terribly . . . I was staying at somebody's house in Hollywood, with Eileen, and we had a big barney. I gave her my money and I went walking the streets . . . for two nights—in Hollywood. I slept under a park bench and I suddenly saw it—and I thought 'God! This has got to stop!' There I was . . . looking at myself . . .

"It doesn't rain in L.A. but it started pissing it down and I found like a bus-stop. I was curled up in there and this guy came up and said 'Hey—come here. D'ya want a cup of coffee?' He thought I was a wino, a vagrant . . . but what it was, I was waiting for my lawyer's office to open on the Monday morning—so I could go in and get some money . . . And there I am, looking like a terrible tramp . . . I said 'By the way—I'm on television next Saturday—look out for me'. He was looking at all his friends, going 'HEY! NO! We gotta right one HERE!' I said 'No . . . seriously . . . 'Saturday Night Live' . . . I'm on next week . . .' 'Yeah . . . very good . . . very good. Have another cup of coffee! . . . And suddenly it clicked."

Soon afterwards the on-off relationship with Eileen came to its final end. "We were still together and then she said she couldn't take the States anymore, so she went back home. She asked me to buy her this house in Sheffield, which I did. And then I go back with my suitcase, and as I walk in she says 'By the way, here's the boyfriend.' I said 'I'm sorry love, I can't deal with that'—and that was it. She wrote me a letter . . . about '80 or '81 . . . with no address on it—just said 'I hope we had as many good times as we had bad times and that all is forgiven.' And it was."

* * *

In the summer of 1978 Joe decided that the time had come to leave Los Angeles. He found a house he liked further up the California coastline, on a ranch above Santa Barbara. Quiet, out of the way and overlooking the Pacific Ocean, it was an ideal retreat from the crazy lifestyle he had known for so long.

Laurel Springs Ranch belonged to film actress Jane Fonda, and was the location for summer camps where children from every social background came to study the performing and visual arts. The last person to live in the house had been singer Cat Stevens who had left some months earlier. But although the house was empty, when Jane Fonda took a call from a realtor who told her that Joe Cocker was interested in renting the house, she told him straight that it was absolutely out of the question.

133

At the time an earlier landlord, from the house in Hollywood, was suing Joe in the courts for damage to his property—including the window removed by the people who took his piano. Reported widely in the newspapers, the matter did not suggest to Ms Fonda that a rock star with an already tarnished reputation was an ideal tenant.

Fortunately for Joe the director of the summer camps, Pam Baker, was a fan of his. She spoke with the realtor and with Jane Fonda and it was eventually agreed that Joe could rent the house for $1500 a month, with an insurance clause in the contract to allay the landlady's worst fears.

Moving to Santa Barbara got rid of a lot of the problems in Joe's life, as Pam Baker, who met him soon after he arrived, recalls. "I think Joe felt real comfortable being there, because nobody hassled him and they left him alone—and were able to protect him because there was a private gate into the ranch. To get to Joe's house you had to drive past all the other cottages and houses on the ranch—so we'd immediately find out who it was and call Joe to say 'Do you want to see this person?' It kept out a lot of people that used to just 'drop in' and eventually they just stopped coming round . . .

I think it was the first time he had a place that was all his own—and he had control over. He knew when he was away that the place was locked up and nobody touched it. He knew that he had some place to come home—and there were people around who he could call on if he needed something. I think it really did have a good effect on him."

Joe moved in at Santa Barbara in early October, 1978 but within a few days he was out on the road, promoting 'Luxury You Can Afford'. It was his first tour of America since the dark days with Stuff, two years earlier. Backed by American Standard Band and Bobby Keys, but with Mitch Chakour replacing Nicky Hopkins on piano, the tour opened in Washington. In an interview with the local *Post*, Joe said he was a little nervous about whether people would remember him—and what for. He spoke of earlier times that he would have preferred to forget, in particular of the time the roadies had played him a tape of a show and he had been unable to believe that the voice singing was his own. He spoke too about the present: "We're not on this tour to make money. We just want to show people we're back and ready to kick ass!"

Playing colleges and clubs, the tour moved East to West Coast and back again—twenty eight dates in all. At Royce Hall in L.A. in late October Joe was called back on stage five times, a few nights later he received a similar reception at the Old Waldorf in San Francisco, and on November 3 arrived at Carnegie Hall for yet another comeback appearance before the rock fans of New York City.

He opened with 'Delta Lady' and threw in 'With A Little Help', but most of the set was from the new album. A tape of the Carnegie Hall show reveals Joe in strong voice, singing well with no signs of strain and with much of the old soul back in his delivery. The horns punch along while Clydie King, Ann Lang and Mona Lisa Young, who were responsible for all backing vocals on the album, are in sparkling form.

The band was supplemented by Jimmy Karstein, introduced by Joe as "a special friend of mine, helping us out for tonight", on percussion, and Phil Driscoll, songwriter and later evangelist, on trumpet. By the end the audience would not let Joe leave the stage—he did four encores before finally calling it a night.

* * *

The promotional tour—"They're trying to tag me as 'The Father of Punk'," Joe wrote on a postcard home—went well, but the album failed to make the impact Elektra/Asylum had hoped. It sold around 300,000 copies and made only number 76 in the U.S. charts, a lower placing even than 'Stingray'. Reviews were mixed: Ben Fong-Torres in *Rolling Stone* thought it Joe's "strongest album in years", Nat Hentoff called it his "most maturely diversified album so far", while in Britain, where the album disappeared almost without trace, *New Musical Express* declared: "Cocker's forte is romancing, not ranting, and there's plenty of that here to confirm his renewed stature". It was the music critic of the L.A. *Herald Examiner* who, having dismissed the album as "uneven and hopelessly boring", voiced some of the most negative sentiments about Cocker's place in late 1970's rock: "Too much has happened since 'Delta Lady'. Everything might have sounded right for those times, but our era is different now. Joe Cocker may indeed be alive and well, but the majority of the music he associates himself with is dead and gone."

'Luxury You Can Afford' proved to be Joe's only album on Elektra/Asylum. After it failed to live up to commercial expectations, the real problems began. The company had given him an initial advance and had then provided a further sum to finance the recording at Muscle Shoals. Steve Wax, the company's president, had arranged the deal and, following his subsequent departure from Elektra/Asylum, Joe ended up being sued for a sum of around $145,000. Without the necessary paperwork to prove that the extra money was non-repayable Joe was liable. Says Michael Lang: "They got a judgement against Joe which we found out about later on when we were doing some dates in L.A. We were right but there was no way we could justify it." Once again Joe was without a record contract.

He was also without money, as the British Inland Revenue discovered in 1978. Joe had not paid any tax since his breakthrough into the rock scene ten years earlier. Since 1972, when he took over as accountant, Bernard Pendry had been fending off the Revenue: "We kept the taxman at bay for years and years. We kept running and giving him bits and pieces hoping

135

that Joe was going to get some money from somewhere to be able to pay it off . . . but like all tax there comes the day when you can't run any further—they've nailed you. You've got to do *something*."

Although he was by now living in America, Joe had to settle with the tax authorities if he was to be able to enter Britain in the future and not face arrest or injunctions preventing him from working. He recalls the situation: "I owed them something like £90,000 and Bernard approached the Inland Revenue and said 'Listen, Joe can't pay this money, but he's getting back on his feet . . . he's making some records . . . if you'll take it in £10,000 instalments'. And they were saying 'You don't make deals with Her Majesty's Government' so he said 'OK then. He's going to go bankrupt tomorrow morning and you won't see a dime from it.' So they ended up agreeing to make this package deal—and I've paid it off . . . I was lucky—whether it was just the way my dad brought me up—it was always to me something terribly sinful, going bankrupt."

In fact Bernard Pendry recalls the agreed sum being £75,000, payable in instalments of £5,000 every six months—but the fine details of his business affairs were never a big concern of Joe's. The accountant also remembers a more amusing brush with the Revenue, over a claim for stage clothes. "They phoned me up and the guy said 'Come off it! I've seen Joe Cocker and all he ever wears is scruffy old T shirts.'"

* * *

After the steady, if unspectacular recovery in 1977 and 78, the following year brought little new development. In May Joe was due to visit Australia for a tour billed—rather ominously, thought the press—as 'The Calm Before The Storm'. Tickets were going well when, only a week before he was due to arrive, it was announced that the tour was cancelled because the American Standard Band were unavailable.

Since helping out on 'Luxury You Can Afford', American Standard had obtained their own contract with Island Records. Their first album was due to be released around the time of the tour and the band's manager, Dan Cole, decided that they needed to be around to promote it. He therefore cancelled their work with Joe who had not time to recruit another band and had to cancel the Australian tour.

"Michael was furious," recalls Kevin Falvey. "He was being sued by the people in Australia and we ended up doing nothing more than opening a couple of record stores. Dan didn't put anything together." American Standard's album got good notices in the music papers, but failed to make much commercial impact. The band—as a separate unit—folded shortly afterwards amidst problems between their manager and Island's Chris Blackwell.

In the late summer of 1979 Michael Lang arranged a package tour for Europe, to commemorate the tenth aniversary of the Woodstock Festival. 'Woodstock in Europe' featured Joe Cocker, Arlo Guthrie, Richie Havens and Country Joe, plus the English blues pioneer, Alexis Korner, who compèred.

Joe did the tour—his first shows in Europe since 1972—with a band formed by Mitch Chakour of musicians from the New England area, who were based in L.A. at that time. Michael Thompson played guitar, Trey Thompson—bass, Jimmy Lang—keyboards, while on drums was B.J. Wilson, the former Procol Harum man who had played on the recording of 'With A Little Help From My Friends'.

The European audiences welcomed Joe back. In Germany there were four open air shows, where, said the Press, "Joe sang everyone else under the table." Apart from one show—there the crowd witnessed a disaster which, even today, causes Joe to wince as he recollects. "It was some amphitheatre where Hitler used to rant and rave. We had these little caravans and the promoter said 'Joe, I've got this stuff . . . I'll let you have a taste if you promise you won't tell your manager' . . . There were varying versions of L.S.D . . . P.C.P . . . I'd take anything in those days . . . He said 'He'll kill me if he knows I've given you this stuff' . . . I said 'OK' and he gives me a gram and says 'All you need is a pin dot and you'll be raving.' He gives me the stuff and I see Michael approaching the caravan . . . and I just picked up this gram and shoved it all up one nostril! Half an hour later he comes up and says 'Joe it's showtime' . . . I couldn't see—it was like I was in a blizzard . . . I'd overdosed terribly.

"Michael went crazy . . . 'Who's given you this stuff?' I told him the truth and the promoter hated me after that . . . I was oblivious. Michael told me I went out there and did four songs and just said 'Good night'. He said it was the worst thing I'd ever done in my life . . . There are some regrettable incidents . . . I'm glad those days are over . . ."

'Woodstock in Europe' was a stop-gap tour for Joe, which he did not really enjoy. Still lacking faith in himself he remained susceptible to the fringe temptations of the rock world, which could destroy months, even years of effort in an instant. Another reason was his dislike at being packaged as a star of yesterday, a relic of the 1960s. Joe Cocker has his faults, as he will admit, but resting on past glories has never been one of them.

* * *

No sooner had the 1980s arrived than Joe began a series of tours that would lead to his acclaim by a new generation of rock fans around the world. Although he would never again conquer America to the same degree that he had ten years earlier, a new following of fans all over Europe, in Israel, Japan and Australasia would ensure sell-out shows and hit records in the years to come.

Not that things looked too bright to Tom Sullivan when he joined Joe as tour manager in January 1980. "We were doing places that didn't seem to me as the sort of places Joe Cocker ought to be in. It was a club date tour . . . a lot of money hassles—you get a lot of money hassles in the bar clubs. I saw Joe in a higher situation than that."

The tour opened at the Royal Oak Theatre in Detroit and moved straight on to a small club in Toronto where the money troubles began, but at least the local *Globe & Mail* reviewer was appreciative: "There is a lot to be said for seeing a dramatic show like Cocker's in a place where fans can plainly view the torture etched on his face as he drags his terse phrases and howls up from somewhere below his kneecaps."

Tom Sullivan had taken over his job from Hobie Cook. "I walked into the room for the first time at rehearsals and Hobie was there. He patted me on the back and said 'Good luck. You'll need it!' and walked off. Even though I knew about Joe . . . I'd heard . . . I really didn't know what he was talking about."

He soon found out. The son of a well-known country songwriter, Gene Sullivan, Tom grew up in Oklahoma City where J.J. Cale and Leon Russell used to come to record demos at his father's recording studio. He was no stranger to rock life having been a roadie for years with Blood, Sweat & Tears, before working for Kiss. But even he was surprised by the numbers of hangers-on and problem people from Joe's past who appeared at all points on the road. "Just a lot of people kept showing up . . . I didn't know who they were—but I soon got to learn. I started seeing these people coming from every direction. They came with their pockets out and expected them to be filled when they left, having had a good time . . . Joe feels sorry for people. He's easily taken in by people who make themselves sound so down for the count. I learned from a lot of bad experiences.

"I don't want to make it sound like everybody Joe associated with in the past . . . it's not all horror stories—there are a lot of nice people out there—but some of the others . . . I've had arguments with people . . . I've had screaming, yelling matches—there was a girl in San Francisco—I didn't know who she was but she seemed a little off-centre. I wouldn't let her get to Joe and Joe didn't want her around anyway. She went up and down the hall screaming that she was gonna kill me . . . she was gonna find Joe . . . she was knocking on all the doors. Things like that . . . I had to call security for them to fetch the police to get her out. I didn't know what she was capable of—she was somebody from the past, that's all I knew about her."

The tour, mainly clubs on the bar circuit, but with occasional theatres or concert halls, took in Canada and the West Coast of America. In the band, Cliff Goodwin and Howie Hersh had returned, following the demise of American Standard, while B.J. Wilson stayed on from the 'Woodstock in Europe' tour.

In July there was another club tour, this time of the East Coast. By now Bob Leinbach was on keyboards while the backing singers were Ann Lang, Beth Anderson and Maxine Green. The highlight of this tour occurred at Central Park, New York City on July 12, before an estimated 20,000 people. It was the biggest show Joe had done in the States for many a year and was celebrated by a live album, released only in Australia and Japan. 'Live In New York' suffers from uneven sound quality but gives clear confirmation of the return of Joe's vocal powers. It also includes two songs never released on studio albums—Bob Leinbach's 'So Blue' and Daniel Moore's 'Sweet Forgiveness', besides a supremely poignant rendition of 'Guilty'.

Hardly rested from the summer shows, Joe went out again in the autumn doing more clubs and then a return to Europe. First stop was Dublin and a great Irish reception at the National Stadium, before taking in Belfast, where sound man Rod Libbey found himself on the wrong side of the security forces as he took photographs on the way to the show. "They stopped the car and pulled the film outa' my camera . . . Somebody had had their head cut off that afternoon, right next door to where we were playing. It was real heavy . . . I don't know whether they were soldiers or cops but they scared the shit outa me!"

The tour moved on to mainland Europe with dates in Italy, France, Holland—and Germany, where, the unfortunate incident in Berlin apart, Joe had given advance notice of his comeback the year before.

On that tour he had been seen performing in Dusseldorf by Peter Rücher, director of the German television programme, *Rockpalast*. Rücher had been sufficiently impressed to book Joe for the 1980 show, to be recorded at the Metropole in Berlin.

Rockpalast 80 was a huge success. From the opening 'Feelin' Alright' the television audience were left in no doubt that Joe was right back on form, rocking through eight of his best known numbers, with a potted history of his career thrown in by TV presenter, Albrecht Metzger. Well-lit, and both visually and musically impressive, *Rockpalast* was a perfect showcase for Joe Cocker and has been repeated many times on German television.

The tour brought yet another change within the band, Larry Marshall replacing Bob Leinbach on keyboards. The new man found early rehearsals rather unnerving. "Joe always used to stare at me, like 'Who is this person?' I asked Mitch—'Everytime I look at him he looks really strange at me' . . . and Mitch said 'Don't look at him'."

Larry Marshall soon settled in and stayed seven years. But on that first European tour he began to wonder whether he had made the right decision.

"I couldn't believe all the crazy things . . . the crazy nights . . . They just got crazier and crazier—I said 'What have I done to my career?'"

One of the stand-out memories for Larry occurred in Italy, after he and Michael Lang had escaped to a bar to try and find some peace. "We're sitting there having a pleasant drink and pleasant conversation and in walks Joe and B.J. and the road crew . . . 'Oh no!' They sit down and some girls come over to our table—and one of them breaks a champagne glass and slits her wrists, right there at the table! So the manager—it's this kinda place—he brings over a new drink and a Band-Aid for her wrist! Then she holds up the glass to her neck and says 'I'm gonna slit my throat!'

"And Joe and B.J. are saying 'Love . . . what's the matter . . . why would you want to do something like that to yourself? You're such a nice girl . . . you've got a lot to live for . . .' But she won't let go. So I grab her by the shoulder . . . I'm thinking . . . photographers . . . and I say 'How dare you bleed at our table! We don't need this shit from you—drop the glass or I'll smack you in the head!' And she drops the glass . . . and Joe . . . he looks at me and goes 'Barbarian!'"

"That's the difference between English and Americans!" laughs Joe. "Michael had rented a Mercedes car and we set off back to the hotel—it was only about half a mile away but we drive and drive and everything gets darker and darker . . . And there's Michael and Larry in the front and B.J. and myself in the back . . . we were incorrigible together for drinking . . . and he's flat out, snoring away. Anyway I finally fell asleep, and I keep hearing B.J. going 'Michael . . . we're lost man. . . . we're totally lost.' There wasn't a lightbulb in sight, it was just darkness. Then sure enough I get this nudge . . . B.J.: 'Joe—be cool.' I'm going 'What?' . . . 'Just be veery cool.' 'Why—what's wrong?' 'Just be . . .'—Next minute there's all this jabbering in Italian and Michael's saying 'Joe—don't start anything will you' . . . and there's guys with repeating rifles and those nasty little guns that can fire off twenty two in a second.

"Michael's saying 'Joe, they want us out of the car' . . . And I'm in one of those zany moods, waking up out of this sleep and I'm going 'Good evening' and these guys are jabber jabber jabber in Italian. 'Spread your arms' 'What?' and Michael's saying 'Joe—just do it. Don't talk to them . . . DO IT!' So we're all against this car and I turned round and I said 'Do you know who I am?' And Michael's . . . 'Not now Joe . . . not now PLEASE!' I said 'No—have you any idea who I am?' And this guy must have known a little bit of English—he points a gun at me . . . I said 'I'm . . . probably . . . the greatest blues singer . . . the greatest white blues singer . . . in Italy . . . Well, in Milan . . . tonight!'"

Whereupon, says Larry Marshall, who, like Michael Lang, had a Beretta pressed against his temple, Joe passed out on the ground. "And these guys look at him and they're going 'Joe Cockair! Joe Cockair!' And they're slapping him and waking him up and getting him to sign autographs! I tell you . . . I felt the bullet go through my head!"

*   *   *

The European tour ended with two shows in early November at The Venue in London, where on the first night there was a row over payment of Joe's fee which caused him to be delayed from going on stage. Insistence on being paid beforehand occasionally led to such situations, but such is the world of rock and roll that to wait until after the show could mean the promoter has already departed with the take. At one club in Philadelphia the band were on stage, playing the intro to the opening song, and Joe was approaching the microphone, when Tom Sullivan ran on and pulled him off because the promoters were holding back with the cash. The band played on for ten minutes, with no idea what was happening, until the fee was paid and Joe returned to the mike to commence his performance.

At The Venue the sell-out audience became impatient and started to jeer, but their attitude quickly changed when, with the money safely collected, Joe went on and gave what the *Evening Standard* described as "a blinding performance with a flawlessly tight band", while an unimpressed *Sounds* reviewer declared a pot-bellied Joe had no right to be on a stage in the 80s. "That did flip me a bit" Joe later said. After the show it was the earlier money hassles that reporters were interested in. "I don't care about money—but that's why my life is so confused," Joe told them. "I'm relieved to have a great manager who stops me getting involved in details like collecting money."

*   *   *

Most of 1980 was spent on the road and a large part of 1981 would be the same. Elektra/Asylum had dropped Joe's contract after the loss on 'Luxury You Can Afford' and with no other companies showing interest there was little else to do but tour, and re-build the following that had been lost during Joe's years in the wilderness.

Michael Lang: "I think we were without a deal for about two and a half years . . . during which time we did some touring . . . did a lot of work out of the country . . . And Joe really started to come back . . . his mind started to come back, his life started to come back. We just really concentrated on that area, but I think that time was well spent . . . we started to build his career back up in Australia and in Europe—to lay some groundwork for what's ultimately come to be."

*   *   *

141

In May 1981 Joe embarked on a tour that would take him all the way round the world. But first, there was an awkward re-union at the Dick Clark Theatre in Terrytown, New York with Leon Russell, whose own career had been launched by his association with Joe in Mad Dogs & Englishmen.

The Cocker party had been gearing up to this one since it became known that Joe and Leon were booked on the same bill. Rod Libbey: "We'd dreaded it . . . we knew it was coming up and then it was 'Here it is! We gotta do it!' It came down to an hour before show time and Joe says 'I'm not opening for him!' I can't believe this is happening . . . And Leon says 'I'm not opening for him!' It was sold out . . . anyway Leon opened . . . he had a weird band with mandolins, country stuff. He did a good show and the crowd loved him . . . Then Joe came out—he had that extra glint in his eyes and he just WAILED! He just LEVELLED the place. And the big thing was if Leon was gonna come up with Joe—but he wouldn't."

They did not play together, but they did speak. Joe: "He was his ever cool self. He just said 'Are you enjoying life? That is the main thing to be here for . . . Are you enjoying what you're doing Joe?' And I said 'Yeah. So so.' And that's the last I saw of him."

The tour took in Europe once again, moving on to Australia, where Joe was invited on to fellow Yorkshireman, Michael Parkinson's TV show. It was an appearance that amazed the live audience and caused Tom Sullivan, watching from the wings, to laugh until tears rolled down his face, from the moment Joe appeared on camera, swatting a passing fly. Joe: "I was trying to be too witty . . . I'd met him in the bar the night before—he could down a few, old Mike. The interview was going well . . . Andrew Peacock was there—he was going up for Prime Minister. He said 'By the way Joe, my daughters . . . I've got two daughters, one's thirteen and the other's fifteen, and they absolutely adore your music.' And I said 'Well, you know me—I'll screw owt, from nine to ninety—if they can't walk bring 'em in a wheelbarrow.' The whole place froze! I could see the horror in old Parkinson's face! The funny thing was, he knew the joke and he sort of lip-synched it with me. So there was this embarrassing silence and it was like . . . 'Well Joe—are you gonna sing for us?' And I said 'Sure' and after the song the producer . . . like normally you'd return and go and sit back on the seat and have another conversation . . . but he said 'Would you mind coming with me . . .' And I'm going 'But . . .' 'No, no—come with me' And he escorted me off the show. It was me trying to be too sharp!"

* * *

The last stop of the tour was Japan, Joe's first visit to a country where he was best known for his performance in the Woodstock movie. There were

142

three gigs in all, at Ngoya, Osaka and Tokyo, where, out in the open at Yoyogi Park, Joe did not let even a typhoon stop him taking the stage. Cliff Goodwin: "I couldn't believe that we were actually playing in such rain—the night before was actually a bona fide typhoon . . . stay in the hotel type of thing." But play they did, before an enthusiastic audience that included an old Sheffield fan, Glyn Senior, who has lived in Japan since the mid-70s. He says: "As far as Joe was concerned, ignorance was bliss—he could have been killed. Anybody in their right mind would have refused to do it."

Larry Marshall played the whole show with his trousers rolled up, and made sure he did not touch any metal. "They were hanging buckets up under the tent roof—filling up in about three minutes and this guy would come across the floor with a big squeezy, right in front of Joe . . . They were gonna have a helicopter up in the air, with a camera . . . and I had a great helicopter sound on one of my synthesizers. So just as Joe's walking out on stage I hit the helicopter button . . . and Rod's maxed it out through the speakers . . . and Joe takes a coupla steps back, ready to dive for cover—he thought it was the helicopter coming for him! There's something about that being a typhoon . . . Those people just stood there and went crazy."

With the tour over Joe returned to Sheffield to spend Christmas with his parents. He visited local pubs with old pals like Ray Stuart and Kenny Slade and gave an impromptu performance at the Pheasant Inn with Frank White, a contemporary from the early days.

Joe had good reason to celebrate the passing year. Apart from his improved health and successful shows around the world he had made a much acclaimed return to record—as featured guest on The Crusaders' album 'Standing Tall'. It had all begun when Joe Sample, the band's keyboards player, sent him a tune, 'L.A. Lights', a year or so earlier. "It was a tricky song to deal with but then they asked me round to their office in L.A. and Joe said 'I've got this tune for you, man . . . called 'This Old World's Too Funky For Me'. He worked with a guy, Will Jennings, who's a lyricist. And then the other song 'I'm So Glad I'm Standing Here Today'—Joe said 'I want you to know—we haven't just written these songs, we've thought about them.' He really put it over to me."

'I'm So Glad I'm Standing Here Today' was the perfect song for Joe Cocker at that point in his life. Will Jennings' lyrics could not have been more fitting and it was a tremendous gesture by The Crusaders to invite Joe to record with them, at a time when record companies did not want to know him. His performance totally justified their faith, but of 'I'm So Glad I'm Standing Here Today' he did later say "I got quite emotional when we recorded that one."

The following February Joe was in Nassau, Bahamas when he heard that 'I'm So Glad', released as a single with 'This Old World's Too Funky For

Me' on the B side, had been nominated for a Grammy in the best gospel record category. He was invited to perform the song with The Crusaders at the awards ceremony and he and Michael Lang flew to Los Angeles. Beforehand there was apprehension in some quarters about whether Joe could cope with such a big occasion, but no one need have worried. Michael Lang: "It was historic, to say the least. When he came out and sang that song he just completely floored everybody there. It was the most emotional thing I've ever seen happen at the Grammys . . . It was more emotional than Tina Turner's big year, or anybody else's—one of those things that nobody expected, nobody had a clue. He just came out and blew everybody away!"

'I'm So Glad I'm Standing Here Today' did not win a Grammy, but Joe's performance, seen on television right across America, was a major triumph. Of the reception he received that night at the Shrine Auditorium, he says "It was a great feeling. Especially when the audience all stood up at the end."

Chapter Thirteen

1982 – 1984

Up Where We Belong

JOE WAS RECORDING his 'Sheffield Steel' album at Island's Compass Point Studios when he received his Grammy invitation. Without a record contract for two and a half years, he had been brought in from the cold by Chris Blackwell, who first became involved with his career back in 1968, after 'Marjorine'. In the aftermath of Mad Dogs & Englishmen Blackwell had dropped out of Joe's affairs, but, long an admirer of his talent, he was now offering a golden opportunity for him to revive his lapsed recording career.

The deal was sparked off initially through a friendship between Joe's guitarist, Cliff Goodwin, and Island engineer, Alex Sadkin. They first met on the sessions for 'Luxury You Can Afford' in Miami, and Sadkin, who moved to Island soon afterwards, helped American Standard Band obtain their record contract. Cliff Goodwin: "I went down on holiday to the Bahamas. I went up to see Alex Sadkin, who was producing a Grace Jones album at Compass Point, and also to visit Robert Palmer, whose album 'Secrets' I'd played on . . . just a visit to friends. And Chris Blackwell said 'How you doing? . . . You still with Joe?' I said 'Yeah' . . . He said 'How is he?' . . . I said 'He's fine'. He said 'Is he still drinking?' I said 'Of course he's drinking . . . he will never stop drinking . . . that's the way he is.' And I think he was struck, to a point, by the honesty. That I didn't try to bullshit . . . I didn't say 'Oh yeah, he's great, man' . . . And before I knew it Joe was down cutting tracks for 'Sheffield Steel'."

'Sheffield Steel' was produced by Chris Blackwell and Alex Sadkin, with the notable assistance of reggae stars Sly Dunbar and Robbie Shakespeare. Cliff Goodwin and Larry Marshall went down to Nassau and played on a couple of tracks—'Don't Talk To Me' and 'Lay Down, Lay Down' but, says Cliff, "Chris Blackwell didn't like what he heard—and took 'em off." Only the exclusive instrumental talents of Island house band, the Compass Point All-Stars, appear on 'Sheffield Steel'.

Chris Blackwell's original idea came as something of a shock to Joe. "He wanted me to sing country and western songs with a reggae feel!" But when Joe went down to meet the Island boss he took a few demos with him, including 'Shocked' and 'Look What You've Done' and as the band tried them out it was clear that when it came to choosing his songs Joe knew best.

The production was another matter. In an interview with Fred Schuers of *Musician* magazine Alex Sadkin said, "What we're doing is featuring Joe, letting everybody really hear his voice, with all that gravel and whines and scars. With interesting instrumental tracks, yes, but without any female backing vocals. It would have been easy, it's such a comfortable thing to have these girls sing along on every chorus. But Chris Blackwell wanted something fresh. It's risky. But it's Joe."

'Sheffield Steel' certainly has a different sound from anything Joe has done before or since. Light on arrangements and heavy on reggae feel, Sly's snare drum and Robbie's bass are to the fore from the opening bar of the first track 'Look What You've Done'. With the exception of two numbers—'Sweet Little Woman', by ex-Free bassist Andy Fraser, and 'So Good, So Right', a cover of the Brenda Russell version—Joe's are the only vocals on the album. Barry Reynolds' fuzzy guitar is effective but never obtrusive on 'Shocked' and Steve Winwood's 'Talking Back To The Night', while the two ballads—Randy Newman's 'Marie' and Jimmy Webb's 'Just Like Always' sound reminiscent of the 1974 'I Can Stand A Little Rain' album

Joe digs up yet another obscure Dylan song in 'Seven Days', while his treatment of 'Ruby Lee' provides great scope for percussionist Sticky Thompson. But the highspot of 'Sheffield Steel' is 'Many Rivers To Cross' on which Wally Badarou's synthesizer wind effects lead into an organ intro for Joe to give a classic rendition of the song Jimmy Cliff could have written specially for him.

The critics, in the main, liked 'Sheffield Steel'. "A triumphant return to the recording studio for the undisputed king of croup-rock" said the *New York Post*. "His best work in years"—*Vancouver Sun*. "A fine Cocker album"—*Los Angeles Times*. "The selections here equal almost anything he's done in the past"—*Los Angeles Herald-Examiner*. Back home in Sheffield the *Morning Telegraph* thought Sly and Robbie's "firm and simple backing provides a better showcase for Cocker's vocal range than he's had for years." It was left to the British music press to put the dampers on—as they had so often in the past. "A singularly rusty and uninspired construct" wrote Charles Shaar Murray, who enlightened *New Musical Express* readers by stating that "This person has never been particularly enamoured of Mr Cocker's particular stock-in-trade."

With 'Sheffield Steel' in the can, Joe turned out for a few promotional dates in America. Mitch Chakour was no longer in the band, his place taken temporarily by Tom Nicholson. Howie Hersh would soon move across from bass to piano, with Artie Funaro taking over the bass for a spell. In May Joe played Perkins Palace in L.A. to a good reception and the following month he was on the East Coast and in Canada, playing Vancouver and the Red River Exhibition in Winnipeg, where ten thousand people turned up on the first night. Interviewed by Denis Hunt of the *Los Angeles Times* he said "I want to do well this time around. This is my first album in a long time. I don't want to louse it up."

The new album was released in June and sold particularly well in Europe, where Joe headed in September. First stop was Sheffield, where he played two nights at the Lyceum—his first show in his hometown for thirteen years. The compère for the two nights was his old friend Ray Stuart, at the time a Radio Hallam DJ, who recalls Joe's acute nervousness beforehand—

"We went to the rehearsal in the afternoon. The band were fine—it was just another theatre in another town to them. They knew they could do it and they knew Joe could do it—but Joe wasn't sure whether he could or not. He didn't turn up until half an hour before he was due to go on—he was in his hotel in Rotherham, but he rang up a few times and said 'Are you sure they're going to like me?' We kept saying 'Of course they're going to like you' but he wasn't so sure! He was apprehensive right up to going on—and then, about ten minutes before he was due on stage his mother suddenly arrived with a big bag of licquorice allsorts—he loves them! All that tension beforehand . . . and when he went on the audience just went crackers."

It was an emotional homecoming from the moment Joe set foot on the Lyceum stage and slipped into 'Look What You've Done'. As his mother watched from the theatre's royal box he went through old hits, songs from the new album, and several unrecorded numbers—'Don't Talk To Me', Jimmy Reed's 'You've Got Me Running' and Marvin Gaye's 'Inner City Blues', which would surface four years later on 'Cocker'. Every song received a tumultuous reception from the audience, many of whom had not heard Joe sing live since the pub days of the Black Swan and Barrow Hill. Afterwards there was a party where Joe met old friends like Phil Crookes, Dave Memmott and Dave Green for the first time in years. "I enjoyed that," he said in a later Radio Hallam interview with Ray Stuart. "I knew just about everybody in the room, going back to being sixteen." Of the two shows—each night he was brought back time and time again for encores—he said, "I loved every second of it—I remember seeing pantomime at the Lyceum, so just walking on a stage like that was a bit euphoric."

Joe and his entourage left Sheffield for Athens and onwards into Germany. Shows there included the Metropole in Berlin—scene of the successful *Rockpalast 80*, Frankfurt, Hamburg and Munich where, with a heavy cold, he played a BR TV show at the packed Alabama Hall.

All around Europe the tour rolled, to Switzerland, France, Holland, Yugoslavia and Italy. In Rome police riot squads had to use tear gas and to fire shots in the air to disperse fans who ran amok, fearing that they would not get to see the show. When Joe took the stage, tempers cooled, only to rise again after the set. Sound man Rod Libbey: "They stormed the stadium, stoned the coach . . . destroyed all my gear, right at the end of the gig. It was a mess. A big mess."

In late October Joe travelled to Australia and New Zealand for yet another tour Down Under. He had no sooner arrived and done a few shows when he learned that 'Up Where We Belong', a duet with Jennifer Warnes that he had recorded as a film theme song, was number one in the *Billboard* Hot 100. Recorded in L.A. in May, for the film *An Officer And A Gentleman*, 'Up Where We Belong', topped the U.S. charts for three consecutive weeks. It was Joe's first ever number one—and only producer Stewart Levine's persuasion had led him to record it. Joe: "I almost didn't want to record that—the demo was dreadful! It was actually three different songs that three different writers had put together . . . Buffy St. Marie . . . she wrote that little 'Time goes by . . .' and so it was like a whole different tune . . . And she's married to Jack Nitzsche, so like they welded that together and then Will Jennings came in and wrote the bridge . . . the 'Up' part, which is what made me realise it had hit potential. It was so unusual—that 'Love lift us up . . .' But the rest of it . . .the demo! And Stewart kept saying 'Well—do you want to do it?'

"They mentioned Jennifer Warnes and I went 'Oh my God . . . she's a country and western singer!' but he said 'No, no . . . it'll work'. It did—when we got in they'd already cut the tracks . . . guessed what key I'd sing it in—D—and we went in there. I'd sat with the words in the afternoon but I still hadn't remembered them so we had to draw 'em up on big blocks of wood and stuff . . . James Brown style. I'll give Stewart his due—he made that record."

But Island boss Chris Blackwell was not impressed. Joe: "He hated it . . . didn't even want to release it. It wasn't R 'n' B and after doing 'Sheffield Steel' it sort of rubbed him up the wrong way. I remember going into their offices in New York. I walked in and I said 'How's the single doing?' and this guy Mike Abrahams, who worked there, he said 'This is how well it's doing'—and the office was piled with returns. 'Joe', he said 'I'm so convinced that this could be a smash that I'm hand-writing notes to every D.J. in the country.' I owe him a lot for that . . . for what he did."

'Up Where We Belong' was Joe's first American hit record since 'You Are So Beautiful' in 1975. In Britain it reached number 7 and Joe, together with Jennifer Warnes, made his first live appearance on BBC TV's *Top Of The Pops* since 1968. A hit all round the world, it brought Joe's name right back into the public eye, amazing many people who had long assumed that Joe Cocker had somewhere along the way faded into rock and roll oblivion.

Joe, having recorded the song, immediately felt it would be a hit. The same feeling that he had experienced when 'With A Little Help' was put down came over him when he heard the playback of 'Up Where We Belong'. "I knew it was a number one . . . Other people were saying 'Well . . . perhaps' but I could just feel it. The song was recorded within a matter of hours. 'Sheffield Steel'—I spent a year on that. And the single eclipsed it overnight."

In February, 1983, at the 25th Anniversary of the Grammy Awards, Joe and Jennifer Warnes' 'Up Where We Belong' won the Best Pop Vocal by a Duo category. The following month they travelled to the Tokyo Song Festival, emerging joint winners with Lionel Richie. While in Japan they also appeared on the Music Fair television show, following a Japanese cover version of 'Up Where We Belong', and Joe and his band played four concerts—at the Kaikai Hall in Tokyo, followed by Yokohama, Osaka and Ngoya.

Back in Los Angeles there was a date at the Academy Awards, where the theme song from *An Officer And A Gentleman* was among the nominations. Introduced by Dudley Moore—not engaged on Derek and Clive business on this occasion—Joe and Jennifer Warnes sang from a balcony while below them dancers, dressed as officers and their ladies, paraded and twirled to 'Up Where We Belong'. If Joe's suit was a concession to the showbiz spirit of the event, his hair style kept everything in perspective—and the song won an Oscar for the writers, to add to the other awards Joe and Jennifer Warnes had already secured.

Seeing her son on the televised Academy Awards show was a great thrill for Madge Cocker. "I'm really pleased for Joe," she told the Sheffield *Star*, "It's great—he's worked so hard this past year he really deserves it." In July Joe went home for a visit, taking the white suit he had worn at the Oscar ceremony for Madge to wash. Having a quiet drink with Ray Stuart in the Ball Inn, just round the corner from Tasker Road, he was invited to sing with the resident pianist and drummer, and obliged with 'Georgia On My Mind'. He then got Ray Stuart up to join him and they went through the old rock and roll repertoire, carrying on until midnight. Ray Stuart: "We ended up with 'What'd I Say' and afterwards an elderly bloke came up and said to the landlord—'Tha wants to book them two, they're alreight!'"

Soon after this return to his roots, while still in Sheffield, Joe was called back to the States for an appearance that was at one time way beyond his wildest dreams. At the Ambassador Hotel in Los Angeles an all-star cast, including Glen Campbell, Johnny Cash, Quincy Jones, Smokey Robinson and Stevie Wonder, gathered to pay homage to Ray Charles in a televised show, *A Man And His Soul*.

Joe has never tried to disguise his adulation of Ray Charles. Denny Cordell recalls accompanying him to see the legendary artiste in New York back in 1969. "We went backstage. Ray was sitting there and somebody said 'Hey, Ray! Joe Cocker's come to see you!' He goes 'Oh Yeah? Joe. I really like the way you sing.' And Joe came down and he knelt at Ray's feet and laid his head on his lap and cried. Tears welled from his eyes . . . He said 'Ray . . . I love you so much . . . just, so beautiful, man.'"

On his part, Ray Charles has long recognised Joe as his disciple. In his 1978 autobiography, *Brother Ray*, he says "Man I know that cat must sleep with my records. But I don't mind. I'm flattered." And in a mid '70 television show he paid Joe a supreme compliment at a time when many lesser people preferred to ignore him.

Denny Cordell: "I was living in Malibu and Joe lived two or three miles up the beach. He came over one night—said 'I want to watch the Sammy Davis Show—Ray's gonna be on.' So Ray does his two or three songs—with Joe cheering him on—and Sammy Davis came on and he said 'Now Ray—you're the Godfather of Soul . . . you're the Genius . . . you're this and that,' he said. 'You've been around a long time—who are the greatest soul singers today?' And Ray said 'Well . . . there's Mahalia Jackson . . . there's Aretha Franklin . . . and there's Marvin Gaye . . . and there's Joe Cocker.' Joe said 'There you are! There you are! He said it! You all heard it! There . . . He said it—you heard it!' It just made him up . . . straight from the man's mouth . . . it was just perfect!"

Now, in 1983, not only was Joe invited on to his guru's television spectacular, but he was to sing a duet with him. It all happened so quickly—getting the call in Sheffield, flying straight back to the States and rushing into the studio—that Joe had not had too much time to become nervous. On the show he introduced the song, telling how he first heard Ray on his transistor radio back in Sheffield and how at that time he would never have believed he would be on the same stage as "The Genius . . . Mr Ray Charles . . . Brother Ray Charles." They then sang 'You Are So Beautiful', Joe standing by the piano as Ray played.

Two years later in West Germany, Joe sang again with Ray Charles in an open-air concert billed as 'The Voices' at the Sportpark, Hannover. They sang 'Baby Please Don't Go' and 'What'd I Say'. Witnesses to the event were highly impressed by the performance, but Joe was left feeling disappointed—"I was dreadful . . . I said to him—'I hated that one' . . .

You have those days. If I was on form I'd love to do a date with him . . . Back home I've got a picture in the bathroom of him embracing me—with his bow-tie on and everything. It reminds me every morning when I get up just what a genius he is."

*   *   *

The Summer of 1983 saw Joe perform several large open-air concerts and festivals in West Germany, the most far-reaching of them all at Lorely St. Goarshausen on August 20 in *Rockpalast 83*. The annual WDR TV show that three years earlier had been the first real milestone in the revival of Joe's career in Germany this time revealed him in full flight to a vast television audience across Europe and into Russia. Sixty million viewers watched the concert featuring Straycats, U2, Dave Edmunds, Steve Miller Band—and Joe Cocker, whose performance was second to none.

Rockpalast 83 was a triumph in the face of potential disaster. On the morning of the show Joe awoke in Eindhoven, where he had played the previous evening, and found himself without any voice at all. Tom Sullivan: "He was worried. He had looked forward to it but he had strained himself a little too much the night before." He was taken to a doctor in Cologne, who specialized in treating opera singers, and given a cortisone injection. Meanwhile the band made their way to the show where they anxiously awaited news. Five minutes before he was due to go on Joe arrived backstage. Bernard Pendry was there: "Nobody knew what was going to happen—and then he turned up—the old scarf round his neck . . . He whispered 'Don't talk'—it was awful! Then he got up on stage and he was absolutely magic! I couldn't believe it."

If the vast open-air crowd had been aware of the anxiety before the show they could not have given Joe a better reception than they did at Lorely that summer's evening. As dusk turned to night he went through a long, hard-driving set, culminating in a frenzied 'With A Little Help' that left the crowd screaming for more. Brought back on stage he sang two more numbers, and was called back for a further encore to do 'The Moon's A Harsh Mistress' and 'I Heard It Through The Grapevine'. Long after he had left the stage for good the crowd were still chanting for more.

Most singers in Joe's predicament would have cancelled their show that morning. None, after requiring cortisone to enable them to sing at all, would have played a long set without restraint and then returned to sing four more songs as encores. Joe would later describe as "magic" the moment he opened his mouth to sing the first notes of the opening number, 'A Girl Like You' and heard a sound come out. *Rockpalast 83* is one show he will never forget.

* * *

To cap a memorable year Joe was invited in November 83 to join Ronnie Lane's American tour to raise money for Action Research for Multiple Sclerosis. In September the former Faces star, who had suffered from the disease for five years, gathered together some of his friends from the rock world to play a benefit concert at the Royal Albert Hall in London. With the help of Eric Clapton and producer Glyn Johns, the greatest line-up of British rock talent ever assembled appeared together on one stage. It included: Clapton, Jeff Beck, Jimmy Page, Steve Winwood, Bill Wyman, Charlie Watts, Kenny Jones, Andy Fairweather-Lowe and Chris Stainton.

The Albert Hall show was a great success and plans were made for a similar venture in the States, with nine shows in four cities. When Steve Winwood had to drop out due to prior commitments, Glyn Johns brought in Joe—"That was a great lift . . . It was mind-blowing that tour—it wasn't long enough for me. I remember walking into the rehearsals and Eric saying ''Ere 'e is! Finally made it!' There was Bill Wyman and all the guys—I was slightly agog with it all. So we tore through all the numbers that I had to sing . . . and I was in decent voice . . . but at the end of it I sort of fell backwards—over Eric's guitar and Jimmy Page's. And I'm thinking 'Oh God! If I've broken these . . .' And Bill Wyman just stood there, cracking up with laughter. He said 'I've never seen anything like that—I wish I had me camera. You fell over in slow motion!'"

The ARMS tour took in Dallas, San Francisco, Los Angeles and Madison Square Garden in New York. As well as boosting Joe's morale in no small measure it provided a happy re-union with his old partner Chris Stainton, Eric Clapton's pianist for the previous four years. Joe had his own spot on the shows, backed by Clapton, Stainton, Bill Wyman and Charlie Watts. A bootleg album of one of the three shows at Cow Palace, San Francisco, reveals him in fine voice on 'You Are So Beautiful', 'Seven Days' and 'Feelin' Alright'. Towards the end of each show he helped out on Clapton's 'Layla', before leading a spirited rendition of 'With A Little Help From My Friends', with the full band, including Eric Clapton, Jimmy Page and Jeff Beck on guitars, plus four drummers.

Tom Sullivan accompanied Joe on the ARMS tour. "There were re-unions with a lot of people—Jimmy Page hadn't seen Joe in years . . . I expected a lot of ego fighting and chaos—I thought this many superstars there would be problems. There were none. It was as smooth as silk . . . an incredible experience."

Rolling Stone, reviewing the third San Francisco ARMS show, declared it "Concert of the Year". Of Joe's 'With A Little Help' Kurt Loder and Michael Goldberg wrote. "Cocker turning in one of his strongest vocals was every bit the equal of the famous Woodstock performance fourteen years ago."

* * *

After the exciting events of the previous year, Joe concentrated on the road in 1984. A new album, 'Civilised Man' was due for release in the Summer, and Europe—greatly impressed by his gripping performance in the live broadcast of *Rockpalast 83*—clamoured for his return. But when he arrived in Germany in late March for a twenty-two date tour, an old face was missing from the band—B.J. Wilson, Joe's drummer, friend and drinking partner for the past four and a half years, had been replaced.

B.J., described as a "fine, English, classical drummer" by one American contemporary, remained something of a legend in Cocker circles long after his departure from the drum stool. Tales of his eccentricities are legion—the freezing November night when the band arrived back at their Berlin hotel to find B.J. sitting outside, pruning the rose bushes with nail clippers . . . the airflight when he fell asleep, set his hair on fire with a cigarette and, waking to the smell of burning hair, muttered, "I'll have to change my socks." Joe: "We were incorrigible drinking partners . . . we were in this famous old hotel in Holland . . . on the beach down Rotterdam way . . . We're sat in the bar and I said to B.J. 'I'm going to put my head down for a bit, ready for tonight.' So he said 'Well I'm gonna get something to eat'. Next thing I know there's a beating on the door of my room . . . 'Meester Cockair . . . please . . . You must come with me . . . your friend—he is in terrible trouble!' . . . 'Who? The drummer?' . . . 'Yes. Please come quickly.'

"And he'd fallen asleep in his soup. It was alphabet soup and there's B.J.—face down . . . he's lucky he didn't drown—as his nose is blowing there's all these bubbles! We picked him up and he's got letters all over his face—B . . . K . . . A to Z . . . stuck all over him and falling out of his hair . . . These guys were so panic-stricken they didn't know what to do. And I'm saying 'Oh don't worry about him, he does it all the time' . . . as there's like four of us carting him off to the elevator—pissed with all these letters all over his face."

In Japan in 1981 B.J. held the band record for bottles of saki consumed— thirty-four, recalls Joe, but by '83, when his drinking began to interfere with his drumming, the situation took on a serious light. Joe: "The band spotted it long before me. If we were due to meet at 7.30 in the hotel lobby, he'd be there at 6.30 and he'd chase down about four doubles. When he was on target he was a magnificent drummer—ballads there's no-one to touch him—but he just got into this crafty drinking . . . always drinking behind closed doors. On stage he'd be dragging time and it got to the point where the band said, 'Hey Joe. Something's got to go. Either

153

us or him.' So it was like five against one. I was trying to pretend it wasn't happening . . ."

B.J. Wilson's replacement was Eric Parker, previously with Steve Winwood and Bryan Adams. He learned twenty-eight songs in two days and then the band left for Europe, along with new bass player, Vito Sanfillipo, who took over from Artie Funaro.

The German tour had barely got underway when Joe heard the grim news that Marvin Gaye, one of his great post-Ray Charles influences, was dead—shot by his own father in a family dispute. Joe had met Gaye only a year earlier, at the Grammy Awards ceremony—"Marvin—he must have embraced me for about ten minutes . . . it was scary! He locked on to me and started swinging me around—and I'm looking at everybody in the room . . . but I was flattered that the guy even wanted to squeeze me."

Joe, deeply saddened by the news of Gaye's death, made a special dedication to him before singing 'Inner City Blues' at that night's show in Cologne. In an interview with the German magazine *Fachblatt*, he said of the Motown star—"He was one of the greatest to me—a tough character, but OK. He didn't receive enough appreciation for his music—his 'What's Going On' album meant very much to me. He was a milestone in black music, though in the music business he was a black sheep. Maybe people understand now what a great talent has been lost."

It is no surprise that Joe felt affinity with Marvin Gaye, whose songs he had first sung back in Sheffield in 1966, when he formed his first Grease Band. Both singers experienced great turmoil in their lives and careers, though in Gaye's case his personal problems were deeply rooted in his upbringing. Both had an uncompromising, burnished-in-the-soul attitude to their music, not always understood by others. And Gaye, like Joe, had seemingly destroyed his career through personal excess—until he raced back to the top of the *Billboard* Black Chart with 'Sexual Healing' in the very same week that Joe and Jennifer Warnes topped the Hot 100 with 'Up Where We Belong'.

In early May, with his fortieth birthday less than three weeks away, Joe could have been excused for believing that the days of craziness and controversy were well behind him. Now, as he frequently told interviewers who harked after tales of drunkenness and drug-taking, putting on a good show was his prime consideration. But while a good reputation can easily be lost, a bad one is hard to shake off. And when an unscrupulous Austrian promoter tried to cover up his own negligence by claiming Joe Cocker was too drunk to perform a concert—he had no difficulty getting people to believe him.

The concert, a late addition to the successful German tour, was scheduled for Vienna on May 1. Although he knew that Joe would not be appearing—and the reasons why—the promoter, Johann Hausner, did not cancel the show. Instead he waited until the 3,000 strong audience were seated in the hall and with excitement mounting, he went on stage and announced that Joe would not be appearing as he was back at his hotel, too drunk to sing.

The audience were not pleased and neither was Joe. He was indeed back at his hotel, but as for being drunk—soon after Hausner's announcement he was examined by a doctor who pronounced him free of any influence of alcohol whatsoever. What the audience had not been told was that arguments had been raging all that day because the promoter had failed to provide necessary equipment for the show to take place.

Joe: "I get up at 12 o'clock in the afternoon and Tom's banging on the door . . . 'Joe—the piano's outa tune . . . the organ doesn't work . . . we've got a thirty watt Vox when we asked for a hundred watt Marshall. We're not even fussy about a Marshall—a hundred watt amp will do.' I just kept sitting on the edge of the bed—waiting. And all afternoon the band kept coming back from the gig. I mean—that's what the contract's about—to say we need specific equipment. So when it came to show time—the gear wasn't right and we weren't going on."

Having been exonerated from Hausner's claim by the doctor, Joe was very surprised at eleven o'clock the following morning to be raised from his bed by the Vienna police and arrested. The accusation was that he had failed to appear at the concert after his fee—$16,000 had already been paid. The German tour agent, Martin Biallis, who had received the money was also arrested and, in the midst of waiting photographers and reporters, the two of them were taken from the hotel.

Once again the name of Joe Cocker appeared in large newspaper print all over the world—for the wrong reasons. Back home in Sheffield, his mother, Madge, who had been half expecting Joe to visit once his tour was over, heard about his arrest on the radio. "It doesn't sound right," she told a reporter from the Sheffield *Star*, "Joe loves to sing and it would take a lot to stop him. There must have been something very wrong."

Sitting in an Austrian police station with no real idea what was happening, Joe became increasingly worried. He had initially been told that he would be released in twenty minutes or so, but without explanation he and Biallis were transferred to a high security prison. "It was horrifying. I was a nervous wreck by this time. They put me in a cell that was so small it just had a toilet and a rusty bed. I thought 'This is it—it's all over', but then they moved me to another cell with two guys, and one spoke a bit of English . . . And they had these little earphones that they plugged into the wall and listened to a radio. . . . And they kept saying 'Oh dear. This is very bad. You are going to be here many months' . . . Then the next thing was 'Ah! People are very angry at you being in here.'"

155

Many telegrams of support were sent to Joe via the court in Vienna—well-known names from the European rock scene like Udo Lindenberg, BAP, Konstantin Wecker, Lazy Poker and Wolfgang Ambros, together with messages from fans all over the world. Eventually, after thirty-six hours in custody, Joe and Martin Biallis were released, with all accusations against them withdrawn. The public prosecutor later announced that their complaint regarding the sound equipment provided by the promoter, Johann Hausner, was totally justified, that it had been consequently impossible for Joe to perform, and that his representatives had every right according to the contract to claim the $16,000 to cover their group's expenses. American lawyers acting for Joe lodged a claim for $6 million damages but he later decided not to pursue the matter, having no desire to return to Austria to testify.

It was a bitter and disturbing experience for Joe. Before he flew out of Vienna he telephoned Tom Sullivan who had returned to America with members of the band in between the show being cancelled and Joe's arrest. Tom: "He must have talked to me for a solid hour, at least. I had to ask him to get off the phone. He was very paranoid . . . he told me that he thought it was me knocking on the door that morning . . . He was extremely down and it had a really bad effect on him—he felt misused by the whole thing."

*　　*　　*

From Austria Joe flew to London, where he filmed a promotional video for 'Civilised Man' at Crazy Larry's Club in Chelsea. The album was released soon afterwards, Joe's first on Capitol. It was originally intended for Island, produced by Stewart Levine, and titled 'One More Time', but Chris Blackwell had not liked it. Joe: "Blackwell hated it, so we had a gentleman's agreement and packed up the deal at Island and I went to Capitol."

Capitol, however, were not totally happy with the album, containing, as it did, so many slow ballads. Another producer, Gary Katz, known for his work with Steely Dan, was commissioned to produce what emerged as side one of 'Civilised Man'. Katz recorded at the Village Recorder in L.A. and Soundworks, New York City. He used Toto's Jeff Pocaro on drums, Steve Lukather on guitar and David Paitch on keyboards, along with bassist Nathan East and piano player Greg Phillinganes, both of whom would enliven Eric Clapton's band in the future.

The Toto men sound particularly influential on the title track, an upbeat number with backing vocals led by Cissy Houston. 'There Goes My Baby' is Joe's version of the old Drifters song, with four-part back-up on male vocals. 'Come On In', composed by synthesizer man Bob Telson, is followed by 'Tempted', from the Squeeze songbook, while Larry John McNally's sad song 'Long Drag Off A Cigarette' features the writer on accoustic guitar and ex Mad Dog Jim Keltner on drums.

Stewart Levine's production on the second side of the album, recorded in Nashville, features such Music City stalwarts as David Briggs, former Area Code 615 keyboardsman; Reggie Young, once guitarist in the Bill Black Combo; and the powerhouse drumming of Larrie Londin, a long-standing member of the Everly Brothers' band. The side opens with Londin at full force on 'I Love The Night', the tempo slowing for 'Crazy In Love', with the Sid Sharp Strings. 'A Girl Like You', which Joe had been singing live for the past year, follows—a dynamic number with Jim Horn soloing on alto sax. 'Up Where We Belong' lyricist Will Jennings co-composed 'A Girl Like You', as he did the following song, 'Hold On (I Feel Our Love is Changing)', music by Joe Sample of The Crusaders. The last number on the album, 'Even A Fool Would Let Go' builds from the David Briggs piano intro for the Sid Sharp Strings to take up the mood of the sort of slow love song Joe sings best of all.

'Civilised Man' marked a new era of Joe Cocker albums. The lean sound of 'Sheffield Steel' had given way to a much fuller style of production, with up-front drum beat and synthesizer on all but two tracks. The old R 'n' B fans might not have been too keen but Joe had entered a new phase—taking advantage of technology to experiment a little and to produce music of the 1980s.

Vocally he was in sterling form, his phrasing sharp and his diction clear on well-chosen material of varied tempo and atmosphere. 'Civilised Man' expanded on the success of his previous album, selling well in Europe and even creeping to Number 100 in the British album charts—albeit for one week. On his fourth label in as many albums Joe's recording future was now secure on Capitol leaving him well-placed for a serious assault on the European album and single charts.

* * *

Joe's sixth tour of Australia was billed 'A Civilised Man Down Under'. Once again he played to full houses and went down a storm on the mainland, moving on for one show in Auckland, New Zealand, where the local press reported he "surpassed his memorable concert of one and a half years ago with a brilliant performance before a large, mainly young audience." In Sydney two days before his fortieth birthday, Joe spoke of imminent middle age, telling a press conference that he now drank less, behaved better and had even tried to exercise! "I never drink before a show, except for a couple of beers," he said. "I'm learning how to save my energy."

After Australia there were festival appearances, television shows and a series of autumn concerts throughout Germany, supported by U2. The

157

following year U2 would achieve their breakthrough and the roles would be reversed. As Rod Libbey recalls "Joe did his set and he'd do about eight encores. Then he'd come out with U2. They loved Joe—they sat on the edge of the stage every gig."

The 'Civilised Man' tour also took in Israel, where Joe had first visited a year earlier. Larry Marshall: "We played Tel Aviv, Jerusalem, Haifa, Caesarea—a real antique amphitheatre where the lions used to go out and get the Christians. The audiences in Israel are just great . . . You go on stage, I don't care which gig, it's like getting off the stage anywhere else. They go nuts—they're just so happy that you're there. The audiences knew every word to every song. There's a kind of energy . . . an electricity in the air."

*   *   *

In October Joe made a short visit to Sheffield. Accompanying him was Pam Baker, the director of Jane Fonda's ranch, whom he had met soon after moving there in 1978. In the intervening years they had become close and now Pam met Joe's parents for the first time.

While home, Joe recorded a programme for Radio Hallam's 'My Kind Of Music'. He played some favourite records from the past, talking to Ray Stuart about each choice. There was the predictable 'What'd I Say' and 'Georgia On My Mind', Jerry Lee Lewis's 'Whole Lotta Shakin' Goin' On' and Aretha Franklin's 'Respect', which he had first heard at the time he was working in the newspaper warehouse. Playing George Harrison's 'Isn't It A Pity', Joe said "I've always respected the man very dearly, always had a soft spot for his simplicity and warmth." He spoke too of the one and only time he saw Elvis Presley in Las Vegas, and was reminded by Ray Stuart of how in the early days they had never missed an Elvis movie. Reluctant to talk about the bad times in his own life, he did mention his recent experience in Vienna, before playing Lionel Richie's 'Hello—Is It You I'm Looking For', which he had heard repeatedly through the earphones on his cell radio. The final record choice was Ray Stuart's—Joe's 'Edge Of A Dream', a theme song which he had recently recorded for the film 'Teachers'.

*   *   *

Two months after Joe's visit, his mother, Madge, died suddenly at home. She had not been ill and her death came as a great shock to her family and friends. Joe was in Memphis, recording tracks for his next album—'Cocker'—when he received the news. He flew home to be with his father, Harold, and brother, Vic, at the funeral.

158

Marjorie Cocker, known as Madge, was often described as Joe's Number One Fan. A small, jolly woman, her support for him never wavered through good or bad times and Joe always knew that whatever happened elsewhere he would be welcomed with open arms back home.

Not that Madge could ever be sure when he might arrive. Never one to write—although not long before his mother died he did buy her a postcard in Jerusalem, but forgot to post it until he got to Paris—the usual warning was a telephone call out-of-the-blue saying he was on his way. And when he did turn up, mostly at Christmas, Madge didn't worry if she saw little of him. "There were always people coming and taking him somewhere," recalls Harold Cocker. "Even Christmas Day—but it never bothered his mother."

When he was at home it was quite usual for the living room at Tasker Road to be full of his friends, just as it had always been before he became famous, yet Madge never turned a hair. Convivial and hospitable, she got on with everyone and, until she died, she corresponded with many of Joe's fans around the world, who at one time or another had turned up on the step at Tasker Road.

When the headlines were bad Madge was philosophical and defended her younger son to the hilt against anyone who dared to be critical on the strength of sensationalised newspaper reports. A popular figure at Joe's British concerts, her proudest moment came at Sheffield Lyceum when Joe brought the house down and came back on stage to sing her favourite song, 'You Are So Beautiful'.

Since their childhood Madge had encouraged both her sons to do the things they wanted to do. Joe chose music and, although she did sometimes wonder if he might have been better off remaining a gas fitter, Madge gained tremendous pleasure from his success. It was most befitting that the album Joe was recording at the time his mother died—'Cocker'—should be dedicated to her when it was released just over a year later.

Chapter Fourteen

1985 — 1987

Massive Crowds
And Great Receptions

THROUGHOUT THE 1980S Joe had spent long periods on the road in Europe. For months each year—from Norway down to Italy, France across to Greece—he had built up an ever-increasing following of ardent fans. There have been no short cuts, success has come through sheer hard slog: long, tiring road journeys in the band bus, early morning flights after a show the night before, an endless round of hotel rooms, snatched meals and the many other hassles that touring entails.

While media coverage, especially televised concerts, has helped reach a wider audience, Michael Lang is in no doubt that Joe's success in Europe has been achieved through the years of live work. "The *Rockpalast* shows in '80 and '83 were milestones—but they didn't really clinch it. What clinched it was being out there, working all those cities all those times. We built it from the roots—that's what did it. It evolved his following . . . people started to love him. We did our own shows—small halls, three thousand seaters and the tours just grew in size. There was a certain market and we built on that."

By 1985 small halls belonged to the past. At Spring and Summer festivals Joe played to huge crowds all over the Continent. "We were playing to 70,000 and then 80,000," says Eric Parker. "And then 100,000. It became like more and more fun seeing how many people were there."

At the Nurburgring, West Germany, on May 25 an estimated 100,000 packed the motor racing circuit, giving Joe a rapturous reception. The following day at the Neckardstadion in Stuttgart Radio Suedfunk 3

160

recorded the proceedings. The day after that he played 'Rock In Munster', another open-air event, with U2, Chris De Burgh and Mink De Ville. In Bad Segerberg Joe played 'Rock Over Germany', moving on to the Olympic Stadium in Munich, more stadiums in Italy, France, Luxembourg and the Barcelona Music Festival in Spain.

In between times there was a rare open-air show in England, at the Glastonbury C.N.D. Festival in June, where Joe topped the bill on the third day. It had rained solidly for forty-eight hours and conditions were so bad that the crew struggled just to get the equipment to the site. "We'd played Brest, done a very dodgy festival in pouring rain," recalls Jim Foster, a member of Joe's road crew. "You shouldn't be out in those conditions. We flew from there to Exeter and when we arrive the dogs are there—and the police. Do we need this? When we got to the site there was nothing that wasn't covered in mud—talking about up to your knees backstage . . . They had to put wooden boards down to get the bus out! What I can remember it was a good gig—but there was no reason for it to have been!"

* * *

Long tours can be tough and gruelling, but the stability within his band during the mid 1980s provided a great support to Joe. There were some line-up changes but the nucleus of Cliff Goodwin, Larry Marshall, Howie Hersh and Maxine Green remained constant from 1980 onwards—while Eric Parker, who joined in 1984 and John Troy, the bassist who arrived two years later, fitted in with ease. In other departments, too, Joe knew he could depend on people—Tom Sullivan, Rod Libbey and Jim Foster—who first helped out at Sheffield Lyceum in September '82 and has worked with Joe on every European tour since. A Sheffielder—for a long time the only non-American in band or crew—he says, "Joe is a nice man. Very, very soft at times. I do enjoy being with him and the set-up—you can't take one way from the other. The people that are around him seem to have absorbed his aura."

In June 1987 Cliff Goodwin, on what would be his last tour with Joe, pondered on the friendly, close-knit atmosphere within the band. "Well . . . a lot of us have put a lot of years in together. It's a love-hate relationship . . . . very much like a family atmosphere . . . life goes up and down and if you were totally enthralled with it all the time, the minute you came upon rough weather you'd have people baling out. Joe is very much part of it all—it's an old style band and the crew's with us. There's none of this rock star bullshit. What we do we do and it's always against the odds—but that keeps us on our toes."

A popular feature of life on the road during these years was the bizarre 'court' held on the band bus and presided over by 'Judge Skip'—real name

Jonathan—Blauner, a New Yorker with a cutting line in humour, who handled the business side of tours for Michael Lang.

Judge Skip's court usually began as the bus drove back to the hotel after a show. Amidst much banter and ballyhoo, the judge's bailiff, 'Rusty', alias John Troy, called the bus to order. "Oyez, oyez, oyez—drop your linen and stop your grinnin' cos it's COURT TIME" was a typical command, followed by a new rhyme which he usually wrote for each court:-

Somewhere the sun is shining
Somewhere hearts are light
Somewhere there is no fining
And no worries in sight.
But we care not for leisure
So dig deep in your pocket
Justice is the court's pleasure
So pray you're not on the docket

After this Judge Skip summoned before him any member of the entourage who, in his keen eye, had overstepped the line in some way.

A band member might be fined five dollars—or the European equivalent—for some minor slip-up on stage that night, someone else for being a few minutes late on the bus. On one occasion a T shirt seller who happened to be on the bus was fined for wearing sunglasses at night—"You don't have to be the smoothest guy around." Joe, band, crew, friends, relatives—anyone who happened to be there—sooner or later Skip nailed them all.

Guilt was decided by members of the crew, who, ensconced at the rear of the bus, formed the 'Well-Hung Jury'. Counsel could be retained to appeal against their decision from the firm of 'Doowe, Cheatem and Howe'—Cliff Goodwin and Larry Marshall—who would proffer most imaginative and impassioned mitigation on behalf of any defendant willing to pay them five dollars or marks. The court enlivened many a long journey and with the fines collected on the 1986 German tour Skip Blauner had a gold disc manufactured, which he presented to the band's regular bus driver, Herbie, insisting that he stop the coach—and the traffic behind it—in a busy street for the ceremony to take place.

*   *   *

Joe's second album on the Capitol label—simply titled 'Cocker'—was released in April 1986. Whereas 'Civilised Man' had two producers, 'Cocker' had five—Capitol trying out on Joe a formula that had brought success for Tina Turner.

The album also featured, for the first time since 'Stingray', Joe's current band, who played on the five tracks produced by Terry Manning. While recording with Manning in Memphis, Joe took advantage of some spare time to visit one of his long-time heroes, Jerry Lee Lewis. It was a disappointing meeting—the controversial rocker who had been arousing outrage and mayhem since long before Joe even formed the Cavaliers, was waiting outside the house when he arrived, driven by Tom Sullivan. Joe: "There he stood . . . in all his enormity . . . I mean . . . I'd seen him that time in Sheffield . . . and he was just . . . standing there . . . on about his fifteenth marriage . . . as we drive up in this black limo . . . I said 'Jerry . . . What can I say man? . . . I love your music'.

'Ah know that!'

'What else can I say?'. . . . Tom's just completely blown away . . .

'Everything cool?'

'Yeah. Everything's FINE!'

And we're just standing there outside the house—there was no way he was gonna let us in! So I go . . . 'By the way . . . my name's Joe Co . . .'

'I KNOW WHO THE FUCK YOU IS!!'

'Yeah. Yeah. Okay . . .' End of story . . . we just got back in the limo and drove away!"

* * *

'Shelter Me', which gets 'Cocker' underway, had been released in advance as a single and maxi- single—the latter's B side bearing two 'Civilised Man' out-takes. A powerful opener—it features some solid Cliff Goodwin guitar work and a rousing sax finish by Mel Collins, late of King Crimson and Kokomo.

The other tracks from Terry Manning, who counted ZZ Top among his previous successes, are 'A to Z'; 'Love Is On A Fade'; his own composition 'Heaven', and 'Inner City Blues'. The song that Joe had been singing long before its composer, Marvin Gaye, was killed gets full justice on record: synthesizer and melodic bass riff teeing up Howie Hersh's jazzy piano solo, while Joe lays out the Motown legend's lament to urban decay.

Three producers had one song each on 'Cocker': Bernard Edwards—'Don't Drink The Water'; Albert Hammond (with co-producer Diane Warren)– 'Don't You Love Me Anymore'—an anguished ballad with rising multi-tracked chorus, and Richie Zito—'You Can Leave Your Hat On'—a pulsating version of the Randy Newman song.

Despite such varied involvement, 'Cocker' does have its own identity, no one number working against the general feel of the album. But Joe was not too comfortable with the recording technique of Ron Nevison, who produced 'Heart Of The Matter' and 'Living Without Your Love'—"He's great at working with people like Heart," said Joe later, "but he had me recording songs not even line by line, but word by word, and then patching it all together. At the end I realised I didn't know the tune!" Times had changed since Denny Cordell laid down a hit and its-B side in one three hour session.

'Cocker' shot up the European album charts—peaking at Number three in Germany, where *Fachblatt* magazine described it as "A document of devotion and fulfilment . . . A declaration of love to his art." 'You Can Leave Your Hat On', prominently featured in the film *9½ Weeks,* was a hit single, topping the Italian charts. Joe was to receive Gold and Platinum Discs for the 'Cocker' album, with over one and a half million copies sold worldwide to date.

* * *

In late April 1986, shortly after the album was released, Joe left America for a tour that would continue until mid November, with only minimal rest along the way. After rehearsals at Bearsville Studios in Woodstock he flew to London and opened at Hammersmith Odeon.

The sell-out show—his only one in Britain that year—was recorded and later broadcast by BBC Radio I. There were three new band members: John Troy in place of Vito Sanfillippo; Carla Vaughn, who took over from Elisecia Wright on backing vocals; and saxist Rick Cunningham, the first sax player in the band since Bobby Keys' last stint in 1978. Joe played eight numbers from 'Cocker' and all the old favourites in a one and three quarter hour set. The Odeon balcony shook as the entire audience stood up and rocked along. Joe was called back twice for encores and the crowd still roared for more, fifteen minutes after it was apparent that the show was finally over.

A fine performance and a wildly enthusiastic audience response were not, however, good enough for the British Press. *The Guardian* dismissed the show as "a night for the diehards", and *The Times* referred to Joe's material as "pleasant, mid-taste, designer soul-struck rock numbers." The *Daily Telegraph* reviewer considered that "a growl was not enough," although he did suggest that this view may not have been that of "the faithful"—presumably the whole audience—"who cheered every number and were still asking for more after the second encore." The most curious review of all came from *New Musical Express*, where, two weeks earlier 'Cocker' had been condemned to oblivion as "EMI's first post-Love Missile tax loss." Describing the audience as "comatose", the *NME* man wrote how they "watched this raucous, energetic performance with a reverent immobility more suited to the English National Opera House." No wonder Vic Cocker says, "I read four papers and I didn't feel I'd been at the same concert."

In Germany, where Joe moved on to play extensively throughout the Spring and Summer, critical opinion was very positive. "Rocksinger Joe Cocker confirms his legend, wrote 'BZ' in Berlin; "Joe seems to be better than ever," said *Esslinger Zeitung* in Stuttgart. "A memorable evening" said the reviews of a show in Fürth, where Joe got out the harmonica for a six minute blues jam.

There were features in *Stern, Music Scene*—"Thank God, civilised as he is, he understands we need him", in *Audio*—"The blues is his life. His voice is his testament", *Stereo*—"He has stayed a musical diamond", as well as numerous interviews including a poignant one in *Pop Rocky* where Joe spoke of his disappointment at not being able to revive his career in England.

Throughout May Joe played concerts in Germany, doing City halls, Sports Halls and open-air gigs as summer approached. There followed several weeks in Italy, where for some of the shows a stripper emulated Kim Basinger's scene from '9½ *Weeks*' and disrobed as Joe sang 'You Can Leave Your Hat On'. Many of the Italian shows were in large football stadiums, with the band playing from the pitch while the crowd watched from behind giant fences, patrolled by soldiers with sub-machine guns. "You notice them," says Eric Parker. "Two hundred guys with Uzis at sound checks! Hey—come to a rock concert and be gunned down!"

Once again Joe combed Europe, playing two large festivals in Belgium, shows in France, Switzerland, Holland, even Sardinia—before returning to Germany where 'Don't You Love Me Anymore' proved a second hit single from the 'Cocker' album. Besides big open-air shows like the Waldesbühne in Berlin there were TV shows, notably *Rock Sommer '86* on ZDF.

In mid October Joe arrived in Australia for a month-long tour—his most extensive Down Under. He opened in Brisbane and moved on to Sydney where the visual accompaniment to 'You Can Leave Your Hat On'—as might be expected—caught the attention of the ever-watchful Australian press. The story of how "veteran rocker" Joe was "stunned by a busty blonde who removed her clothes in front of 7,000 screaming fans" was widely reported in the Australian media, who always liked to introduce a little sensationalism into a visit by Joe Cocker.

Joe: "I went on this daytime chat show and the guy was obviously disappointed. "So there's no chance of ever seeing the Mad Dog back again?" It was like—why, do you want me to go berserk? I said 'Well I'm sorry to disappoint you but these days I'm more concerned about doing a good show' . . . And it was 'Oh dear!' . . . But really it was good press the whole tour. Pam went with me and they got this picture of us walking down the street . . . 'THE NEW COCKER . . . settled down'."

* * *

Joe had not toured in America for several years. His only real market there lay in the bar clubs, which he was not at all keen on. "Too many difficulties, too many arguments on the bar circuit," says Michael Lang. "We don't ever want to have to do that again." He had, however, consistently—if not too regularly—appeared on American television over the years—shows like *Saturday Night Live* and *Don Kirshner's Rock Concert* in the early days of his revival, and more recently *Solid Gold* and *David Letterman*.

In 1986 Joe guested on two major rock broadcasts—the Apollo Anniversary show and a sixties reunion with former Fillmore impresario, Bill Graham, besides playing a show in New Orleans for the National Association of Broadcasters, during a break in his European tour.

The Apollo show, a marathon event, featured a seemingly endless roster of stars: Mary Wells, Four Tops, Commodores, Stevie Wonder, Smokey Robinson, Temptations, James Brown, Rod Stewart, George Michael, Sammy Davis Jnr, Lou Rawls, Diana Ross and many more. Joe's contribution was a duet with Patti La Belle, 'You Are So Beautiful', with Billy Preston accompanying them on piano. Their magnetic performance brought a standing ovation and a request for an encore from compére Bill Cosby—on a show in which many performers had to cut their songs.

The sixties show, an HPL TV Special, was recorded in September '86—again during a brief break from Europe—at the old Fillmore West in San Francisco. It included many of Joe's early contemporaries—John Sebastian, Donovan, Lovin' Spoonful, Santana, Sly Stone—and Joan Baez, who duetted with Joe on 'Up Where We Belong'. Given a warm introduction by Bill Graham, Joe opened the TV show with 'The Letter' and returned at the end to sing 'With A Little Help', all the other performers joining in. Kevin Falvey, former American Standard man, played in Joe's backing band for the show. He says, "There was a lot of interesting things in that show, but Joe far and away was the best."

* * *

At the end of the Australian tour Joe returned to Santa Barbara for just a few days before flying off again to Germany in late November. While there he promoted a new single, 'Now That You're Gone', a song he had co-composed with German musician Karl Lage for a film, *Zabou*, starring Götz George. But the highlight of the trip came in Berlin when he was presented with a Gold Disc for 'Cocker' on a live television show. "Simply the best rock singer in the world with the best album he has ever made," said the Berlin issue of *Journal für Musik*. "Joe is like old whisky. He is getting better and better."

166

*   *   *

For the first five months of 1987 Joe remained in America, spending the early part of the year at home. He no longer lived on Jane Fonda's ranch, having moved to the first home he could totally call his own. Built to his own specifications—including a music room—and situated up in the mountains near Santa Barbara, it provided a perfect refuge from the road, a place to relax and at last enjoy the hard-earned fruits of success.

In February he travelled to the Club Taboo in Detroit, where he recorded a Cinemax TV Special hosted by James Brown. Always popular with Detroit audiences—connoisseurs of true soul—Joe sang the old Percy Sledge hit, 'When A Man Loves A Woman', and duetted with James Brown on 'I'll Go Crazy'—a song Joe had first covered as Vance Arnold back in the Sheffield pubs. The duet has since been released on a Polygram album, 'James Brown and Friends'.

With Capitol and his fans eager for a new album, the next two months were spent recording at the House of Music in West Orange, New Jersey. Although 'Cocker' had been very successful, the next album returned to the concept of a single production team—Dan Hartman and Charlie Midnight.

Dan Hartman first made his name as a member of the Edgar Winter Group in the early '70s. A vocalist and multi-instrumentalist he recorded extensively with Winter and others before releasing his first solo album, 'Images', in 1976, and later moving into production. Charlie Midnight, also a vocalist originally, led his own band before concentrating on songwriting and teaming up with Hartman. Together they composed all the songs for James Brown's 'Gravity' album—which Hartman produced—the record which resurrected Brown's hitherto ailing career.

Joe found working with the new team an enlightening experience. Charlie Midnight produced the tracks, with Dan Hartman credited as executive producer when the album—"Unchain My Heart"—came out. Joe: "Charlie's a singer and it was the first time I've ever had a producer who's been a vocalist . . . who has a vocal-backed nature. So he understands what pains I go through when I'm out there. If I sing off tune they tell me in a second—and a lot of people don't. But what they liked about my singing was that I can do . . . four takes . . . pretty much identical on my phrasing—because that's the kind of singer I am . . . and most singers these days do like twenty odd takes . . . or they just build them a phrase at a time. I'm not trying to give the teenage secrets away but it's like I can FEEL my expression going back."

*   *   *

His album ready for mixing, Joe embarked on his by now annual tour of Germany and Western Europe. There were a couple of line-up changes in the band—Janice Singleton joining Maxine Green on backing vocals while the long-serving Howie Hersh had departed for pastures new. His replacement, Charlie Giordano, was an accomplished blues pianist who had worked in New York clubs with visiting celebrities like Lowell Fulson and Chuck Berry, in between stints with Pat Benatar's band.

The tour opened in Walldorf on June 12, with an open-air show in Heppenheim the following night. Joe then flew to Sweden, back to Frankfurt, up to Norway and back again to Karlsruhe in South West Germany, all in the first week. It was a tiring, but not uncommon, schedule, described by one of the crew as "dartboard touring". More stadiums and large halls followed in and out of Germany, to Switzerland where Joe greeted the audience, "Nice to be in Montreux but I wish you'd do something about the dogshit on the pavements!" The same show, at the famous Casino, saw bluesman James Cotton get up to jam with Joe on a couple of numbers.

Athens at the height of a heatwave brought problems. Rod Libbey: "That was almost a disaster. Bob Geldof had been there three days before and they'd left the piano out in a field—for three days and nights! It was 110 degrees and people were dying every day . . . And they said 'Will you need a tuner?' A guy turned up . . . like Chopin . . . he started yelling and screaming—trying to tune the piano!

"That was the show where they put us on a stage, playing towards the end of the stadium—with enough P.A. to do maybe five hundred people . . . but there were people all the way round the stadium and nobody could hear. It was oversold by about ten times—they were turning cars over in the streets . . . people were going wild outside, it was oversold so badly. There were people behind us—they couldn't hear, but they loved him. They stormed the stage, came over the security barriers. They were climbing up the towers and all over the P.A. system!"

Meantime Joe made a lightning trip to London for the 'Island Party', a celebration of Island Records 25th anniversary, televised live in Britain on July 4. Due to his schedule he had to pre-record his spot on the show. He congratulated Chris Blackwell on his achievement and then sang 'Sweet Little Woman', from 'Sheffield Steel', backed by Sly and Robbie, Wally Badarou and Barry Reynolds, before flying back to Essen, Germany, where he had a show the same night.

Shortly after the 'Island Party', Joe had a call to say that Alex Sadkin, who had produced 'Sheffield Steel', was in a coma after a car crash in the Bahamas. They had first met in Miami when Joe was recording 'Luxury You Can Afford', and had become good friends in the ensuing years. Joe:

"I said a prayer for him . . . but then I got another call to say he was dead. He lived music—all the time. I mean, I can go home and watch movies for days—Alex lived music." Joe's already-recorded album, 'Unchain My Heart' would be dedicated to Alex Sadkin—"A man who lived for music, and a good friend."

Through Holland, Belgium and Denmark the tour rolled on, to Nurburgring in Germany and finally to Italy. In Salo at an open-air show in late July, a wedding party somehow became entangled with the Cocker party, and the bride and groom, in all their finery, ended up on stage with Joe and the band. There were more shows in Vio Reggio and Milan, before the last date in Naples, where Joe broke a finger and then dislocated it trying to pull a button off his shirt.

*   *   *

The tour had been highly successful—massive crowds and great receptions. Exhausted and in some pain, Joe headed back to Santa Barbara, where his finger required an operation. No sooner had this been done than he was on his way back to Germany to collect a Platinum Disc for 'Cocker' and to win the Best Male Singer of the Year award in a televised show from Berlin. Making a rare appearance in a tuxedo—and dicky bow—Joe celebrated the award by singing "Unchain My Heart" live to a backing track; all the other performers on the show mimed.

From Berlin Joe flew to England where, after a few days in London and a visit to his father in Sheffield, he was joined by his band for an EMI Convention in Brighton. He played a storming set before record company executives from all over the world, performing 'Unchain My Heart' for the first time with the band, and featuring a range of material from albums old and new.

Called back for encores he ended—fittingly—on 'Up Where We Belong', Maxine Green and Janice Singleton sharing the verses that Jennifer Warnes sang on record. Joe and the band were in great form, as evidenced by the number of people, EMI top brass and others, who filled the dressing room after the show, offering their congratulations.

*   *   *

On October 11, nine years after they first met, Joe and Pam Baker were married. Pam had played a big part in Joe's recuperation from the dark days of drink and drugs and without her intervention Jane Fonda would not have been persuaded to rent Joe the house on her ranch. That she did allow him to rent it was a major factor in Joe's escape from the craziness and bad company of L.A.

169

It was her admiration for Joe's music that led Pam to speak up for him at that time—they did not get to know each other until later. Soon after he moved onto the ranch, Joe went out on tour and in the following two years Pam was away for long spells doing political work for Jane Fonda and her husband, Tom Hayden. Their friendship blossomed after she returned to the ranch to take over the children's camps in 1981, and five years later when Joe decided the time had come to have a house of his own, Pam moved with him. Now, with Joe having popped the question in Athens, on his recent tour, they were married—by the local plumber who doubled as a part-time vicar.

Best man was Mark Aglietti—chief roadie on the 1972 tours and one of the earliest friends Joe had when he first went to live in America. Famous names like Jim Keltner, Jimmy Karstein and Ian McLaughlan of The Faces were among the guests, together with Joe's band and their wives, and the producer of his soon-to-be released album, Charlie Midnight.

Joe's father, Harold, did not make the wedding. Interviewed by the Sheffield *Star* he said "I have never liked travelling and have never been abroad and now I never travel outside Sheffield. I thought at eighty I was too old to start." Harold was, however, very pleased by his younger son's marriage and fully approved of his new daughter-in-law, who he had met for only the second time on Joe's visit home the previous month. "I'm very happy for them" he said. "Marriage will be a steadying influence on him . . . she will keep him on the right lines."

* * *

The newly weds' honeymoon was spent in Europe—promoting Joe's recently released album 'Unchain My Heart'. Tougher and more direct than his previous Capitol records, it was recorded with a basic band comprising some of New York's hottest session musicians.

David Beal, a studio veteran though still in his early twenties, played drums. He had played on an earlier Cocker session when 'Love Live On'—theme from the film *Harry And The Hendersons*—was recorded in Dan Hartman's home studio. Bass player T.M.Stevens' musical beginnings were in funk bands. His varied career includes a spell with the Mahavishnu Orchestra, an unreleased album with Miles Davis, a stint with The Pretenders and all the bass work on James Brown's 'Gravity' album, written and produced by Charlie Midnight and Dan Hartman.

Phil Grande was responsible for the overall guitar work on the album. A member of the Charlie Midnight Band which supported Joe on some dates in the Southern States in 1981, he had subsequently worked on many Midnight record sessions. Jeff Levine, keyboards player, arrived via an audition. A background in R'n'B and gospel, at nineteen he hit the road with The Chambers Brothers, staying four years and later working with such luminaries as Sam and Dave, Bo Diddley and Wilson Pickett. Of his first meeting with Joe Cocker, Levine says "I just immediately felt that Joe has a natural appreciation of music—for music. Strictly on that basis—forgetting social value or anything else. And that's sort of where I come from too—music for the sake of good music."

*   *   *

The album's title track, an '80s treatment of an early 60s Ray Charles song, begins with a striking piano intro from Jeff Levine. The renowned Clarence Clemmons from Bruce Springsteen's E Street Band is featured on a tenor sax solo, while the Uptown Horns punctuate Joe's vocals, aided by the album's main backing singers—Tawatha Agee, Vaneese Thomas and Benny Diggs. The idea to record 'Unchain My Heart' came from Michael Lang—"For years we'd tried to think up some oldie . . . some great old song. We were on a plane coming back from L.A . . . most of the album was done and we were still trying to come up with something. And the song just popped into my head. For such an old song it's the perfect vehicle . . . Joe heard it immediately and he said 'OK—let's do it.'"

Even more spontaneous was the choice of 'Isolation', which arose out of a conversation on the studio floor. Phil Grande: "Joe and I were just talking about John Lennon . . . reminiscing . . . and he said 'There's one song I've always wanted to do.' I sort of jumped on that and we ran to the piano—while everybody was having dinner . . . And when he started singing it I hit the ceiling! I said 'God—if anybody could do justice to this song . . .' We just turned off the lights in the room and we cut that in two takes . . . It was just a very magic moment."

One of the few songs not recorded live was Dan Hartman and Charlie Midnight' composition "A Woman Loves A Man". Phil Grande recalls how this came about: "That was done, first of all, with the drum programming. It was built brick by brick and it pieced together along the way. It was late in the sessions and everybody was very in tune with each other's playing. Actually we wanted to do 'When A Man Loves A Woman' but Percy Sledge had just re-released it."

Hartman and Midnight also composed the upbeat 'Satisfied', while Midnight had a hand in 'Trust In Me', where Renee Geyer makes an appearance as guest vocalist. Both producers provide handclaps on 'The River's Rising', while 'The One', a slow ballad, is complemented by Phoebe Snow's ethereal vocals.

There is a definite air of optimism around on this album, especially in the new songs. In the past the lyrical content of Joe's albums often reflected the problems of his life at particular times—"the painful pertinence of the material" as *Rolling Stone* observed of 'I Can Stand A Little Rain'. Here, with a bunch of songs written for him, the mood is one of a man mellowed by the change in his life—with backward glances serving only to re-inforce the happiness he found in recent times.

Nowhere is this more noticeable than on the three compositions by Canadian songwriter Eddie Schwartz: 'Two Wrongs (Don't Make A Right)', the bouncy, cheerful 'All Our Tomorrows', and 'I Stand In Wonder'. Of Schwartz's ability to write such pointedly suited lyrics, Joe simply explains "He's a fan. So he understands."

For the musicians who played on the "Unchain My Heart" album, working with Joe Cocker was a rewarding experience. "It had such a good feeling," says T.M. Stevens. "There was a good blend in the studio." David Beal was amazed by the ease with which Joe could cut tracks live. "That album was real smooth. We went in, cut it and came out. We were all in one room and Joe was in the vocal booth. I've never done that before."

Joe gives much of the credit for the album to producer Charlie Midnight, a feeling shared by Phil Grande. "See, Charlie relies on the human element—the soulful element, more than the whole technical thing. We wanted it to get back to guts—heart and soul—not a lot of overdubs. We kept it very pure, very simple, with the power of each player coming out . . . the individuality—but supporting Joe at all times. I think that's why it's really worked."

*   *   *

The promotional tour for 'Unchain My Heart' began in Milan six days after Joe's wedding, moving on to Germany and London where he did numerous press interviews and appeared on ITV's *Live At The London Palladium*. Introducing him on a show that included many other prominent acts—The Communards, Donna Summer and Barry White among them, compère Jimmy Tarbuck said, "My very favourite—a man who's been to hell and back. If I had twenty Palladium shows this guy would be on every one!"

After more television and press interviews in Rome, Joe and Pam flew back to New York where Joe guested once again on a TV show in honour of Ray Charles—a special Grammy award for a lifetime's achievement in music. Broadcast in December 1987, Joe duetted with Cissie Houston on a medley of Charles hits—'Hallelujah I Just Love Her So', 'Yes Indeed' and 'Unchain My Heart'. "I'm a bit like a child when I'm around him," Joe told N.Y. journalist Lisa Robinson. "I don't say too much."

In between the recording and broadcast of the Ray Charles show, there was a short tour in the States with the band. Opening in San Francisco Joe did a handful of dates, ending up at the Beacon Theatre and the Ritz for his first New York City shows in six years. Both sell-out shows, the audience at each venue was reluctant to let him leave the stage.

'Unchain My Heart' crept into the bottom end of the American album charts—nothing spectacular but nevertheless Joe's first album entry for a long time. In Germany it reached number two, and all over Europe and Australasia the album—and the single, which also enjoyed success—built on the progress already achieved in the '80s.

Further recognition came when the 30th Annual Grammy Award nominations were announced for 1987 and Joe's 'Unchain My Heart' was nominated for a rock vocal award. Bruce Springsteen won it, but Joe was not complaining. The nomination alone confirmed his own belief, shared by those around him, that "Unchain My Heart" was his strongest album in many a year.

Chapter Fifteen

1988 – 1990

Full Circle–To Earth

IN A ROCK AND ROLL career spanning three decades Joe Cocker has had more than his share of ups and downs. Hit records, prestigious awards and a huge following around the world have at times been clouded to the point of despair by management hassles, tussles with authority and drink and drug problems that would have finished off a lesser mortal long ago.

The chubby, fresh-faced lad who had to pay to gain admission to his first gig and went on to become one of the most distinctive voices in popular music has travelled a long hard road. As the *International Herald Tribune* said of the successful 'Cocker' album: "He has gone up and down too often for it to be called a comeback. Joe Cocker's life has been one continuous comeback. It was a long haul to get somewhere to come back from in the first place."

It was an eight year haul round the Sheffield pubs. Even by 60's standards Joe Cocker took a long time to make it. Many people would have given up and found something else to do, but for Joe there was never anything else he wanted to do. Music is the only thing that has ever really mattered.

His singlemindedness has no doubt helped him through some of the bleaker times. Of the mid 70s when drink ruined his career and nearly his life he says, "I really just lived a wayward existence . . . but music has always kept me together." In a *Daily Mirror* interview at the time of 'Up Where We Belong' he gave a profound insight into his feeling for his own music. "I don't go out to make hit records. I get my satisfaction from creating the sort of music, singing the sort of songs and producing the emotions that appeal to me."

That uncompromising approach singled him out among the white blues giants of his generation, but also led to the eventual decline of his record sales, culminating in 'Stingray'. "It was self-indulgence," Joe would later admit. "I'd do ballads because I like ballads, with no thought for the sales. I always assumed that if you turned out something good it would sell. Not so." Nowadays he might "try to keep an ear open to what people want to hear," but the restoration of Joe Cocker's career—especially in Europe where they have always had a penchant for the blues—has nevertheless been achieved very much on his own terms.

Joe: "I think the reason I've done so well in places like Germany and Italy is because I get more personal contact with the crowd. It's like all the waving the arms about stuff—when you've got to get yourself over to 40,000 people you have to sorta extend your presence . . . but it's not like I'm trying to be a star. In Europe they love things natural."

Joe has always had a natural feel for his work, an inbuilt sensitivity that he can communicate to audiences, however large or small. Phil Crookes, his first musical partner, met up with him again in the late 70s while on holiday in America. "I saw him in a little club in L.A. and he got up with the resident trio and sang 'You Are So Beautiful'. He'd got some kind of magic—and he's always had that magic. You can't put your finger on it . . . it reaches people."

The same magic was in evidence at a small, sweaty club in Newcastle-upon-Tyne, England in October '87. Joe, worn out from a tiring round of press interviews and television appearances promoting 'Unchain My Heart', was persuaded to make an unpaid guest appearance at a party given by Tyne Tees T.V. Earlier in the day he had recorded a spot for their *Roxy* pop show. Looking utterly exhausted Joe dragged himself up on stage and, backed by a less than mediocre local band, gave a performance that can only be described as spellbinding.

In seven years with Joe, Larry Marshall witnessed many against-the-odds performances: "He has a magnetism. There has never been a night when I've been working with him that he hasn't at least once given me goose bumps. He'll just do something a certain way and I'll go 'Phew'. This might be on like 'You Are So Beautiful' that I've done hundreds of times—but he still gets me."

Eric Parker, the drummer who replaced B.J. Wilson: "Joe's very sensitive about the feel of it. Certain nights I would think he probably didn't hear this one song I maybe made a mistake on, or whatever . . . it didn't feel right. But the next day he'd say 'Oh by the way . . . that song . . . the bridge should be a little different.' He's all ears, he really hears that stuff . . .

"A lot of guys go up there and they couldn't care less what's happening behind as long as the lights are on them. Joe's a different breed altogether . . . Like a lot of performers he's pretty shy . . . he's quite a gentleman. I've played with so many bands where the guy's quite big—and they let you know. Every day. 'Pardon me, but I'm the star—don't forget that.' People of a much lesser stature than Joe."

"The Voice of the Common Man," said Leon Russell. "A man of great finesse"—Denny Cordell. Even those whose associations with Joe ended less than happily have no hesitation in praising his talent. Tommy Eyre, summarily sacked from the Grease Band at the end of '68—"The guy's got one of the best voices in the world . . . he's still my favourite white singer after all these years." Says former manager Nigel Thomas "One of the great, great talents. Joe Cocker should be an enormous star. All he cares about is music."

Jerry Moss, who together with his partner Herb Alpert, has recently celebrated 25 years of A & M Records says "Joe Cocker is the greatest white singer I've ever been associated with . . . probably in the world. He meant a lot to me, personally, and he was a big transition artist. We did very well in the mid 60s with Herb Alpert and Sergio Mendes and then all of a sudden the market changed and got into so-called rock and roll—and Joe was the guy we changed the company with. He was the guy we bet on and he came through for us in a big way. Personally and professionally it was a very rewarding experience. I loved the association and I have nothing but the warmest feelings in my heart for him."

Star status is something with which Joe Cocker has never identified himself. Of his early reservations that people would not like him, he still maintains, "It's something that's followed me through my life—I just never compared myself to star category. It's because I'm aware of my limitations. I don't play an instrument and I don't have the best vocal range in the world . . . I just do the best I can with what I've got."

His wife Pam: "Joe is obviously a star but he never acts that way—in any situation. I've known a lot of stars in my life and there is a certain attitude that they project, even to their closest friends and the people around them . . . to make you aware that you're always in the presence of a star. Joe just hasn't got that."

What he has got is an unassuming warmth and humour that inspires great affection. A discussion among band and crew about sponsored tour clothing—"I'd like to know, when we get all these charitable benefits," says Joe, "how it is I end up with a size 54 waist jacket, a pair of shoes that would fit a gorilla and socks that come up to my asshole—and you all walk round looking like Prince!"

Kevin Falvey recalls a plane flight on the 1977 Australian tour. "One of the weirdest things that ever happened to me . . . We're sitting on a plane, going somewhere and all of a sudden we hear Joe's voice coming over the intercom. 'This is Joe Bangooni. Will all the ladies please discard their used underwear under the left wing . . .' And they all got up and looked round!"

Jerry Moss posed one of the greatest challenges to Joe's sense of humour. "You know, Jerry was one of those guys, it was very hard to get a smile out of him. And I always wanted to—just to see the man change, or to shock him or something. And I could never do it . . . But one night I went out to a restaurant with him . . . and I'd bought this pair of red shoes, and with them they'd given me some bright red leather boot polish . . . So we're all having dinner and while no-one's looking—I was a lunatic in those days—I scooped a handful of polish and put it in my mouth, then wiped my hand off. And I'm sat there . . . and I went 'Ugh . . . uuuurgh' . . . clutching my stomach in agony. And everybody's saying 'Jesus! Joe! What's wrong?' . . . while Jerry's just sat there. And I let all this red stuff flow down my face—and Jerry just calmly said 'By the way . . . you know the next album . . .' Just as if nothing had happened! Everyone else thought I'd burst an ulcer or something but it just didn't faze him at all. I just wiped it off my face and said 'Still can't get you!'"

Shock tactics of a different kind were employed on Leon Russell, when Joe went along to see him one day with Denny Cordell. It was around the time of 'I Can Stand A Little Rain' and Cordell, whose partnership with Russell in Shelter Records was soon to end in considerable acrimony, met Joe by chance and took him along. Cordell: "Leon was a big star now, he was in this new pad with a bigger and better studio, all that sort of stuff and we went along there—but he was pretty uptight. Very tense and frosty. He tried to make small talk but Joe wasn't having any of that. He kept saying 'Go on Leon luv. Do something. Really knock me out for a change. Do something . . . Go on!' And Leon wouldn't have any. So we hung in there . . . Leon still trying to make small talk . . . and he says 'Now tell me Joe . . . how's Jim Price getting on?'
'Jim Price luv? Fuckin' hate Jim Price.'
'You hate him Joe . . . Now that's not a nice way to talk about your brother.'
'Brother luv? I fuckin' hate him! I hate his wife . . . I hate his kids—and I hate his fuckin' dog!'"

Joe bore no ill will whatsoever towards Jim Price, whose production efforts were responsible for such Cocker classics as 'Guilty' and 'You Are So Beautiful'. He was merely trying to shock the ever cool Leon Russell. And, says Cordell, he succeeded. "The only trouble was, when you were out with Joe and he hit form, you never knew where the line was going to be drawn!"

Denny Cordell knew Joe better than anyone back in the years immediately following his breakthrough. He witnessed the triumphs of '69 and the tribulations of Mad Dogs the following year. He also witnessed many scenes that makes Joe's survival the wonder that it is. "Joe thought he was indestructible . . . any form of drug proffered—no problem luv, straight down the gullet and carry on as if nothing had happened. He had that sort of Northern pride—nothing can knock me down, I can climb the highest mountain, swim the deepest ocean. I remember—we were in New York on that '69 tour. Freezing cold. Real New York give-you-a-headache-in-five-minutes cold. We were going to walk back from the club and I said 'You'd better put a coat on Joe because it's cold out there.' He was wearing a tiny little T shirt . . . I've got a big coat on and I'm freezing. So he stomps out . . . I said 'Joe—you'll freeze to death.' He said 'I don't need a coat luv' and he took his T shirt off and stuffed it in his pocket and he walked up 8th Avenue bare-chested. That was Joe!

"He was a very nice cat. A very sweet, gentle man. And of course he was a big star. He turned a lot of people on so he was adored—and of course everybody would bring him their offerings—always some form of drug. He's a pretty vulnerable cat and all things like career and stuff didn't interest him—he just wanted to sing."

Joe's single minded attitude meant that all business matters were left to others—whose motives were not always in his best interests, as he later discovered to his cost. But for a man whose career at one time seemed blighted by management hassles he holds remarkably few grudges. "What good is it gonna do? What it comes down to is that I was to blame for making goofs—never reading contracts . . . I've wised up since. If I'd been hipper . . . like Spencer Davis—take him for instance—he was the sharpest businessman ever . . . Frank Barsalona would say 'I go to pick up the money and Spencer's already picked it up!' I'm saying 'Wise man'—but that's before I learned the ropes of anything . . . I'll tell you what the mentality was back then . . . I'd say 'Hey Dee—where's my money?'

"'Whaddya mean?'

"'Where's my dough . . . from the tour?'

"'Why? What d'ya want? D'ya want a house? D'ya want a car?'

"'Not particularly . . . I'd just like to have my money'—In a bunch and they just couldn't grasp it.

"'Well why, Joe? Tell us what you want . . . D'ya want a pair of roller skates?'

"'I WANT MY MONEY'

"And they just couldn't grasp that. They would buy me anything in the world but they wouldn't come to that understanding . . . They'd say 'You're a rock and roll singer . . . You're not supposed to ask shit like that . . . Hey Joe—that's not cool! Asking for MONEY?' They'd rather give you ten grand . . . I think it's from that old black school . . . like

Marvin Gaye . . . these cats loved to go round with twenty grand on the hip . . . big deal, right?

"The point is . . . the brighter you are with that stuff the more headaches they give you. It's like—'Joe! You supposed to be a singer!' 'Yes . . . well, I try to be you know.' 'Well then . . . why don't you just be a singer . . . stop trying to be a businessman . . . Let me look after stealing your money from you.'

"But I get to know these people so closely . . . that I can never fall out with them. . . . Again, after all these years if I met these people tomorrow I could go out and have dinner with them. Why? Because it's rock and roll. This world is what it is and the rock and roll world is like no other."

* * *

Joe's happy-go-lucky attitude to money meant that in the past when he did receive any it soon went—frequently to the benefit of hangers-on and so-called friends, rather than himself. That was assuming he had actually cashed the cheques. Nigel Thomas: "When I took over Joe there were two cheques that he'd lost over the previous eighteen months. One was from Warner Brothers for the Woodstock record and one from A & M for record royalties on Mad Dogs. He'd received the cheques—he was living with his mother—and he'd simply lost them. It came to light when Jerry Moss called me one day and said these cheques had never been cashed. I said 'That's impossible'—but they hadn't."

On such stories are myths created—but this one is absolutely true. In September, 1987 Harold Cocker was rummaging in a record cabinet in his living room. The contents had remained untouched for longer than he cared to remember. In there—among dozens of Joe and Vic's long-forgotten 78 r.p.m records, including Lonnie Donegan, Chas McDevitt, Eddie Cochran and Jerry Lee Lewis; the sheet music for 'Makin' Whoopee'; two books—'The Right Way To Play The Chromatic Harmonica' and 'Ray Charles—24 Songs', and three unopened invoices from a New York dentist—were two cheques. One was issued by A & M dated 4 June 1971, for the sum of $197,054.51; the other from Warner Bros for $26,000. They had arrived during Joe's period of Post-Mad Dogs seclusion and he had put them on one side and forgotten all about them.

Today, older, wiser and grateful for what amounts to a second bite at the rock and roll cherry, Joe takes a little more interest than he used to in business and financial matters. Now too, the spongers and scroungers are kept at arm's length. Of the mid 1970s he says, "A lot of people trod on my life in those days. I was misused—I know that."

Some of them took a long time to shake off too. Tom Sullivan: "You know, when I first went with Joe there were times when I would come off a

tour and I would have more money than him. He would lose so much money
. . . various things . . . I don't know just what was going on to be honest
with you . . . That was another thing about the ARMS tour—walking in
that room that day with all those people. Looking round that room and
realising that here were all those millionaires—and Joe. He's had it all and
it's slipped through his hands in all kinds of different ways."

* * *

It is no secret that considerable amounts of Joe's money went on drugs.
Even after he kicked the heroin habit in 1973 he continued to dabble and
experiment with other pharmaceutical delights for some years. In 1979 he
explained to an incredulous Bart Mills of *The Tribune* his experiences with
PCP—conventionally used as a rhinoceros tranquillizer. "Anything that
changes your angle on the music," he told him. "You take a drug like
that—it bends your ear. Even though you recognise that it harms your
brain. I mean . . . you hear machine guns going off in the back of your
head."

Drugs led many giants of Joe Cocker's generation to an early grave. He
survived to realise the futility of it all. A man with few regrets, he has
occasionally expressed the wish that he had looked after himself better in
the past. "We thought we were invincible, but it all took its toll—physically
and mentally," he told an interviewer not so long ago. Today, of the
difficult but successful battle to stay away from temptation he can afford
to be pleased by what he has achieved.

"I don't want to know. I can be sitting in a bar in Holland or somewhere
. . . It's late and I'm on my own and somebody'll appear—'Hey Joe! You
wanna come up to the room for a good time . . . Coke?' Like clear off!
I don't want to know . . . But I'm pleased I can cope with that now."

What is still hard to cope with at times is the way some interviewers want
to talk only about the old drug days, to the detriment of the music and
everything else. "It gets very wearing. The say 'Do you still take drugs?'
—'No' 'What was it like when you did?'—'Well, I try not to think about
it.' 'Why don't you do anti drug commercials?'—'I don't do any kind of
commercials.' 'Have you a message for today's kids?' —'What can I say
. . . Don't do it. You'll only come down the same old road you went up.'
It gets you down a bit at times . . . It's like that's sometimes all they want
to hear."

His legendary drinking has been curtailed too. A heavy beer drinker
since his teenage years, Joe, like many people who come off heroin, turned
increasingly to alcohol to blot out the blues in his life—and to alleviate his
nervousness before shows. And as with drugs there was never a shortage
of 'well-wishers', each eager to be the person responsible for relieving Joe

Cocker of his senses. Mick Weaver recalls an incident in 1974. "We got to one hotel, checked in, and the hotel clerk puts this bottle across the counter, says 'Hey Joe, that's for you.' It was a bottle of grain alcohol, about 120 proof . . . Just a present, thought he'd like it. I'll tell you though—I've never seen anybody who could put it away like Joe could—he's as strong as a horse!"

Jerry Moss was astounded to receive medical confirmation of Joe's strong constitution. Around the time of the 'I Can Stand A Little Rain' sessions, Jim Price had called him in the early hours one morning, alarmed that Joe appeared to be vomiting blood. "We got to Joe's motel room and he's asleep on the floor . . . we rouse him, he's very groggy, and get him to the hospital. By now he's starting to sober up . . . 'Like, what's going on man?' and just then the doctor walks out through the door. Joe says 'Who are you?' and the guy says 'I'm the doctor' and with that it all gets hysterical. I feel like I'm in some Marx Brothers movie. So Joe goes out in the corridor and by now he's feeling great . . . he's feeling terrific, but he told me he would stay there . . .

"The doctor called me about two days later and he said, 'He's got a circumstance within his system where if he does a tremendous amount of alcohol he has a tendency of throwing it up.' I said 'Really doctor. Well how long can a man live with a condition like this?' And he said 'He can live to be ninety-eight years old . . . this is one of the strongest guys I've ever seen in my life! He's got one of the most rugged constitutions I've ever run across!' He's a marvel!"

Michael Lang: "Jerry Moss could never confront him about his drinking, because he'd react when he was that into it. So I would wind up doing things like . . . if there was a bottle of scotch I'd have to drink a bunch of it . . . just so there'd be less to drink . . . There were a lot of those things that sort of gave him the room to get himself back together . . . but he deserves most of the credit for it. He hooked himself up from his bootstraps."

A visit to a Harley Street doctor, arranged by his English accountant, Bernard Pendry, convinced Joe of the need for moderation. "I sent him up there because he was in a terrible state. He gave Joe a proper physical and he didn't pull his punches. He told him 'Your liver is shot to pieces . . . If you don't stop drinking you're gone.' After that he seemed to cut out a lot."

Hazards, however, still lurk, especially on the road and not always in the most expected places. "There are so many jerks," says Larry Marshall, "who, because of his reputation say 'Well—let's see the drunk Joe Cocker—that's the one we've all heard about. Let's get him drunk.' And it's not only booze—it can be anything. 'Right—let's see him really out of control.' It's criminal. Specially some of his friends—in quotes—Joe's old buddies that come by . . . but airline stewards presenting him with a bottle

. . . even some promoters have done it—and then all of a sudden they're real shocked if Joe's a little loaded on stage!"

In the 80s such incidents became rare, due to Joe's increasing stability and to the vigilance of Tom Sullivan, rarely away from his side. His job was not an easy one. "I had no intention of being here this long," he said in June 1987, into his eighth year on the road with Joe. "I made it pretty plain when I came off that first tour that I didn't want to be around anymore. It was hard to deal with some of those situations . . . I didn't want people to dislike me but I found out along the way that I had to learn to live with that. Why? A lot of it had to do with the friendship that Joe and I developed."

Tom Sullivan left Joe's employment at the end of '87, preferring home life in L.A. to the rigours of touring Europe. Shortly before he departed Joe commented on his difficult role—"Tom's more than just a roadie . . . we have a rapport . . . he's the man-they-love-to-hate. If he's not there people will say "Joe . . . do this . . . or do that . . . You're not doing anything else" . . . but Tom just says 'Hey—he needs his rest'. He knows just how to do it."

Nowadays Joe does not drink before a performance. "The show's the main thing. In the old days I used to be too busy drinking but now I'm just concerned to do a good show." Afterwards he can relax, likewise on nights off during a tour. But the days of staggering about the stage, slurring his words and throwing up in front of the audience are well behind him.

* * *

Early in 1988 Joe decided that the time had come for changes in his band. Towards the end of the previous tour he had spoken of his feeling that the old set-up had become rather cosy, and of his need for fresh inspiration. "In the past I've felt that I was not achieving what I wanted, musically—and I still do. I need a fresh buzz, something that's going to give me a kick up the backside."

He had been greatly impressed by the musicians who played on the 'Unchain My Heart' album and, when in late February he arrived in Italy to begin another European tour, the New York session men formed the nucleus of his new band.

It was a completely fresh line-up, with the sole exception of backing singer, Maxine Green. The former Ikette—"my all-time angel" as Joe has introduced her on stage—had seen many musicians and fellow backing vocalists come and go since she joined Cocker in 1980; now she was the only survivor in an otherwise clean sweep.

Joe's decision to part with the old band was not made without a great deal of soul-searching. The hardest part came when he had to tell long-serving guitarist Cliff Goodwin: "I broke the news very nervously . . . I could hardly talk to him about it. He'd been with me over ten years and he took it really hard, harder than anyone else. But I said to 'em all . . . I think in the long run—it's not a bad track record to say you've worked with me for a few years."

The new band comprised the musicians who had played on the album—Jeff Levine, keyboards; David Beal, drums; T.M.Stevens, bass and Phil Grande, guitar—supplemented with a second guitarist, Jeff Pevar, saxist Marty Kersich and Danny Louis on trumpet and keyboards. Renee Geyer, who had guested on the album, started out as Maxine Green's vocal partner, to be replaced after a few weeks by Carla Vaughn.

The tour opened with an appearance at the San Remo Television Festival and a week-long stint on the afternoon DOC TV show in Rome. Live concerts began in Paris before a capacity audience at Le Zenith. Holland, Belgium and Spain followed in successive days, then on to Switzerland and West Germany.

For the next four months he stormed through Europe, with only a few days off along the way. Everywhere audiences went wild, the new musicians—unleashed from the constraints of recording studios—generating an atmosphere and excitement not seen in a Cocker show since Mad Dogs and Englishmen. Visually, as well as musically, the band brought a new edge, while for his part, Joe had rarely looked so relaxed and confident as he sang through the high-energy two hour set. "An assurance never previously seen" commented one Dutch reviewer; "Joe is turning into a turbo version of himself" said *Berlin Morgenpost*.

In Hamburg, halfway through the tour, Joe spoke of his satisfaction at the way the new line-up was working out: "It's still in the experimental stage but the element I feel with this band . . . I get out now and I don't feel that I have to lift their morale as I go along—which was getting to be a strain with the old band. They don't have that attitude—Oh we're playing somewhere off the beaten track so we can have a quiet one, we don't have to worry.

"I don't want to sound like I'm having a go because they worked hard for me during those years. And there were nights, I admit, I'd go out and they'd be on good form—and then I'd have my work cut out . . . but there were just nights when they'd say "Hey Joe—it's only so and so" . . . we should try and give 'em a crack wherever we go.

"It's a lot more consistent with this group. I go out and I know that everything's gonna be full weight. It's all there."

The new band members made no secret of their delight at being out on the road with Joe Cocker. "To get the opportunity to work with somebody who's touched your heart over the years . . . just to be onstage with him every night. It's just a beautiful feeling," said Phil Grande, admitting that he could have earned far more money staying at home and playing sessions. "Working with Joe?" said David Beal. "It's a riot . . . a great experience. In the studio everything's got to be precise . . . and new, that nobody's heard before. Out here you can just play rock and roll. Joe is just amazing at what he does."

T.M. Stevens, having completed the 'Unchain My Heart' session some months earlier, was touring with Little Steven when he met up with Joe quite by chance at the Town and Country in London. "I didn't even know he was there and he didn't know I was there. I came out and did the show . . . it was a hot night, the place was packed—we rocked. We went up for a press party and I saw Joe there. Well—I didn't do any interviews that night: And his wife said 'You're gonna play with Joe?' We laughed about it—now here I am. Joe is so humble . . . and that's a lesson for all of us. I mean, when I look at him . . . he's paid some dues."

In early June Joe made his first trip behind the Iron Curtain, to play two open-air shows sponsored by the East German government. An East Berlin show attracted an estimated 100,000 people. In Dresden, where a government official told Joe he was the first international artist to appear for over forty years, 125,000 were present—"people as far as the eye could see." Back in 1969 Joe had played to huge crowds at the summer rock festivals in America. Those events had numerous star attractions on the bill. In East Germany the people gathered for one man—Joe Cocker.

Two highspots marked the end of the European tour. On June 6 came an appearance at London's Royal Albert Hall for the 1988 Prince's Trust Rock Gala, before the Prince and Princess of Wales. Backed by Midge Ure's All Stars Joe sang 'The Letter' to tumultuous applause. For the show's finale he led the rest of the bill, which included Eric Clapton, Mark Knopfler, Peter Gabriel, Phil Collins and The Bee Gees, on 'With A Little Help From My Friends'. Televised later in the month the show brought Joe his best exposure in Britain for almost twenty years.

The other big event was the Nelson Mandela Birthday Concert on June 11. Wembley Stadium was filled with 80,000 people and a reported billion television viewers around the world watched the ten hour show. Joe sang "Unchain My Heart" in the afternoon soul set, backed by Jeff Levine and a large band directed by H.B.Barnum.

Late summer brought more touring, with a short series of well-received shows in America, beginning in Los Angeles. Montreal, Toronto and Atlanta were among the stop-offs, while in New York Joe played the Pier on one of the hottest nights of the year. The *New York Post* was impressed: "He harshly gargled his hits and equally excellent album tracks in the emotional manner which continuously endears him to successively younger generations."

For the seventeen American shows, and the ten Australian dates which followed, Joe brought none other than Chris Stainton back into the band—playing additional keyboards to Jeff Levine. Ever since the ARMS tour of December 1983 he had talked of getting together with his old pianist and now it finally happened. The re-union came about through Michael Lang contacting Stainton, who some time earlier had departed Eric Clapton's band and was filling time in London's West End, playing in the orchestra of Andrew Lloyd-Webber's 'Starlight Express'. Fifteen years since it fell apart, the Cocker/Stainton partnership was back in business and Joe was delighted—"We were always so close and it's been a pretty emotional thing getting back together. And the whole band have such a high regard for him. Musicians being what they are they soon sensed that Chris is extraordinary. I've worked with some marvellous players, but he's something unique."

*   *   *

Through the winter Joe worked on his new album, 'One Night Of Sin'. Once again Charlie Midnight produced, and the band that had first been assembled for "Unchain My Heart", with Chris Stainton added to the ranks, provided accompaniment.

With a balance of rockers and ballads, 'One Night Of Sin' opens with Bryan Adams' 'When The Night Comes', the Canadian star playing rhythm guitar on the track. Joe: "Yeah, like his special way of doing it . . . He was a little bit reluctant to give me the tune at first because he probably could have made it a hit himself, but I was grateful." As it happened, Joe made the song a hit on singles charts across Europe and reached the *Billboard* Top Twenty in America for the first time since 1982, peaking at number 11.

Joe's choice of songs on the album is a mix of the old and the new. Gerry Goffin's 'Got To Use My Imagination' gets the heavy sax/trombone treatment, while 'Unforgiven', a Tim Hardin song stored away for nearly fifteen years, has only piano and a sax solo behind it. "We'd had that song since way back when I worked with Rob Fraboni on 'Stingray', says Joe. "No one had ever done it and it seemed like a good idea. It's a heavy kind of tune."

Michael Lang suggested 'Fever', which features a strong arrangement and the presence of the Uptown Horns. Made popular by Peggy Lee in the 1950s, the 78 rpm version that Joe first heard as a schoolboy still lies in the record cabinet at his father's home in Sheffield.

Producer Charlie Midnight gets writing credits for 'Letting Go' and 'Bad Bad Sign', which precedes one of the best tracks on the album, 'I'm Your Man'. Joe: "I've always liked Leonard Cohen. I've got a new tune of his tucked away somewhere. Again—that was Michael's idea. Leonard sings in such a strange key you can't really tell if a song's got any melody or not, but it worked out pretty good."

'One Night Of Sin', the title song, was Charlie Midnight's idea. "We're

185

both old blues fans and he thought it would be cute to put it on. Elvis had a hit with it but he called it 'One Night With You.' I guess at that time, being image conscious, the sin element had to go, but this is the original version by Smiley Lewis. One night of sin's destroyed my life."

Recording the album in New York was tough going, at the height of winter and Joe with a heavy cold, but one of the most satisfying aspects was the inclusion of a self-penned song, the first in six albums and fourteen years. Co-written with Chris Stainton and Jeff Levine, 'Another Mind Gone' came about when Joe heard that his old drummer B.J.Wilson was on a life-support machine, having tried to kill himself. "I got stirred . . . B.J. worked with me for a long time, he was a friend of mine. It just angered me and I guess the lyrics had a lot to do with it. There are a lot of rock tragedies, but that's a heavy one."

'One Night Of Sin' shot straight into the album charts all over Europe before its America release in late summer 1989. By Christmas it had sold more than a million copies world-wide and was well on course to surpass the previous best, achieved by 'Unchain My Heart'. As Joe rightly commented during a BBC Radio I interview, "It's not bad for a forty-five year old guy singing the blues, is it!"

In February 1989, shortly after the album was completed, Joe was invited to the White House in Washington to perform at an inauguration concert for the new President, George Bush. Several years tussling with immigration authorities about his right to a Green Card was only one irony. Joe: "I'm not really a politician but if I had any leanings I'd probably be more of a Democrat. Most of the neighbours on the mountain were surprised I did it, but to me it was an honour I suppose, being asked by the President to perform for him. Trouble was I ended up singing so much at the rehearsals I had no voice when it came to doing the show. But he came along and he looked me in the eye and said 'Weeell?' And I said 'Congratulations Mr President' and he went 'Alright!'"

June saw the beginning of yet another touring stint, that would continue to the end of November and take in over eighty shows. The first leg was Europe and open air festivals in the usual stadiums, bull-rings, on the beach before a 50,000 crowd at De Panne in Belgium, and in Salzburg, the Town Square. "Mozart's home town—there was a huge thunderstorm, a bit like Woodstock, marvellous colours in the sky. The Town Hall couldn't agree who to let play in their Town Square for the first time and they chose me. It was a big kind of family deal, a lot of fun."

Later Joe returned to Austria to play seven more shows, the success of which was measured in sales of the new album. "I was amazed. When you think only six years ago they wanted to lock me away for ever, we sold going on 150,000 records. Quite something when you think of the size of the place."

In the band there were changes from the previous year: Chris Stainton was now a regular member, and Steve Holley—ex Wings—had replaced David Beal on drums. The sole horn player was Deric Dyer. Originally with the American Standard Band who toured with Joe in 1977 and 78, he had recently achieved distinction with Tina Turner. Maxine Green was still there on backing vocals, but with another new partner—Doreen Chanter, of the Chanter Sisters. In Europe and the following American dates Glenn Nightingale played rhythm guitar, only to be replaced by Keith Mack before the Autumn dates.

In America Joe played mostly 5–6,000 seater venues, opening in Seattle on September 8 and winding up in Wilkes Barr. P.A. a month later. On several dates the band was supplemented by the Memphis Horns—Wayne Jackson, Andrew Love and Gary Gazoway, when shows were recorded. The results can be heard on the "Joe Cocker Live" album—from the October 5 show in Lowell, Massachusetts.

Back in Europe the final stint of the tour was titled '5½ Weeks Of Sin'. Opening in Budapest on the eve of the dissolution of the Hungarian Parliament, Joe filled the Sporthalle with 12,500 people. This was a time of political ferment in Eastern Europe, climaxed by the breaching of the Berlin Wall. In the ensuing celebrations Joe was expressly invited to head the hastily arranged Konzert für Berlin on Sunday, November 12. "We were in Hamburg on the Friday when we heard the news of this massive event but we had a show in Denmark on the Sunday night. Anyway I agreed to do the show at the Wall in the afternoon. We flew into Berlin that morning but because the journalists had taken all the available hotels we were way on the outskirts. We drove in and Udi Lindenberg and BAP and all the big German names were there. . . . I had quite a soft feeling in my heart to run out on stage . . . seeing all those people, I think most of them were East Germans. It tugged my heartstrings." There were 10,000 people in the Deutschlandhalle and an estimated 100,000 outside, listening to the show live on radio. On TV news bulletins all over the world millions of viewers saw just a snatch of the concert—Joe's leap into the air at the end of 'With A Little Help From My Friends', as the camera cut away to outside the hall. Joe: "Yeah, it looked pretty good on the news—like I was leaping the wall!"

The culmination of '5½ Weeks Of Sin' was the last night of the tour at Sheffield City Hall. Ever since he played the Lyceum in 1982 Joe had talked about returning to his hometown, now he did it. This time there was no sign of the nerves that had preceded his earlier visit—it was a confident, powerful Joe that walked out on stage as the audience erupted to 'Bad Bad Sign'. "There shouldn't have been a dry eye in the house as homecoming hero Joe Cocker gave his heart and soul" said the *Sheffield Star*.

A hectic schedule means that Joe does not get back to Sheffield so often now. He seldom plays in England and his Green Card difficulties in America—now resolved—meant restricted movements in and out of his adopted homeland for a number of years. None of which bothers his father, Harold, still at Tasker Road and very active and alert for a man in his eighties. "People sometimes ring me and they think I'm kidding when I say I haven't heard from him for so long. He'll ring me occasionally—from Australia or Germany or somewhere and then he'll suddenly appear. I don't hear a lot from him because he's not much of a one for either writing or telephoning. But I always used to say where our John's concerned no news is good news! So I never worry myself unduly when I don't hear from him."

Harold Cocker had not wanted Joe to leave the Gas Board back in 1964, and the trials and tribulations that came in the wake of his success a few years later served only to convince Harold that rock and roll was a less than ideal occupation. "I was quite clear in my mind that there was no future in it, that he'd have been better off a gas fitter . . . I kept some of his tools for a long time—our John used to laugh when he came up—'Fancy you saying that I might go back to gas fitting!' I don't know that I've ever really changed my mind. I still have that feeling that he'd have been better off as a regular worker—although would he, the way things have turned out? Unemployment in all walks of life . . ."

Vic Cocker has no such doubts about the course his younger brother chose to take. "There aren't many people who really have the courage to do what they want to do. And Joe did. People see others become famous and they think it's just good luck. But you've got to believe in yourself—and you've got to believe in yourself when nobody else does."

It is no coincidence that the revival of Joe's career has occurred alongside a greatly increased stability in his personal life. Joe gives much of the credit to his wife. "I'll be honest, Pam's a lot to do with it. She's done a lot for me. I mean, when we got together I was just . . . a piss artist. But when I get out on that stage these days I feel better. . . . I've got more confidence than I had a few years ago. And I think the fact that I've been continually working over the last few years has restored that faith in myself."

Pam also lends an ear to the difficult task of choosing songs for his albums. "He gets sent millions of tapes and I usually end up listening to them before Joe does. There's no way that he could do most of them but I feel honoured that we have this collection of demos and songs that we can listen to and nobody else ever hears. There's one song that we've both loved for several years—that he's tried to get on the last two or three albums. It means a lot to us—it's called 'She Keeps Me In One Piece' but no one that we play it to can hear it. Yeah—he does listen to my opinion—but I certainly don't make or break them."

"I have to go by my own instinct," says Joe. "I really do—no matter who I trust. But my old lady, Pam, she's a vital inspiration. I pick those songs and if she's unimpressed I'm upset. But we are very rarely off skew."

*   *   *

At home in California Joe leads a quiet life. "I must have sung in every bar in Santa Barbara when I first moved there, but I just had enough of it. It was never a case of 'Joe—if you'd like to get up'—they'd announce me and I always felt terribly obliged. I don't go out much now for that reason."

Instead he tends his dahlias, does a little painting and watches a lot of movies, via a TV satellite dish. Far away from spotlights and stages he goes back-packing in the mountains and fishing with local friends. "They're not interested in the rock and roll side of my life. When I get back home they'll ask me how it's gone, but they don't want to know about rock and roll. It's more like 'Hey—did you know the drains are leaking at number forty nine!" He also reads a lot—on the road as well as at home. Joe's knowledge of current affairs and his perception of political and social issues can come as a surprise to people who meet him for the first time—perhaps expecting some sort of burned-out wild man, as the sensationalist press have so often portrayed him.

*   *   *

After a series of unsatisfactory relationships with managers in the first half of the 1970s Joe has remained with Michael Lang for over a decade. A successful partnership, it has not always been smooth going. Lang: "I wouldn't call it easy . . . it's easier now because he's bright and he's had such a weird history with management in the past, and so many people have taken advantage of him. It takes a long time to build up a trust . . . I think we probably have it, although at times . . . Yeah I think that's pretty much where things are coming from. I mean, for years I supported the whole production—put tons of money into keeping things going. We didn't have anything going . . . so those things register you know."

Joe: "I think it was just before 'Sheffield Steel', Michael came up to Santa Barbara. We had an earnest talk and I said 'Let's go for it . . . if you promise me you'll work hard, I'll work hard for you too.' So we made a pact and it's been a slow sort of progression—but it's paid off in the long run, leading up to today." Looking back at the state of his career when Michael Lang took him up, Joe agrees. "Yeah. I do owe him a lot in that respect . . . he works hard for me there's no doubt about it. Michael's a workaholic."

Kevin Falvey, once of the American Standard Band, before becoming involved in management with Michael Lang, has been well placed to observe the Cocker/Lang relationship. "Michael just really loves Joe . . . it's an interesting relationship because Michael is such an individual character himself. He and Joe have not always in the last few years hit the stride together . . . but at the same time, business-wise, it's always worked. It's such a really difficult relationship, manager and artiste . . . When you're slogging round Europe and things are going wrong—because of the promotion, or just the organisation—no matter how you look at it it always filters back onto management."

* * *

The "Unchain My Heart" album in 1987 and a new band heralded another episode in Joe Cocker's continuous quest to further his musical direction. Shortly before the album was released he spoke of his great satisfaction at working with producer Charlie Midnight. "I never knew his cast were around . . . whether we sell a lot of records I dunno, but at least I'm getting a new angle on where I want to go . . . You know I'm R 'n' B—but I love my soul music."

He went on to speak of the influence of his first producer, Denny Cordell, now retired from the music business and breeding racehorses in Ireland. "He's a fascinating cat, Denny, I do owe him a hell of a lot. We had some strange times together but as a producer he's immaculate. Denny introduced me to a world of music I didn't know existed. I dunno—I just had such a hard taste, I was black . . . My mind was black—all the way. And it still is."

It was his acknowledged debt to black music that caused Joe to turn down a lucrative engagement in South Africa's Sun City. "I heard about this place being an oasis in the middle of Africa—and they offered me a million dollars for about four days work. My accountant was saying 'Joe—you've got to be a lunatic not to take this on.' I said 'Don't you know about apartheid?' and he said 'Oh my God! I never knew you were socially conscious!' But I grew up at school resenting the apartheid thing, where they had this rule that white people who associated with blacks were put in jail. I always thought . . . what terrible people—to be so anti-black."

Similar principles apply to his refusal to do television commercials. "It's prostitution . . . They say 'Hey—look at the money' but I just won't do it." There have been plenty of offers. "By the score," says Michael Lang. "Some nice ones . . . Kodak, a telephone company . . . if he were inclined to do them they were classy enough to do. But he just says no and you have to respect that."

As to the future, in the short term there are plans for a real assault on America, where Joe's following slid away over the years. He could have broken into a new market after "Up Where We Belong", concentrating on ballad material, but that was not what he wanted to do. Joe likes to sing some ballads but his is a rock and roll audience who want to hear him sing rock and blues.

That should be high on the agenda in the Summer of 1990, with a long tour of the States on a double bill with guitar hero Stevie Ray Vaughan. Playing slightly larger venues than in '89, the plan is for Joe and the Texan bluesman to switch top billing depending on the strength of the local following. "He's a bit closer to the blues than I am so I hope our audiences will be compatible," says Joe.

His success in East Germany in 1988 and the more recent breaking down of political barriers have opened up vast new areas of potential work. "When you think, it's quite intriguing that suddenly sixteen million people are there. I've been asked to go to Czechoslovakia and Russia's always been in the offing for the last couple of years. Suddenly it's like there's more places to play than you can actually do in a year's work."

In the long term Joe and Pam have thoughts of opening an English style pub in Santa Barbara. "Modelled on the Yorkshire style pub—a games room, backgammon and darts. We'd have a nice lounge, plush seating, really do a proper job on it. I've even got people willing to financially back it . . . Maybe when I get to fifty or so . . . I've said to Pam . . . I don't want to end up going to Las Vegas like Tom Jones or Engelbert . . . It's very lucrative, but that idea of doing two shows a night . . . your greatest hits . . . just doesn't suit me . . . It would be nice to have a little concert room and I could just do a gig when I wanted to . . ."

So, for the time being there are no signs of a let-up on the gruelling schedule of touring. Not that it gets any easier—he has difficulty sleeping and eating on the road and his great success in Europe has meant ever-increasing demands on his time, with little opportunity to relax. "As long as being on stage is fun," he says. "As long as I enjoy that part . . . still get that buzz out of performing . . . then I can put up with the miseries of getting up at five in the morning and all the rest. But if the stage ceases to be fun . . ."

He ponders on what it is that motivates him to keep up the pace, to spend long periods away from home. "It's not about money . . . it's not about money at all. It's like Ray Charles made all that money . . . he got so many millions for doing one coffee commercial. Yet something possesses Ray to still go out there . . . It's like the limo driver who picks me up at the airport in L.A. and takes me to Santa Barbara. Not so long ago . . . I'd just come off a long tiring tour . . . hadn't eaten or slept . . . and I was in real pain with a broken finger. And he said 'Hey Joe—it's your DUTY! I don't know . . . it's a heavy duty sometimes."

* * *

It is a source of great wonder to many people in the music business that Joe Cocker is still around today. It is a source of greater wonder that he releases albums that turn platinum, has a following that spans two generations, and has found a stability in his life that few who knew him in the dark days ever thought possible. Albert Lee, today one of the world's top rock guitarists, was with Joe through some of his bleakest times in the mid 70s. He speaks for many when he says: "I'm amazed that he pulled it all together. Delighted, but amazed . . . If ever there was a candidate it was Joe."

Chris Stainton, closer than anyone to the chaos and confusion that nearly finished Joe in the post-Mad Dogs era, marvels at the way his old friend has survived. "I just don't know how the guy goes out and does it every night" he said at the end of their most recent tour. "We've done something like eighty dates and he's up there for two hours or more. And it's not like the old days—everything's so precise now. He's amazing."

Rita Coolidge admits that during the darkest days she did not go out of her way to see Joe. "I heard such horror stories—it was breaking my heart. I have had conversations with Joe over the years where he would get loaded and I'd have no idea what he said . . . I'd get bits and snatches here and there. And then I guess it was about 1982 Joe played in Los Angeles and he came over to the house afterwards. We sat in the kitchen and talked until about 6 o'clock in the morning—and I understood every word he said. I was just so amazed at the clarity of his memory about things that went on. He would tell me things I had totally forgotten and quote word for word what someone had said to him and what I'd said. It was then I knew he was gonna be alright."

Jerry Moss never doubted that Joe could regain his career. "I'm just happy that the guy's doing great. He's a survivor, that's for sure. He just needed somebody that would keep him going, in a professional sense, and I think Michael Lang did that. He deserves a lot of credit, cos I know how tough that is."

For Michael Lang Joe's revival has brought great personal satisfaction. When they got together in early 1977 Joe was disillusioned, dejected and almost permanently drunk. His life, as well as his career, seemed in ruins. Today he is positive, enthusiastic and at last able to enjoy life for what it is. Michael Lang looks back on the intervening years. "I must say it was a heroic feat for him . . . And he deserves it you know, he was always too nice. You watch him come thro' things where he's finally learned to take command of the band . . . Over the years he's started to have more and more control of things . . . He's really got his life back. And Pam has been a tremendous help in that . . . it's just so good to see. He's got a career—it's not like he needs a hit record to survive . . . it's a real career as a great artiste should have—because of his talent. You hear so many of those stories that have cowboy endings . . . This is one that seems to have really come full circle—to earth."

British Discography

SINGLES

Re-releases and singles from previously released albums not included.

1964
Decca F11974   I'll Cry Instead/Precious Words

1968
Regal Zonophone RZ3006   Marjorine/The New Age Of The Lily
Regal Zonophone RZ3013   With A Little Help From My Friends/
                                      Something's Coming On

1969
Regal Zonophone RZ3024   Delta Lady/She's So Good To Me

1970
Regal Zonophone RZ3027   The Letter/Space Captain
Fly Bug 3   Cry Me A River/Give Peace A Chance

1971
Fly Bug 9   High Time We Went/Black-Eyed Blues

1972
Cube Bug 25   Woman To Woman/Midnight Rider
Cube Bug 28   Pardon Me Sir/She Don't Mind

1974
Cube Bug 47   Put Out The Light/If I Love You
Cube Bug 57   You Are So Beautiful/I Get Mad

1975
Cube Bug 61   It's All Over But The Shoutin'/Sandpaper Cadillac

1976
A&M AMS7243   The Jealous Kind/You Came Along
A&M AMS7257   I Broke Down/You Came Along

1978
Asylum K13138   Fun Time/I Can't Say No
Asylum K13148   A Whiter Shade Of Pale/Watching The River Flow

1981
Cube Bug91   Let It Be/Marjorine

1982
Island WIP6708   Sweet Little Woman/Look What You've Done
Island WIP6802   Many Rivers To Cross/Talking Back To The Night

1983
Island WIP6830   Up Where We Belong/Sweet Little Woman (A-Side
                                      with Jennifer Warnes)

1984
Capitol CL333   **Civilised Man/A Girl Like You**
Capitol CL347   **Edge Of A Dream/Tempted**

1986
Capitol CL362 (Maxi-single)   **Shelter Me/One More Time & If You Have Love Give Me Some**

Capitol CL404   **Don't You Love Me Anymore/Tell Me There's A Way**

Capitol CL413   **You Can Leave Your Hat On/Instrumental**

1987
Capitol CL465   **Unchain My Heart/The One (B-Side with Phoebe Snow)**
MCA MCAS1219   **Love Lives On/On My Way To You**

1989
Capitol CL535   **(Maxi-single) When The Night Comes (ext.version)/ Ruby Lee (live version) & When The Night Comes**

1990
Capitol CL572   **What Are You Doing With A Fool Like Me/Living In The Promiseland**

A 1967 Sheffield University Students' Rag EP included two tracks by Joe Cocker's Blues Band—I've Been Trying & Saved.

A single—Joe Cocker with The Crusaders—I'm So Glad I'm Standing Here Today/Standing Tall (B-Side Crusaders only) was released in 1981, MCA 741.

Other singles *not* released in Britain are: Threw It Away/Easy Rider (Island 499) 1983; Now That You're Gone/Don't Drink The Water (Capitol 1563.7) 1986. Both were released in Europe.

ALBUMS

As released in Britain. Does not include compilations or re-packaged material.

1969 **With A Little Help From My Friends** (Regal Zonophone SLRZ 1006): Feeling Alright; Bye Bye Blackbird; Change In Louise; Marjorine; Just Like A Woman; Do I Still Figure In Your Life?; Sandpaper Cadillac; Don't Let Me Be Misunderstood; With A Little Help From My Friends; I Shall Be Released.

Joe Cocker! (Regal Zonophone SLRZ 1011):
Dear Landlord; Bird On The Wire; Lawdy Miss Clawdy; She Came In Through The Bathroom Window; Hitchcock Railway; That's Your Business; Something; Delta Lady; Hello, Little Friend; Darling Be Home Soon.

1970 **Mad Dogs And Englishmen** (A&M AMLD 6002—Double Album):
Honky Tonk Women; Sticks And Stones; Cry Me A River; Bird On The Wire; Feelin' Alright; Superstar; Let's Get Stoned; Blue Medley—I'll Drown In My Own Tears, When Something Is Wrong With My Baby, I've Been Loving You Too Long; Girl From The North Country; Give Peace A Chance; She Came In Thru' The Bathroom Window; Space Captain; The Letter; Delta Lady.

1973   **Something To Say** (Cube HIFLY13)—
Released in late 72 in USA as JOE COCKER: Pardon Me Sir; High Time
We Went; She Don't Mind; Black-Eyed Blues; Something To Say; Midnight
Rider; Do Right Woman; Woman To Woman; St. James Infirmary.

1974   **I Can Stand A Little Rain** (Cube HIFLY18):
Put Out The Light; I Can Stand A Little Rain; I Get Mad; Sing Me A Song;
The Moon Is A Harsh Mistress; Don't Forget Me; You Are So Beautiful; It's
A Sin When You Love Somebody; Performance; Guilty.

1975   **Jamaica Say You Will** (Cube HIFLY 20):
(That's What I Like) In My Woman; Where Am I Now; I Think It's Going To
Rain Today; Forgive Me Now; Oh Mama; Lucinda; If I Love You; Jamaica
Say You Will; It's All Over But The Shoutin'; Jack-A-Diamonds.

1976   **Stingray** (A&M SP4574):
The Jealous Kind; I Broke Down; You Came Along; Catfish; Moon Dew;
The Man In Me; She Is My Lady; Worrier; Born Thru' Indifference; A Song
For You.

Live In L.A. (Cube HIFLY23)—
A belated album of material recorded during 1972 shows at Long Beach
Arena and Hollywood Bowl, Los Angeles, and at New Haven, Connecticut.
Released by David Platz's Straight Ahead Productions: Dear Landlord; Early
In The Mornin'; Didn't You Know You've Got To Cry Sometime?; St. James
Infirmary; Hitchcock Railway; Midnight Rider; What Kind Of Man Are You?;
High Time We Went; Love The One You're With.

1978   **Luxury You Can Afford** (Asylum 6E 145):
Fun Time; Watching The River Flow; Boogie Baby; A Whiter Shade Of Pale;
I Can't Say No; Southern Lady; I Know (You Don't Want Me No More); What
You Did To Me Last Night; Lady Put The Light Out; Wasted Years; I Heard
It Through The Grapevine.

1982   **Sheffield Steel** (Island ILPS 9700):
Look What You've Done; Shocked; Sweet Little Woman; Seven Days; Marie;
Ruby Lee; Many Rivers To Cross; So Good, So Right; Talking Back To The
Night; Just Like Always.

1984   **Civilised Man** (Capitol EJ240139 1):
Civilised Man; There Goes My Baby; Come On In; Tempted; Long Drag
Off A Cigarette; I Love The Night; Crazy In Love; A Girl Like You;
Hold On (I Feel Our Love Is Changing); Even A Fool Would Let
Go.

1986   **Cocker** (Capitol EST 2009):
Shelter Me; A To Z; Don't You Love Me Anymore; Living Without Your
Love; Don't Drink The Water; You Can Leave Your Hat On; Heart Of The
Matter; Inner City Blues; Love Is On A Fade; Heaven.

1987   **Unchain My Heart** (Capitol EST 2045):
Unchain My Heart; Two Wrongs; I Stand In Wonder; The River's Rising;
Isolation; All Our Tomorrows; A Woman Loves A Man; Trust In Me; The
One; Satisfied.

1989 **One Night Of Sin** (Capitol EST 2098):
When The Night Comes; I Will Live For You; Got To Use My Imagination; Letting Go; Just To Keep From Drowning; Unforgiven; Another Mind Gone; Fever; You Know It's Gonna Hurt; Bad Bad Sign; I'm Your Man; One Night Of Sin.

1990 **Joe Cocker Live** (Capitol ESTSP 25—Double Album):
Feelin' Alright?; Shelter Me; Hitchcock Railway; Up Where We Belong; Guilty; You Can Leave Your Hat On; When The Night Comes; Unchain My Heart; With A Little Help From My Friends; You Are So Beautiful; The Letter; She Came In Through The Bathroom Window; High Time We Went; What Are You Doing With A Fool Like Me*; Living In The Promiseland*. (*Studio tracks)

An album of Joe's 1980 Central Park, NYC show was released in Australia, title LIVE IN NEW YORK, in 1981 (Liberation 5002) Tracks: Put Out The Light; Look What You've Done; So Blue; Guilty; Jealous Kind; Hitchcock Railway; Sweet Forgiveness; You Are So Beautiful; The Letter; With A Little Help From My Friends.

FILM SOUNDTRACKS FEATURING JOE COCKER

1970 **Woodstock**—With A Little Help From My Friends

1982 **An Officer And A Gentleman**—Up Where We Belong (duet with Jennifer Warnes)

1983 **Teachers**—Edge Of A Dream

1986 **Wildcats**—We Are Alone

1986 **9½ Weeks**—You Can Leave Your Hat On

1987 **Zabou**—Now That You're Gone

1987 **Harry And The Hendersons**—Love Lives On

1988 **Bull Durham**—When A Woman Loves A Man

1989 **An Innocent Man**—When The Night Comes

MISCELLANEOUS

Joe Cocker is credited with contributions to the following albums:

1970 **Leon Russell—Leon Russell.** A&M

1971 **Delaney And Bonnie—Motel Shot.** ATCO

1974 **John Lee Hooker—Free Beer And Chicken.**
Duet on 'Five Long Years' and 'The Scratch'. ABC

1976 **Bo Diddley—The 20th Anniversary Of Rock 'N Roll.**
Background vocals on 'Ride The Water' (Parts I & II) and 'Not Fade Away'. RCA

1981 **The Crusaders—Standing Tall.**
Guest vocalist on 'I'm So Glad I'm Standing Here Today' and 'This Old World's Too Funky For Me'. MCA

1987 **James Brown—James Brown And Friends.**
Duet on 'I'll Go Crazy'.

Index